THE BIG IF

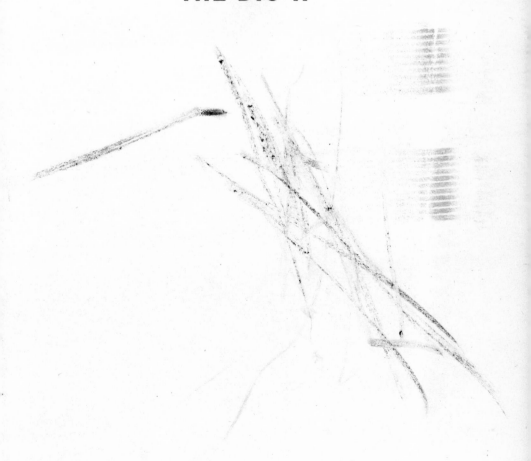

Rick Broadbent

THE BIG IF

The Life and Death of Johnny Owen

MACMILLAN

First published 2006 by Macmillan
an imprint of Pan Macmillan Ltd
Pan Macmillan, 20 New Wharf Road, London N1 9RR
Basingstoke and Oxford
Associated companies throughout the world
www.panmacmillan.com

ISBN-13: 978-1-4050-5298-6 HB
ISBN-10: 1-4050-5298-8 HB
ISBN-13: 978-0-230-01406-0 TPB
ISBN-10: 0-230-01406-2 TPB

1 3 5 7 9 8 6 4 2

A CIP catalogue record for this book is available from
the British Library.

Typeset by SetSystems Ltd, Saffron Walden, Essex
Printed and bound in Great Britain by
Mackays of Chatham plc, Chatham, Kent

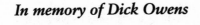

In memory of Dick Owens

'I ain't ever liked violence'

Sugar Ray Robinson

ACKNOWLEDGEMENTS

This is not intended as an apology for boxing, but the writing of this book, the sad subject matter notwithstanding, did evince a rich seam of good running through a much maligned sport. Dick and Kelvin Owens were generous with their time and memories, especially given that many of them are difficult ones, and I am grateful. Likewise in Mexico, Lupe Pintor was friendly, hospitable and humble, while Juan Pablo Alcocer Lamm deserves special mention for his excellent research.

Among the others who were kind enough to help in a myriad of ways, in no order of importance, I am particularly indebted to Edith, Vivian, Susan and Shereen Owens, Dai Gardiner, Don James, Idris Sutton, Byron Board, Graham Walters, Martyn Galleozzie, Jeff Pritchard, Billy Vivian, Jesse Harris, Ken Bryant, Heddwyn Taylor, Gareth Jones, Colin Hart, Harry Carpenter, Matthew Roberts, Gavin Emmett, Virginia, Coti and Jesus Pintor, John Beyrooty, Marty Denkin, Don Fraser, Gerardo Aceves, Lalo, Alberto and Brianne Davila, Jose Camarillo, Rick Farris, Dougie Fischer, Sue Connolly, Brian Doogan, Eric Armit, David Avila, Alex Ramos of the Retired Boxers Foundation, David Luxton, and Richard Milner at Macmillan.

Many newspapers, books and magazines were consulted, but the archives of *The Times*, the *Los Angeles Times*, the *Observer*, the *Western Mail*, the *Merthyr Express* and *Boxing News* were most useful, along with *Boxing* by Bertram Job and *Aberfan: Disasters and Government* by Iain McLean and Martin Johnes.

The photographs used come from the family archives of the Owens and Pintors. Where possible, credits have been included, but I apologize for those we have been unable to source.

Finally, I would like to thank Debs and Erin for their help, and Sam for the drinks.

Contents

Prologue

It was fight night in Merthyr Tydfil and Dick Owens kept a sentry position by the drawn curtains. The thin drapes were his veil of secrecy. Inside, the front room had been rearranged for the clandestine exercise. The bowl of fresh fruit had been taken from the sideboard and secured at a safe distance. The sofa had been shoved against the rear wall and the dining table had been lifted away from its ancient location, leaving a small square of breathing space on the mottled carpet.

Marilyn pulled on the pitted gloves, shook her arms and raised her fists. John smiled, his eyes glistening with anticipation.

'Right, then,' she said. 'Let's have you.'

He edged forward, his anchor foot planted deep in the carpet, ungainly arms tapping at his sister. She pushed him back and smirked, and then rushed at her brother, striking him with a firm jab and then pounding relentlessly. She caught John on the bridge of his nose, but he did not care and he trundled back for more. This time Marilyn placed a glove on his forehead and held him at bay, his spiralling arms clawing the air. She was ten and she knew how to make her extra three years count.

Dick glanced through the crack in the curtains. Seven stages of youth were in this humble room. From baby Dilwyn, naïve and innocent, to John, flushed with blissful ignorance. And now as Vivian, his nine-year-old son, floored John and the walls reverberated to the sounds of anger and mirth, he felt satisfied.

'Come on, John, is that all you've got?'

He bobbed forward again, seven voices merging. His only thought was to attack. Push him back. Keep on top. A crisp prod to his jaw and John felt the carpet again. Kelvin was now bouncing up and down on the sofa, and beating the soft rumps of his clenched fists into Vivian's back. John came at him again. Vivian grabbed him and the three boys fell in a heap.

Dick huffed a laugh and ruffled the hair of little Susan. It was a trial raising a flock of seven children, but also a joy. No gain without pain; that was a tenet of life in the valleys, whether it be remembering to breathe under the fear that the coal seams might run dry or plotting the course of a novice boxer. Suffering could nurture as much as every late-night bottle-feed and, to the boxer, the need to suffer was as fundamental as a need to skip rope and pound the streets with soles worn to a wafer. Pain was merely a mile post on the way to reaching the higher plain. And the best, the greats, could make an art form out of suffering, as Ali would do when he bound George Foreman with those loosely slung ropes in Zaire.

'She's coming! Quick! She's coming!'

The melee disentangled. The threads that strung them together unravelled and each child helped return the room to its original state. The sofa was pushed and pulled, John making sure the feet covered the scuff marks of time. Dick handed Dilwyn to Marilyn and he and Vivian lifted the table. They scurried sidewards like a wooden crab and angled it correctly.

The latch shifted and they felt the first salvo of cold, outside air. It must have been a disappointing night at the bingo, Dick thought as he glanced at the clock. The scratchy sound of a bag being placed on the side meant they had seconds before their deception was exposed. Dick straightened the cushions and Vivian hid the house's two pairs of gloves behind his back.

Edith surveyed the scene with palpable suspicion.

'What's been going on here?' she asked, tracing the faces for giveaway guilt. 'You look out of breath,' she said as her gaze landed on John's angular features. His eyes circled their sockets.

'They've been playing,' Dick said. 'You know what they're like.'

Edith fixed her husband with a knowing glance. She had already noticed the crack in the lampshade and the telltale swirls on the carpet. She had also noted that the fruit bowl had mysteriously moved. She did not miss a trick, but she knew that she could not stop it. So, instead, she restricted herself to loading her words with innuendo.

'Oh aye, I know what you're all like.'

Several hours later Dick Owens lay in bed, staring at the ceiling, letting his thoughts drift into the future. He knew his wife hated the idea of the children boxing, but it was just sport. He knew she hated it when the front room, the showpiece for any family, was abused. 'The kids should be out playing, not boxing in the house,' she had said, but he saw it as a release, a safe haven for all that pent-up energy.

'You know what,' Dick mused in a warm, ursine growl, as the voices from the children's rooms finally dissolved, 'I don't know why I'm saying this, but when John grows up I know he will look after us.'

Edith stirred. 'He's just a boy, Dick,' she said.

'I know that, love,' he whispered. 'But he'll look after us. I know it.'

*

Fast forward seventeen years to fight night in Los Angeles. The boy is now an extraordinary man, a boxer stripped to his core. His legs are fragile, spider limbs, his arms as thin as breadsticks. The body is a rack of ribs, the flesh pulled taut over the skeletal framework. When he takes off his robes the crowds laugh and gasp, forgetting that when you strip away the flesh, the bone and the maw of boxing, you are left with its soul. And the boy's soul was strong. It is 19 September 1980, and the WBC World bantamweight title is on the line.

For Johnny Owen and Lupe Pintor, what should be just another day in the annals of sporting history will change everything. On this day, outrageous fortune will strike mortal blows and expose the combatants as both triumphant figures and vulnerable men. Ordinary men who are too extraordinary for their own good. This is boxing. Some say it is a morality play in a roped ring, but it is really life whittled away to an ugly, simple truth.

This is the boxer's story.

1

THE BIG IF

The Olympic Auditorium was a snarling cesspit of bias. It throbbed with the sweaty sabre-rattling of hopes and dreams. Johnny Owen, the Matchstick Man, ignored the cans of urine hurled by spiteful hands and the savage mien of the hateful crowd. This was his moment, this was his destiny.

The previous night, 18 September 1980, in their humble room at the Gala Inn Motor Hotel, Dick Owens had held his son close to him. The iron bars on the window locked out downtown Los Angeles. The police cars sounding another night of chaos faded. The guns and the drugs and dimly lit dangers shimmered like rippled memories and, for a brief moment, father and son were back in Merthyr Tydfil. Dick's eyes glazed over. The days of torturous runs through saturnine streets, of chopping wood with a blunt axe, the interminable pounding of a bag bearing the scars of ingrained fantasies all crystallized into proud satisfaction. This was journey's end.

'Come on, Dad,' whispered a soft, calming voice. 'Don't get emotional.'

The following day the Mexicans had left the laundromat, the kitchens, the car washes and the factories and headed for the Olympic, where 10,000 lives merged.

At the side of the ring sat Rick Farris, an American who had been a boxer. He had exchanged a few words with the challenger the previous day and had been taken by his prosaic grace. Now he looked at the scrawny body of the Welshman moving awkwardly in his corner and crossed his fingers.

Byron Board, Johnny's biggest fan, took his place and surveyed the scene. He was still shaken. As usual he had walked in front of his boy, carrying the trademark skeleton standard, but he had been shocked by the hostility of the crowd. He had been scratched and pushed and spat at. He remembered Almeria the previous year and how they had grown from their experience in that rancorous bullring. He thought about how they were robbed on that occasion, about the wintergreen oil, the trouble over the purse and how old Harry Vines, the boxing official, had been carried from the ring before being roughed up by La Guarda. He sighed and hoped they would not be victims again.

The press row was full. A dozen journalists had made the trip from Britain. Gareth Jones, who had got to know the Owens family while working the boxing beat for the *Western Mail* in Cardiff, was sure the Mexicans would not have it all their own way. Even though he was doused by the sports writer's natural cynicism, he nevertheless felt the magic coursing through him that night. This was a world title fight and he had known Johnny Owen since he had tentatively made his first telephone call, ringing him at the *Mail* office to inform him of an early victory. A few seats away was Hugh McIlvanney of the *Observer*. The previous year McIlvanney had christened Johnny 'the virgin soldier'. In that article he recalled someone turning to Dick Owens at a fight and telling him that his son should be put in a shawl, carried home and given a good basin of broth. The Americans were similarly deceived by his size. Jim Murray, of the *Los Angeles Times*, had labelled him 'the world's biggest pipe cleaner with ears' in the edition that was being sold on the news-stands outside. He had also suggested, in a protracted Charles Dickens analogy, that the boxer was 'Tiny Tim without the crutches' and a 'classic victim of the industrial revolution'. At least that was better than the image conjured up by his colleague, John Hall, where the challenger had 'the skinniest limbs this side of an ostrich farm'. Both expected him to lose.

Back home in Merthyr they listened and formed pictures in their minds' eyes. In the tiny council house on the Gellideg estate, Kelvin Owens felt his brother would do well. He knew the champion was good and had even beaten Carlos Zarate, a genuine legend, but his brother was special. When there were street fights on that blackened Merthyr canvas, its edges daubed with blood and alcohol, it was Johnny who was the peacemaker. Everybody loved him. And he had the stamina. By God, he had the stamina.

Jesse Harris knew about that. A Welsh schoolboy champion, Jesse had long since succumbed to the sirens that wreck all but the most dedicated of fighters. He had lived atop an elephantine hill, chased horses and pounded a bag hung in a stable. Johnny had looked after him when he first went down the hill and into the frantic world of a valley gym, and had even stood in his corner at the Welsh championships to massage his confidence. Jesse now fiddled with the radio and battled against the fizz and crack of the airwaves.

The sisters could barely imagine the Olympic, but they were there in spirit. From the Gellideg estate, its greying council houses bleached by incessant rain, they tried to picture Johnny. Susan sat and drank her tea. This time there was no need to put her hair up tight, dress as a boy and speak in a comically gruff voice to get into the working men's club to see him fight. Shereen went about her daily routine, killing time with the familiar, and then rose to go to bed, wondering whether her brother would be a hero when she woke.

There were lots more people thinking about Johnny Owen that night. One of them was Eddie Thomas, the ruggedly handsome former welterweight champion. Since he had stopped boxing, Eddie had become embroiled in the other side of the sport that had given him his status and the squat nose, like a melted candle, that parted his rough-hewn features. His gym in Penydarren High Street was famous for spawning two world champions, Howard Winstone and Ken Buchanan, and Eddie's place in Merthyr folklore was cast in the cement foundations on that steep, arcing road.

Thomas poured a whisky and recalled the night Buchanan had fought Ismael Laguna at Madison Square Garden in New York in 1971. The world lightweight title was at stake and Ken's eye was puffed up like a balloon. The glory was slipping away and the referee was frowning at the eye, teetering on the verge of a shattering decision. That was why Eddie had taken out the razor blade and slit the swelling early on. Sometimes destiny needs a helping hand.

'Fuck me, Eddie, that's sore!' Buchanan had cried. 'Who's side are you on?'

Thomas stifled a smile as he pictured his man lasting the fifteen rounds and taking a unanimous verdict. That was nearly ten years ago, before he had fallen out with Buchanan.

Don James had grown up with Winstone. He had been standing a matter of yards away from him when he had lost the tips of three fingers in Line's toy factory. He was with him when Thomas had collared them for fighting in the lanes, ringed by pebbledash and the gnarled angst of a rival gang. James had been an amateur champion himself before he trained Johnny in his amateur days. 'The problem wasn't getting him in the gym, it was bloody getting him out,' he would tell people with one of his panoramic grins. Some of his friends had flown to Los Angeles, but James had stayed at home, tending to the grass roots and letting his mind wander from the days of Winstone to the night of reckoning before him.

Many others who had taught and sparred and fought in the name of boxing carried on with their own courses. Some spent the night drinking in the pubs and Labour clubs, escaping the ennui of their existence; others waited for news with uneasy breath. There was Martyn Galleozzie, Johnny's friend, recovering from his own fight against George Metcalf up at the Elephant and Castle three days earlier. Galleozzie had lost. A good puncher with a knockout left, Galleozzie's heart was drifting out of the sport. His wife was pregnant and he had promised her he would stop when they had children. As he felt the tenderness of his cheek with the back of his hand, he backtracked to the previous winter when thick snow had stilled Merthyr. Fires had burnt and pots boiled as an entire town waited for the thaw. But then, as Galleozzie looked through the window of his lounge and out along the snowscape, he had become aware of something in his peripheral vision. A tiny figure was moving up and down, struggling with the knee-deep powder and the masked ice. He watched and smiled. Trust Johnny, he thought. Training in this weather. He was different. Now, as Galleozzie traipsed up the stairs, he rubbed his face once more and knew his own days were nearly over.

Idris Sutton was finishing his shift at the Ukrainian Club in Swansea. He had lost touch with Johnny but still followed his progress with a paternalistic interest. The world champion? Imagine that. The bar hummed with conversation and chinking glasses. Sutton emptied the slops bucket. Some of the Ukrainians had fought against Britain in the war, but you forgive and forget. And they liked to talk boxing with Sutton and he liked to tell them how he became the army champion while stationed in Hong Kong; how the bandages were wrapped in and out of his fingers and over his knuckle to make up for the missing digit. The Gurkha was tough and durable, as Sutton had found when he broke his hand on the side of his head in the first round. He had returned to the corner confused and panicked.

'I've done something bad to my hand,' he groused. 'I don't know if I can carry on.'

Sergeant Major Hooker had barely batted an eyelid.

'Well, you've got two choices,' he'd said. 'In there it's legal. Out here it's illegal and I'll kick you to bloody death.'

Sutton had the punchline down to a fine art.

'I said I'd stay in.'

This was boxing. It had given him so much, and tonight just might be the best moment of all. He washed the last glasses and called time.

There were the Pickett brothers, Les and Mike, and Billy Vivian, who had been there on the night the lights had gone out in Londonderry. These people made up the boxer's world and it was a million miles away from Little Mexico, the Olympic Auditorium and its pungent atmosphere.

Heddwyn Taylor was not happy. He had come a long way since the days when he used to take time off school to sell coal dust. Now, instead of a horse and cart, he had his own mine and a gleaming Rolls Royce. He was a wealthy man, an envied success among a litany of hard-luck stories, but he had lost the right to stage Johnny's title fight. Afterwards, he would tell people he had all but agreed a deal with the Mexicans to come to Wales, but then Mickey Duff had come on the scene with his silver tongue and silk purse and now the bout was being held in

Los Angeles. He sat in his valley palace with a drink laced with bitterness and wondered what had gone wrong.

The American promoter, Don Chargin, was more content. The Olympic was full and his deal with Rogelio Robles, the owner of a chain of tortilla plants, and the 'Dragon Lady', renowned boxing promoter Aileen Eaton, was paying off. For the past twelve weeks they had been transmitting fights live to Mexico City. He knew the challenger looked like gossamer next to the champion, but he also knew it was a good match.

'Don't get the idea he is going to faint from fright,' he told the local cynics. 'We can't laugh off the threat of the empire any more.'

If anyone raised an objection, Chargin pointed out that three Britons – Alan Minter, Maurice Hope and Jim Watt – had become world champions in the past year and a half. Chargin made fifty fights a year. He could not afford a mismatch.

Chargin looked around. The Olympic was rocking. A small slither of Welsh supporters struggled to make themselves heard. They wore cheap red and white T-shirts with the boxer's name emblazoned across the front. They were proud and stubborn. Keith Davies, his floppy fringe parted in the centre, led the resistance, momentarily stopping to ask himself why there were so few policemen in the arena. The Welsh barman counted only four. Then he saw Johnny, the beer kicked in and he joined his band of brothers in another song, unaware that in a matter of hours he would become their unofficial spokesman as the world's media asked what had really happened.

Marty Denkin, referee for the evening, made sure his bow tie was straight and sucked in the dead air. He had been in plenty of situations like this. He was on his way to being inducted into the Hall of Fame and was working on the *Rocky* films with Sylvester Stallone. He would even have a role in

Raging Bull, the most vivid and realistic boxing film of them all. What Denkin did not know about his sport was not worth spit. He was an expert on all the tricks – the way fighters clenched an arm with a cocked elbow and then complained that they were being held, the rabbit punches, the play-acting when a punch wavered on the low side. He knew instinctively when a fighter was in trouble or if he was gone, if he was a pure flame or a fall guy. Sure, it was a world title fight, but for a referee like Denkin this was just another night at the office.

In the corner that night were Dick Owens and Dai Gardiner. They had been a great team when Owens had first sought out Gardiner to manage his son, but the relationship had ebbed and flowed and was now diverging around immovable obstacles. Gardiner was speaking quickly like he always did. It had been his vision to take a fighter to the very top and here he was. Just one more Herculean task, one more bout. Nobody would criticize him for putting Johnny in the ring if he was the champ.

America had been a strange experience. Dai and Dick had clashed over sparring, hotels, money and television requirements. Now thoughts of those disagreements disappeared as Dai glanced across the ring and met the cold eyes of Guadalupe Pintor, *El Indio de Cuajimalpa*. One look at that igneous physique and it was obvious this fight would be tougher than all the rest. But Johnny was used to defying odds, and if he could do it again then maybe the fractured friendship with Dick Owens would be mended by the camaraderie that comes from shared pain. After tonight the three of them would be unanimous again. Everything would be fine.

Dick Owens was proud and confident. Nobody knew Johnny like him. He was already a legend, and a loyal son. He did not need to prove anything. Earlier that day, during an indulgent moment, he remembered the first time he had seen Johnny box.

He had taken off his top and stood there like a ghost before bursting into life, wiggling his hips while his hands remained perfectly still, as if inventing a strange new dance. The Labour club had broken into a collective laugh at that.

'Attack from the start,' he said. 'Keep on top of him.' Johnny nodded and gave one of those almost imperceptible half smiles.

Lupe Pintor felt sure he would retain his title. It was only three months since he had defended his crown against Eijiro Murata at the Budokan in Tokyo. It had been a tough winning draw against the unbeaten Japanese fighter, but he had good powers of recovery and was over it now. He was in his prime. It was only the previous year when he had put the great Zarate into premature retirement on that heady night at Caesar's Palace. So what if some people said he was lucky to have got the decision? He was the WBC world bantamweight champion. He crossed himself and said a silent mantra. His opponent did not look capable of causing him trouble. He looked in vain for the bulging biceps and the pumped-up pectorals. He was not like the Latino fighters who flooded the gyms in Mexico and LA. Pintor tapped his red gloves together and drew on the energy of the crowd as they chanted his name.

It was late in Merthyr, and Vivian Owens tried to banish the image from his thoughts. It was stupid. Superstitious nonsense. Much more important, it was getting towards fight time and he still could not find anything on the radio.

'Give him one from me.'

That had been the last thing he had said to his brother and he hoped he would. But the dream kept nagging away at him, gnawing at his subconscious, and the more he tried to banish it the more lucid it grew. Shutting his eyes did not work. Nor did the staccato backbeat of the radio. And there he was again. Standing in a large, darkened room. The family was present.

Dick and Edith and all his brothers and sisters. All were dressed in mourning suits. Vivian wore a black tie. They were all there, motionless, unspeaking, as if the room was preserved in amber. All of them except Johnny.

In his corner the challenger was ready. This was what it was all for. This was the chance he had craved. Pintor would be strong and powerful, but nobody had ever hurt him badly and Johnny could outlast them all. Friends, family and Wales. That was who he was fighting for and he would do his best. Attack. That was what Dick had said and he was right. Push him back, pick out the weaknesses and wear him down. The later rounds would be his rounds.

Two days earlier Johnny had made an entry at the back of his tiny green pocket diary, the one secret he held from everyone. He had taken out a pencil, its end chewed to a yellow stump, and begun writing. Somehow it helped to pull the words out of his mind and put them down in black and white. He paused and listened to the night's cacophony. Another ambulance attending another crime. He was looking forward to going home.

The bell sounded. Johnny Owen climbed off his stool and raised his hands. He was on his own.

2

THE TOOTH FAIRY

It started with the Tooth Fairy. Dick was in the Harp Inn enjoying a pint when Nan, the landlady, beckoned him.

'Your daughter's outside,' she said.

He wondered what could be wrong, took another swig and wandered out of the bar into the night's chill. Marilyn, his eldest daughter, grimaced against the wind.

'Mam wants you home.'

Dick sighed. It was the holidays and he liked his time in the pub, but if Edith wanted him then he knew he had to go.

The house hummed with disorder. Vivian was holding his head while John sat innocently on the sofa. Edith wore the exasperated look of a mother nearing the end of a well-worn tether.

'He's shoved a tooth down his brother's ear,' she snapped. 'And we can't find it.'

Dick held Vivian's head, tilted it to the light and looked down the reddening ear-hole.

'I don't think there's anything in here at all,' he quipped.

They caught the bus to St Tydfil's Hospital and the story, if not the tooth, came out.

Vivian had lost a tooth and placed it under his pillow in

anticipation of a night-time visit from a fairy. There might even have been a silver coin for his trouble. John had snatched the tooth and a row had broken out. Vivian had threatened to tell his parents and John had responded by ramming the molar into his brother's ear.

'He wanted the fairies to come,' Vivian remembered. 'He pinched my tooth, and when I went to get it back he forced it right down my ear. I ended up in bloody hospital, sitting on a stretcher with my head on one side, trying to dislodge it.'

The hospital receptionist smiled. So did the doctor. But for Vivian, now jumping off a table, head cocked to one side and with a flat palm banging his other ear, it was no laughing matter.

'If we keep this up the kid is going to be punch-drunk,' his father mused.

It was agreed that surgery would be needed the following morning, whereupon a drained Vivian announced that the rogue molar had finally come loose. By that time it was so late that the buses had stopped running and the Harp Inn had closed for another night. The family group traipsed home through the fading streets. It was John Owens's initiation into the cause and consequence of fight night.

It had been the fundamental will to fight that had driven the Owens to Merthyr. Originally they hailed from Llanidloes to the north, but they were sucked into the region by the carrot of a new start. They settled in a village called Penwaunfawr in Dowlais in 1840 and, like hordes of others nursing dreams, optimism and extended families, worked in the mines and ironworks.

Merthyr was no Promised Land, though, and had a history

rich in strife and bloodshed. The memory of the Merthyr Riots in May 1831, when the greed of the ironmasters had spawned a deathly schism, festered. It had been only nine years since the reformers had settled on land behind the Castle Inn. One of them, Lewis Lewis, had been hoisted aloft by the crowd as a totem of their defiance and fight night began. Soldiers were bludgeoned and stabbed before their colleagues inside the inn opened fire, and within a matter of minutes the street ran red with the blood of both sides. Sixteen soldiers were injured and twenty-four rioters were killed. Barely an hour from the first shot, women were working their way through the carnage and picking over the bones of the dead to find their loved ones.

There were more skirmishes before the iron war ended and the authorities took their retribution. The trial of the rebels began on 13 July. Richard Lewis, known widely as Dic Penderyn, was hanged from the gallows after being found guilty of stabbing Donald Blake, a soldier, with a bayonet. Lewis Lewis, a more prominent cause of the mayhem, was found not guilty of the same charge but was convicted for attacking a house and deported to Australia. Forty years later a man named Ieaun Parker confessed on his deathbed that he had been the one who stabbed Blake. In those blackened days of political strife, the notion was formed that a clenched fist can provide catharsis even if it might struggle to bring resolution.

This was Merthyr in the nineteenth century. The River Taff had been appropriated by the ironmasters as a dumping ground and there were frequent outbreaks of cholera and typhoid. The mortality rate was the highest in Britain and, in the first half of the century, more than 60 per cent of burials in the town were of children under the age of five. It was a hard place reflected by its people.

Industrial growth caused its own problems. There were

clashes of class and culture, all played out against a backdrop of ever-increasing heaps of funereal debris. The harder the Penwaunfawr workers toiled, the bigger these mounds of waste would become as the industrialists sucked the life out of their rats and then almost buried them beneath monuments to their avarice. Few stopped to wonder if the pace of change was too fast to sustain.

The factories thrived while the people merely survived. From John Owens's great-grandmother working underground as a spragger, putting sheaths of wood between the spokes of a tram's wheels to slow it, to Will John, his great-grandfather, who worked in the ironworks and boxed in the booths on the Bont, everyone was fighting in one way or another.

Boxing was a natural by-product and Merthyr would go on to boast an incongruous number of champions, given its small population. Its people were hewn from the mines and ironworks and tested their mettle in the bloody booths. The best of all was Jimmy Wilde, who went by the unwieldy nickname of the Ghost with the Hammer in his Hand. Born in 1892, he started life as a miner and never forgot the day he first heard the cage slam shut and the sensation of falling.

'The descent seemed slow at first and then bewilderingly fast,' he said. 'Daylight disappeared like a quick dusk. Then my stomach seemed to want to leave me. The breath had been knocked out of me. My first impressions were of water, deafness and blackness.'

A flint-faced colleague named Dai Davies, who doubled as a bare-knuckle fighter, soon began to tutor Wilde in the tiny bedroom of his home, away from the disapproving eyes of his mother. He taught him that power comes from timing as much as muscle, and that speed of foot is as important as sleight of hand. It was not long before Wilde was earning pocket money by stopping boys sneaking under the tent at the back of Jack Skarratt's boxing booth. So successful was he, sometimes taking on a dozen opponents, that Skarratt quickly realized he would be better off employing him inside the tent. There is a grainy bill from his days in the booths depicting Wilde in a boxing pose. Small and puny, with an ashen gravity that looks more in keeping with a bookkeeper, the wording beneath the picture must have been a red rag to many a brawny bruiser. It read: 'The seven stone champion of Wales: open to box anyone in the world at 6–10 stone.' Many came, most fell, all were beaten.

His progression to the professional ranks almost never happened when a steel rope pulling a tram gnawed into his trapped leg. He recovered, and the accident stiffened his resolve to leave mining behind. He had gone four years and 101 fights without tasting defeat when he fought Tancy Lee for the British and European flyweight titles in 1915. In the seventeenth round, Wilde's corner threw in the towel. Drained by an illness, Wilde was a shadow of his normal self, but he was nevertheless incredulous that his corner should have conceded defeat and warned them never to do so again.

'From that night onwards I asked Mr Teddy Lewis, my manager, never under any circumstances to throw in a towel on my behalf. If any boxer can beat me let him do it. I would not grudge anyone the full credit of a victory to which he is entitled when it is won fairly and squarely.'

He gained his revenge against the Scotsman in eleven pulsating rounds the following year, Wilde using the momentum of his opponent to bolster his punches, and became the first official world flyweight title champion when he beat America's Young Zulu Kid on 18 December 1916. Having lost his seat on the *Titanic* through flu in 1912, Wilde now toured America and was fêted everywhere he went. He lived the high life, dined with Hollywood greats and gorged on his fame. But the incredible number of fights took their toll. By the time he stood across the ring from Francisco Guilledo, fighting under the pseudonym of Pancho Villa, at the Polo Grounds in New York in 1923, he had been inactive for two years and was making the long descent from the summit. That night, the cage door once again slammed shut.

'Villa fought like a wild cat,' Wilde's wife, Elizabeth, said. 'Back-handed punches were his speciality. Every blow cut Jimmy to ribbons. Jimmy fought in a state of coma, although his hands seemed to respond to the working of his brain.'

Even in the first round it had been evident that the hammer was weakening. The bell sounded for the end of the second, and then Villa threw a punch after the second round ended as Wilde was turning away, and that punch dismantled the defenceless champion. Later, Wilde would say he could not remember going out for the third, fourth, fifth and sixth. His face a bloated, purple pulp, he was counted out in the seventh round.

The crowd was incensed that an era had been brought to such an ugly end.

'Me not want to hurt him,' Villa mouthed as he pushed his way into Wilde's dressing room afterwards. 'Not me do that.'

There were rumours of Mob influence on that night, the theory being that Villa was told to win at all costs. He had not wanted to cheat but had no choice with high-ranking New York mafiosi in the crowd. Later that night, as Wilde crossed the Hudson river to his base, lightning strikes killed two of his boatmen. Some interpreted the tragedy as an act of God. The Wilde nights were over.

Four days later Elizabeth saw blood begin to trickle from his split mouth.

'He's dying, he's dying,' she screamed.

In fact Wilde outlasted Elizabeth. When he passed away in 1969, the victim of a beating at a Welsh railway station, his Alzheimer's disease was so advanced that he was unaware that his wife had been dead for two years. One story goes that Wilde's assailant was an alcoholic who was never served another drink in the whole of Wales.

During his latter years Wilde was visited by the Kray twins, the notorious London gangsters who were fans and proud owners of *The Art of Boxing*, Jimmy's self-penned manual. As with much of Wilde's colourful history, there is an apocryphal ring to some aspects of the legend, but it may be that this Welsh will-o'-the-wisp, who never weighed more than 108 pounds, was simply too good to be true. It is little wonder that he became John Owens's hero.

Wilde never blamed anyone for his fate. It was, perhaps, the natural consequence of such an unnatural talent. He had taken a fight, on average, every eight days of his professional life and, like so many, he hung on for one too many. It was, however, understandable; his purse, £13,000, was more than John Owens would get for his own world title bout some fifty-seven years later.

Wilde died with a record of four defeats in 149 contests. It is a tally that compares favourably with anyone from the modern era, including Ali, who ended up with five defeats from sixty-one fights. He was also a character. David Wilde, Jimmy's great-grandson, said: 'He was fighting up in Sheffield one night and was up off his stool at the start, but the other guy was slow coming out. Jimmy went over and said, "Excuse me, would you mind hurrying up. I've got a train to catch in ten minutes."'

By the time of his death, nobody knew that the baton had been passed from Jimmy Wilde to a schoolboy labelled Flappy and Jug Ears by crueller peers, that as a nation mourned a man who had ignored mere flesh and bone to become a romantic ideal, John Richard Owens was taking the first tentative steps towards the fight nights that would form a timeline back to his hero.

Wales had plenty of other boxing heroes, from Peerless Jim Driscoll, who once put off a world title fight because he had promised to box in an exhibition for Nazareth House Orphanage, to Tommy Farr, the former miner from the Rhondda.

Dick Owens was a young boy when Wales ground to a halt as Farr took on Joe Louis, the Brown Bomber, for the heavyweight title of the world in front of 32,000 partisans in New York's Yankee Stadium in 1937. Louis was a legend in the making, despite being a black man in a segregated country, and would not lose a fight for another thirteen years. Farr was a more prosaic figure, the lines on his back betraying his rugged upbringing in the mines. When Louis asked where Farr had got those marks, the Welshman dead-panned: 'Wrestling tigers.' After fifteen gruelling rounds, Louis could well believe it, albeit he was a decisive points winner. 'My face looked like a dug-up road,' Farr lamented after the bout, but his place in folklore was established.

Dick Owens walked down Lower High Street to his uncle's house in the early hours that day.

'He had a wireless and I had to listen to the fight,' he said.

He was hooked on the sport. He had heard Farr's comment that, faced with a life of working beneath the ground and in the boxing booths, he considered fighting 'the lesser of two evils'. He started subscribing to *Boxing News* when he was eleven and had a few amateur bouts himself, but it was not until his boys started throwing punches themselves that he became really immersed in the sport.

He met Edith at a dance in the Miners' Hall in Merthyr.

They courted for two years before they got married at the local register office in 1948. It was the year Joe Louis announced his retirement after beating Jersey Joe Walcott, and the year a new heavyweight called Rocky Marciano was starting out in the pro ranks on Rhode Island. The paths of those two men would cross three years later when Marciano would finally end Louis's illustrious career after the Brown Bomber had been tempted out of inactivity for one last hurrah. And on the undercard of 1948 boxing feats, there was Eddie Thomas, the Merthyr Marvel, beating Gwyn Williams in London to become the Welsh welterweight champion.

The Owens had their wedding reception in the local pub in Abercanaid and lived in Edith's home town for a while. Then they moved to Dowlais before arriving on the Gellideg estate. Edith was a busy woman after getting married. In 1950 she gave birth to her first child, Phillip. Three years later came Marilyn, followed by Vivian in 1954 and John on 7 January 1956. The next to arrive was Kelvin, followed swiftly by Susan and Dilwyn. Then she had a rest until Shereen provided a full stop to her labours in December 1966.

It meant there was rarely a dull moment in the little council house the family had moved to in Heol Bryn Selu. Vivian was the family tearaway, absent-mindedly throwing stones over a neighbour's wall. On one occasion a missile came back and struck John squarely on the side of his head. He could feel the dampness of the blood and the throb of pain, but he ignored it.

'Vivian would always get into trouble,' his father said. 'But John didn't cry and he never said a word. There was no emotion. He went to hospital and had a couple of stitches.'

Phillip always kept animals. At any one time he would have a small menagerie, but his was not an unqualified love of nature.

'He had everything,' Kelvin remembered. 'He had pigs,

horses, chickens. He used to keep chickens out the back of our house. One Christmas we were going to have one for our lunch and he went outside to kill it. I didn't want to look because I'd heard how they can run around with no heads. He cut its throat and hung it on the drainpipe. All the blood was dripping out. I caught a glimpse and it was horrible. When it was finally served up, we all looked at it and thought the same thing. Nobody touched it.'

On another occasion, Phillip was bitten by a horse. His response was to bite it back.

'He had club feet when he was little and had to have braces on them,' Dick said of his eldest. 'He must have had a dozen operations. They said he couldn't go in the water, but we'd strip his legs and let him go in with the others. Then we'd take him back to the doctor so he could put the braces back on. They used to call us rotten for that, but we couldn't treat him different to anyone else.'

It was in this boisterous household of two adults and eight children that John proved the prescience of his father's suggestion that he would take care of the family. A sensitive, quiet soul, he was deeply in tune with the moods and needs of those close to him. It was why, when he was only seven, he would do the weekly shop, trawling from store to store to save even a halfpenny, and why he single-handedly nursed his ailing brothers, sisters and parents as they were all struck down with a particularly virulent strain of flu one Christmas.

'We were all lying about the living room, too ill to go to bed, and if it wasn't for John then I don't think we'd have survived,' his father said. 'He fed us soup and made sure we all had our medicine. He looked after us.'

His appearance belied his resilience. Almost anorexic, his ribs were worn on the outside like a bone waistcoat. He looked frail and half-formed, as if the spell he had spent in St Tydfil's when just eight months old, with tubes attached to him and doctors baffled by his condition, had handicapped him for life. Yet he had recovered from spending those two months in hospital with a mystery illness and was now the strongest of them all.

His hero Jimmy Wilde had also dragged remarkable strength out of a puny body. 'Once or twice a promoter did not scruple to tell me I was consumptive and ought not to box at all,' Jimmy Wilde said of his early days in the ring. But those who came from mining country knew that looks were skin-deep; fire came from within.

Pranks were the daily bread of this motley crew. As their father threaded a brush up the chimney to clean the flue one day, he was called into the kitchen by Edith. When he returned he was struck by the guilty silence. Peace in an overcrowded terrace was generally a precursor to chaos, a telltale quiet as piercing as any confession. In that solemn hush, Dick went back to the chimney only to find the rods had all been loosened with the effect of provoking an avalanche of soot when he grasped the lowest one. He shouted for his children to line up against the wall and asked them, one by one, who was responsible for the foolishness. No one said a word. They were many things, but they were not snitches. Some hours later, with a loop attached to the end of the pole, Dick finally got his chimney brush down.

This was the harsh but happy boyhood of John Owens. Money was scarce and corners were cut, but the honour and respect that would make him unusual in the self-aggrandizing world of boxing were instilled in those frenetic days.

It was never an easy life, though, and this tight family unit came close to being torn asunder when John was just seven.

At that time his father was working as a moulder at Dunlop's boot factory. It was a good job with reasonable pay and a far less testing vocation than working in the pits. After thirteen long years, Dick Owens had finally turned his back on mining, but he found himself having to take an increasing amount of time off from the factory because of Edith's poor health. She had suffered complications during the birth of Susan and the problems continued to plague her. When his wife was hospitalized it made life virtually impossible. Dick sat up into the early hours, trying to come up with a more appealing solution, but kept returning to the only one he could think of. It hurt him to his core, but he was on good wages at the factory and the prospect of losing his job would send shudders through the family. And so he stifled the last vestiges of pride and decided that to keep them all together he would drive them away.

'I had to get back to work, but how could I with Edith in the hospital?' he said.

'So one day I called all the children into the front room and asked them whether they would go into homes until their mother came out. It was an awful thing to have to do, but I needed to keep my job. They all said they would, so I phoned the children's clinic in town and made an appointment for that afternoon. I got the children ready and we caught the bus into Merthyr. We went to the offices to see the lady, but I couldn't tell her that I wanted to put them into homes because I was crying so much.'

The council official told him to go home and that she would come and visit him the following morning to make the arrangements. It was as if someone had draped him in a dark shroud that evening. Marilyn, at ten the eldest girl, helped him make supper for the other children, but the normal symphony of shouts and screams was replaced by an anxious hush. Marilyn and her father put the others to bed and a traumatic day became the longest night. The pain of losing his offspring almost doubled him up. It was an acute, searing sensation of emptiness that would revisit him almost two decades later.

'I didn't sleep a wink that night,' he said. 'I tossed and turned and my mind was in turmoil. I never stopped crying and my eyes ached.'

At 7 a.m. the sun cast a lustrous welcome in the mournful bedroom. The wall was slowly coloured by coruscating rays and Dick might have felt a glimmer of defiance. Before he could harness it, John was in the room, those sunken cow eyes softening his harsh features.

'We have to go into the homes today, Dad,' he said. 'Don't worry. I'll look after the little ones.'

Soon Kelvin shuffled into the room, followed by Marilyn and the others. There were seven children sitting on his bed. It was a snapshot that broke his heart as he contemplated the day ahead.

'I looked at them and thought, No way am I going to let them go, job or no job. I said to them, "If you all help and be good, then maybe we can stay together." They said they would.'

The council official arrived at 9.45 a.m. Dick made her a cup of tea and she explained that she would have trouble keeping the children together. Some would have to go to Brecon and some to Cardiff. Dick had already made up his mind, but the news that his children would be separated strengthened his stance.

'I told her I would not be putting the children into homes after all,' he said. 'She told me that it would be an awful lot of work and that she could get someone to come in and help me. I told her I could cook, wash, iron and clean and that the only thing I needed was to keep my job.'

The woman from the council asked where he worked and a smile crept along her lips.

'The personnel officer there is a friend of mine,' she said. 'Don't you worry. I'll make sure your job is safe.'

Two days later, Dick received a letter from his bosses in a brown envelope and a weight lifted from his shoulders.

Gradually Edith grew stronger. She was allowed home and life returned to normal, although the pain of that period never left her husband.

One year the family took a holiday in the Brecon Beacons. This was a time for the rigours of daily life to be forgotten amid the lush hills and mountain streams. Up in those fecund fields, free from the claustrophobia of being crammed into two box rooms, they could breathe. A waterfall ran down into the Neuadd Reservoir, giving the place the feel of an idyll for idle times, and the children would often go swimming. All except Kelvin.

'I can't swim because I have a perforated eardrum,' he explained. 'I have great balance until I'm in water. I remember when we were at junior school we went swimming to the local baths. We'd always been brought up never to show your fear, so I got in and held on to the bar. Then they said they were going to take the bar away. Well, no way was I going to let go. Every time I looked out of the water it seemed like I was going uphill. I jumped out and started crying my eyes out. I went and got changed. That was the end of it. I didn't swim.'

On that camping holiday his brothers and sisters egged him on. And so, in a show of bravado and masking his fear with deep gulps, Kelvin went to what he deemed to be the safest point of entry. He checked his footing to be sure of the depth and then pushed off.

'What I didn't know was I was standing on a submerged

ledge,' he said. 'I went straight down like a stone. I was in a major panic and extremely frightened.'

As Kelvin broke the surface, coughing and spluttering, arms flailing at nothing in blind panic, John strode through the depths.

'I felt him grab hold of me beneath my arms and then he lifted me above him, clean out of the water, and walked back to the side,' Kelvin said.

'You saved my life,' he told his brother.

'Don't go soft, Kel,' John replied, and he gave a half-smile. It was no big deal. It was his role to carry the family.

But this was Merthyr and trouble ran through it like a rip tide. From the mining accidents to the street fights, it was a ragged old place, snagged on its bloody past and in constant danger of coming apart at the seams. All Dick Owens could do was try to keep his family safe. It was a basic struggle that was highlighted in every household throughout Wales in October 1966.

It was the last day before half-term and John, aged ten, sat in his class at Gellideg Junior School, eagerly anticipating the holidays. A short run over the hills in Aberfan, another teacher at Pantglas Junior School was preparing to take the register when she heard a noise. It was a low, guttural roar at first, but then it grew to a crescendo of ear-splitting thunderclaps. Her first thought was it must be a jet plane and that it was going to land on the school.

'Get under your desks,' she snapped at the children who were frozen in their seats, transfixed by the darkening windows.

Mr Davis had written some sums on the board and the class had started to toil with them when the distant rumbling began. Then, within seconds, came the screaming peal and sonic boom.

'Everyone was petrified,' said one of the children.

Up on the coal tip there was a sense of disbelief. Some of the charge-hands were shouting useless warnings. They yelled as loudly as they could but their mouths moved in silence. There was no telephone to ring down below. There was nothing they could do other than save themselves and watch the avalanche scorch the hillside and rip through the embankment behind the village. Windows and doors were smashed in Moy Road by this sea of sludge. Inside a classroom, a teacher saw a giant spinning boulder double and treble in size until it crashed into the bricks and concrete of the wall, razing it to the ground and sending him flying across the floor.

Nobody was killed in that classroom, but they were lucky. In total, 116 children and twenty-eight adults died in the Aberfan Disaster.

'I was there for about an hour and a half until the fire brigade found me,' one boy would recall. 'The desk was jammed into my stomach and my leg was under the radiator. The little girl next to me was dead and her head was on my shoulder.'

A pupil who had survived returned to find his new jumper. He had four siblings and his only concern was that he would get into trouble for losing the mustard top his mother had knitted for him. Lew the Milk, a dairy farmer, clasped his son tightly. He had been working when he heard the news and had rushed to the scene. He had formed part of the human chain of grief as miners, fathers and policemen passed the tiny corpses between them. All around him he could hear weeping, wailing, shrieks and sobs. And then he had been passed his own son. His heart sunk to the pit of his stomach and Lew broke from the chain and carried David towards the road where the dead bodies were lined up. Then a nurse had breathed hope and uttered those immortal words: 'This boy's alive!'

In Merthyr, Dick and Edith Owens sympathized with the

grieving parents of Aberfan. They had seven children and Edith was seven months pregnant with Shereen. They could only imagine the sense of loss and anger, but they said their prayers for the bereaved. It was a shocking accident that left indelible scars. There was the grief of those mothers who had sent their children to school when they had not wanted to go, and the guilt of the miners whose toil had stoked the malevolent wave. As they read the newspaper reports about Aberfan, the Owens sympathized with those who had lost a child to freakish fate. Everyone was affected by the tragedy. Everyone knew it could so easily have been their children who had been taken away.

The streets and pubs were quieter than usual and, when the fog of shock and sadness slowly lifted, every parent not directly involved was thankful for what they had.

'It hit the whole area,' Dick said. 'Everybody was speaking in whispers for a while. It knocked the stuffing out of everyone.'

Four days after the carnage, the Owens watched footage of the mourners gathering to bury their dead children in a hillside.

Drive to Aberfan from Merthyr and you see the gravestones dotted on a green slope. Go over the stream and up the single road through the tiny place and you come to a fork – left for the cemetery, right for the garden of remembrance. The tragedy is inescapable. The children's graves form two neat lines, each capped by a stone arc. To the rear is the resting place of Robert Coffey, a boxer whom John had become friendly with. Although he was four years older, Coffey had been nice to the novice fighter. 'It was such a waste,' Dick said. 'They were pals and the accident hit John like the rest of us.' The television and newspapers were crammed with pictures of blackened, broken people. It was as if the valleys had been winded by a celestial body-blow.

It would be trite to suggest boxing suddenly became part of the area's therapy, but it remained a natural step for young boys in Merthyr and Aberfan. The tragedy hung over the region, the insensitivity of the National Coal Board pricking away any scabbing, and mired it in depression. Boxing had always been an escape route and perhaps now it could be more so.

Phillip, the eldest Owens boy by four years, had been the first to try his hand. He went along to Eddie Thomas's burgeoning gym. Thomas had hung up his gloves the year Vivian was born and was now establishing himself as a businessman and a world-renowned cuts man. Vivian, John and Kelvin did not join Thomas's gym and instead went to Merthyr Amateur Boxing Club. It was housed in a ramshackle green hut on Plymouth Street and was run by a brace of big-hearted men named Danny Galleozzie and Billy 'Punchy' Davies. When the Owens arrived in single file, the hoods of their duffle coats pulled tightly around their wind-bitten faces, Galleozzie always came up with the same response. In a loud, affectionate voice he would cry: 'The mice are in, boys. The mice are in.'

In Merthyr there were two streets where the Italian influx settled. They had come for the steel, although the first Galleozzie in Merthyr was a craftsman who made figurines for the Catholic churches. Like so many families in the area, boxing was the sap of the Galleozzie family tree. Galleozzie's father had even been the champion of India for seven years. He died when he was still in his fifties, with the flat nose he had earned from the years of bouts causing a brain haemorrhage.

Galleozzie did not show his emotions, but he loved boxing. His son, Martyn, who became a close friend of John, said:

'Dad would come home from a day shift working in the pit at 3.30 p.m., have dinner, go to bed for an hour and then he'd be down the gym. He put all his spare time into it. It amazes me to think how much he and Billy did for all those boys. He had always been into it. Even when he was fifteen he was boxing at a very good level. He used to box under a different name because he was so young, but eventually they caught him and made him buy a licence. In effect, they made him go professional. He boxed one of the Turpins before the colour bar was lifted in this country. My father thought he had won the fight and so did his trainer and there was a huge row over the decision. They even called my father before the British Boxing Board of Control and banned him for three months. My father said, "I've got two exhibitions. Let me do those and I'll never box again." That's what he did. His last exhibition was against a young Eddie Thomas. Eddie was seven years younger and up-and-coming. Afterwards my father gave his shorts and shoes to him. Eddie always said the first pair of proper boxing shoes he got were from Danny Galleozzie.'

His generosity extended to his young charges, but in those rookie days John Owens did not stand out as being exceptional. He was a quiet, reticent boy who wanted to do his work and then go home. That suited Galleozzie fine.

'People respected my father,' Martyn said. 'He didn't give a shit and if something had to be said then he'd say it. He didn't care about the consequences. He had no favourites. You know, I'm his son and there was a show one night in the Swansea Road club when he went in the other boy's corner. I lost the fight and my father was laughing. He was a hard man, but he loved John.'

People turned to boxing for a release. It was, like Farr said, a lesser evil, or, as Martyn Galleozzie maintains, a choice born from desperation.

'Boxers were born out of adversity, poverty to a certain degree,' he said.

These were mean streets for tough people. There was the misery of the mines, of Aberfan, of a lack of choice and dwindling optimism.

'It was dangerous in the mines but that didn't enter your head,' Dick Owens said. 'There might be a fall and someone might get killed, but you never imagined it would happen to you. You just shoved it away, like boxing.'

The Owens had moved to the estate in the late 1950s, a few years after it had been built. They lived in a house with a long garden, over which the boys would hurdle and play in the woods. Then, in 1962, they moved up a street for an extra bedroom. The green that fronted the new home became the scene of free-for-all football matches.

'It was 30-a-side and there weren't many rules,' Kelvin said. 'John was a defender and I fancied myself as a goalkeeper. Occasionally the nurse's car would draw up and I would have to run inside, drop my trousers and she would stick a needle in my backside for my asthma. Then I'd go back out and we'd carry on. They were brutal affairs.'

John was a Manchester United fan while Kelvin supported Leeds.

'They would have terrible rows about football,' their father said.

Later the focus would turn to music. John's favourite band was Slade, the amalgam of sideburns, gargled Black Country vocals and bizarre millinery, while Kelvin liked David Bowie.

'He used to say Bowie looked like a girl,' Kelvin recalled.

There was great excitement when the Owens became the proud possessors of the first television set in their street. That meant their house doubled as a local cinema and there would often be lines of neighbourhood children sitting in front of the flickering box. Yet, more and more, it was not football, music or television that started to take up the boys' time, but boxing. And so they moved the furniture and broke the lampshades, and Dick filled an old army bag with sand. Edith hoped they would grow out of it, while Marilyn's all-action windmill offence taught the boys to move fast.

'She really thought she was Cassius Clay,' Vivian said of his sister. 'She thought she was better than all of us.'

All five boys stayed with boxing for varying lengths of time, but not all lasted the course. The rebel yell of adolescence often tempts boys from the gym, and Dilwyn, the youngest, would quit early. 'I'm too pretty to get knocked around,' he said. 'Bugger boxing.' The others took longer to turn their back on the squared circle, but John's passion for it never wavered.

In those early days they would all attend the annual Welsh schoolboy championships. Hundreds of boys would line up and the weighing would start at 9 a.m. A scratched sign bearing the words 'NO GAMBLING OR SWEARING' hung in the hallway. It was an arduous process and matches would be made, putatively on weight and experience, but often in a more arbitrary fashion as officials groaned at the queue snaking towards them like a pimpled python.

'We always packed food and tea because there were no cafés on the road in Wales, and some of the boys would be starving,' Dick said. 'We'd leave at the crack of dawn and the fights might not be over until the early hours of the next morning.'

What happened at one of these scrambled events led John to a mountain-top epiphany. By the age of ten he had developed some rudimentary ringcraft and already had the boundless energy that would be his signature in the professional ranks. His punches were light but his effort huge. For John the champion- ships at Cymmer Afan were more than a day out. He was in it to win it, and, when the verdict went against him, he was disconsolate. He stormed from the ring and marched to the dressing room, the squeak of boots on canvas and the soft thud of leather on flesh tapping away in the background. Dick had never seen his son react in such a manner. His bottom lip quivered and he sunk his head deep into his shoulders.

'Never mind, John,' Billy Punchy said in his warm brogue. He patted him on the head and John bristled. 'You forgot your certificate,' Billy added. 'I'll get it.'

'Not bothered,' John spat sulkily.

Dick wiped his hands on a towel and studied the scene. Perhaps he realized it was a pivotal moment, if not in a career, then in the maturing of a child. Billy Punchy returned from the pandemonium of the hall and handed the certificate to John, but the boy snatched it and threw it away.

'I told you, I don't want any loser's certificate,' he groused.

On the way home the other boys talked excitedly about their own bouts, bragging of any success and blaming others for their failings. John was quiet. There was nothing unusual in that, but his father knew this was driven by more than his natural inclination.

'I've decided,' John said.

His father did not flinch as he focussed on the road.

'I've finished with boxing.'

The other boys fell silent as the swish of the windscreen wipers and the soft punches of the night's rain sounded the passing bells to another fallen boxer.

Sunday departed with John having spent much of it in his room. 'Don't say anything to him,' Dick told his wife. He hoped that John would come to his senses and realize his petulance was misplaced. Monday arrived and Vivian and Kelvin got their training bags from beneath the stairs.

'You coming, John?' Vivian shouted up the stairs.

The silence gave him his answer. He shrugged his shoulders and wandered out.

Dick had endured enough. He looked at the multicoloured Romanian eggcups on the shelf. They were the first things his son had won from boxing. He rubbed a thumb over a tiny silver cup no bigger than three inches, and put it back on the shelf. He called John downstairs and told him they were going for a walk up the mountain.

Surveying the view from the top, Dick considered how beautiful this desperate land could be. Everything was huge. The height, the depth, the slag heaps, the towering brick turrets of the mines. It was a big place for a little boy to be heard.

'It's not fair, Dad,' John sighed. 'I won that fight. Fair and square. They gave it to the wrong boy.'

Dick chose his words carefully. He had toyed with them for most of the past day.

'Look, son, I think you won the fight, too, but you behaved very badly. In life we would all like to be winners, but someone has to lose. You have to learn to lose like a gentleman because everyone gets bad decisions. That's life.'

John stared across the valley. Even the smoke from the chimneys was suspended up here, as if someone had just pressed a pause button.

'You must never show emotion in or out of the ring,' his father continued. 'If you have to do that then it is better to do it when we are alone together.'

John did not answer and the walk down the mountain was completed in silence. On Wednesday he went to the cupboard beneath the stairs and pulled out his bag. He went back to the gym and did not stop training for the next fourteen years.

ROUND ONE

The seconds after the bell are debunkers. The hype, the glory and the vitriol are suspended. The current of moving heads is stilled. Managers talk, promoters shout and journalists write, but in the midst of the baloney and the phoney war, there are only two people. When the bell rings, the cast is broken and the boxers emerge. It is man versus man, alone in their own world in front of 10,000 rancorous voyeurs.

The preamble had been subdued. Lupe Pintor was not a showman. He boxed because he had to. Once it had been to stop people stealing his ice, and now it was to plot a course to a better life. Except he wasn't thinking that. He just thought about hitting and not getting hit, fixed on the dirty, black hardness of the moment. This was not a show to be trivialized by gold lamé gowns and grandiose entrances. These were his people and he was a transmitter for their angst. He knew the Mexicans wanted a show of courage, hearts on sleeves to be battered and bruised to the brink of horror, and Pintor could do this. It was his gift from the gods and his gift to the weak.

Johnny Owen felt nervous. Although his entourage would talk of his unflappable nature, he felt the same nerves that have afflicted every man who has ever stepped inside a ring. To get into the Olympic the fighters had to walk up a flight of stairs and then drop down into the auditorium. For a brief moment it was like being a bystander at your own party. All of this was for you – the packed aisles, the queues for beer, the boil and bubble of expectation. Some of the crowd had seen Owen before he had got to the top and they had gone for him. On reaching the summit, he bounced up and down and raised a hand in the air.

'I was a very proud man,' Dick Owens said. 'Little did I know that within the next hour I would be a very sad man and my whole world would collapse around me.'

There was no premeditated stare-down. This is the moment when the referee brings the fighters together and the weeks of training and trash-talking are moulded into a single point-blank glare. It is a psychological test of will. Look, don't blink. It is the last chance to score a mental point before the rack and ruin of physical torture takes over. The combatants tonight were silent.

In the commentary seats, the Americans were ready. Tom Kelly had called hundreds of fights, while Danny 'Little Red' Lopez was a former world featherweight champion. Allan Malamud, the sports editor of the *LA Herald-Examiner*, completed the trio. They talked about Owen's physique and checked the microphone. It was time.

Marty Denkin, the referee, calls Lupe Pintor and Johnny Owen to the centre of the ring, spoke Kelly, the lead. *Johnny Owen has heard all the thin funny-men jokes you can think of, but they say he's a lot tougher than he looks, not to be taken lightly.* Was that another joke? *His big problem will be to withstand the body shots that you know will come his way from Pintor. Denkin is the third man in the ring and we're ready to go for the WBC world bantamweight title. Scheduled for fifteen. Pintor is a decisive betting favourite at ringside.*

Marty Denkin loved the Olympic. This simple box rising into the LA smog was a mecca. The word Grand, painted on the exterior in red paint, was a reflection of size rather than elegance. This was a bruising, ugly architectural leviathan. Opened in 1924, hopefuls and no-hopes, greats and gangsters, film stars and fading stars had all passed through its doors. It was a hulking mess of pitiless concrete, the backdrop to films such as *Requiem for a Heavyweight* and *Rocky*. Looks, as would be proved in its ring tonight, can be deceptive, though, and to Denkin the Olympic was one of the great boxing venues.

'Your ambition was to get a four-rounder at the Olympic,' he said. 'Then a ten-rounder. Then a title fight. Like they say in the Mob, if you got the Olympic you were a made man. You know, the fans in that place didn't like anyone coming in the way of their excitement.'

Denkin put his head between the fighters in his care and spoke loudly in his New York tone.

'I respect you for getting in the ring, but respect is a two-way street and you respect me by listening to my words. Respect the rules. If I see a rabbit-punch I'll warn you. Do it again I'll deduct a point. Foul consistently and I'll disqualify you. Now let's all do our job.'

Owen and Pintor touched gloves and the Welshman shrugged the corners of his mouth by way of acknowledgement. He had moved his eyes between the floor and Pintor's face during Denkin's brief. He had bowed gently to each corner of the cauldron and had been consumed by boos.

The bell sounded. An alarm bell. A clarion call. And so it began.

The first exchange of blows is a show of ego. Who has the power and the advantage? Who has the passion and the controlled fury?

Pintor with a left. Owen in red trunks with the stripe, Pintor in white. Owen's right on top of Pintor now. He's beginning to land some good shots. Owen with that long left hand, then a right, an uppercut. Pretty busy round.

Owen ducked down with his hands covering his face. His tactic was to get inside and force Pintor backwards. It could look ungainly, given the height difference, but it worked, Pintor's stocky legs unhinging and his feet shuffling to the ropes. When he felt their touch on his swarthy back, he unleashed a mighty left hook to the body. Those at ringside winced. Pintor struck again. He reasoned that a frame like Owen's could not deal with his wrecking balls. Spotlights flashed. Sounds echoed in the fighters' heads. Time and motion stopped for their dance. Pintor caught Owen squarely on the jaw, but he responded immediately and wobbled the flesh on the Mexican's cheek. The roar softened to a far-off monotone.

You wonder where Owen gets any strength. He is atrociously thin, but he's obviously very tough. He's taken some pretty good shots to the body already in this round and it's been a busy round for both of these men. Oh, a great shot to the liver, but Owen did not seem to mind at all. 1.45 to go in round one.

Johnny Owen was already earning respect and leaving egg on the faces of those who had succumbed to easy metaphors. Pintor's tall mat of black hair was sending eddies of sweat into his eyes. They were eyes that recalled the way Jack London, the novelist and boxing aficionado, had described Felipe Rivera, the hero of *The Mexican*, his story of a deathly, slender boy who fights with his fists to pay for guns for the Revolution. Savage as a wild tiger's. Pitiless as steel.

Owen's armour was fashioned from accuracy. He had power, as his sparring partners and opponents would testify, but he lacked Pintor's mighty blow, the punch that he could summon up from the threshold of humiliation to save himself. It was, as Angelo Dundee, Ali's trainer, had said when asked to fathom the depths within these men, as if they had an 'innate reservoir' from which they drew something new. 'Normal people just don't have this,' Dundee said.

It did not surprise Dick Owens or Dai Gardiner to see Owen smite Pintor with a flurry of left jabs. They knew it was a solid punch, firm and frequent. Owen was encouraged and pressed Pintor, who responded by sending lefts to the body and jaw. He used his lack of inches to hit home with an uppercut, breaching Owen's defence and making his head rock momentarily backwards.

The British writers who are here to cover this fight, and they are considerable in number, say this is probably the biggest fight this man will ever have. He's almost a prophet without honour in his own country, gets very little headlines, almost no press. This would be the biggest thing that has ever happened to him. Pintor with a good left to the body, but Owen again took that and came back with one of his own.

The first three minutes debunked the myths. It was Johnny Owen who was the spirit of the revolution, unpicking every snigger with his strength and skill. The bell sounded. It was his round.

3

FIRE AND ICE

The veins of Mexico have been rupturing since the time of the Aztecs. When these inveterate warriors won a battle in the early fourteenth century, they celebrated by sending their paymaster eight thousand human ears as a token of their efficiency. Coxcox, the ruler of Culhuacan, was so delighted with his memento mori that he consented to his daughter being made an Aztec goddess. Life was sweet and the leader and his mercenaries enjoyed mutual affection, right up until the night Coxcox attended a banquet held in his honour and noticed a dancer performing in the flayed skin of his daughter. Unfortunately, she had been killed to appease Huizilopochtli, the god with the insatiable blood lust.

Human sacrifice, cannibalism and betrayal are consistent themes in Mexican history. The Flowery Wars of the fifteenth century were conducted with the principal aim of securing enough prisoners to murder in the name of Huizilopochtli and thereby keep the sun in the sky. Over the course of four days in 1487, it is claimed that the Aztec king had twenty thousand people sacrificed as part of the dedication ceremony for a new temple. It was a hot summer.

It is this attitude to life that has so fascinated historians.

These were a people who were culturally and industrially sophisticated, and yet they believed there were thirteen heavens and nine hells. Warriors could be assured of a place in the heavenly firmament, but others would spend four years enduring a painful journey under the vast northern deserts before coming to the ninth layer of hell, where they vanished to be replaced by skeletons. The place of the skeleton in the iconography of Mexico endures. It is a symbol of a life lived badly and a lost soul. For some younger Mexicans it has little resonance and is akin to a voodoo charm, but for others it is a reminder to be true to oneself. All these years on, Kelvin Owens appreciates the mixed messages sent out when his brother marched into the Olympic Auditorium in 1980 with his trademark skeleton standard brandished proudly to the fore.

The arrival of Hernan Cortés in 1519 signalled the end of the Aztec dynasty, although it took two years of internecine warfare and relentless violence to consign it to the past. The Spanish desecrated the Aztec idols, raped a people's history and rode roughshod over indigenous beliefs to influence everything from language to architecture. Four centuries later the Mexican Revolution claimed another two million lives before it stuttered to an unsatisfactory conclusion in 1920.

In the years following it Mexico exhaled. It was restorative to breathe without being strangled by another battle cry and another lost cause. The population exploded as skyscrapers sprung up and the populace refrained from its tradition of self-mutilation. Yet the peace was rarely confident and the economic boom left the minions trailing in its wake. The poor were marginalized and pushed to the wastelands on the periphery. Shanty towns doubled and trebled in size, scorching the earth with their poverty. It was into this bewildering environment that Guadalupe Pintor was born on 13 April 1955.

The stories of Merthyr and Mexico City are linked by their violence. The homes of John Owens and Lupe Pintor were both built on blood and conflict, but the early lives of these two combatants were very different. Owens lived in a council house on an estate built on the side of a drizzle-damp hill, but it was a happy upbringing. The boyhood of Pintor, although he also came from a similarly sprawling family of five brothers and one sister, was more troubled.

When I met Lupe Pintor for the first time in 2003 I had no idea that his story was such a remarkable one. His life has been governed by the quirks of providence. His warmth and willingness to help with this book revealed an avuncular kinship, but occasionally the marble eyes would narrow and he would fix me with a look that went deep into the past. It was at those moments that I remembered the words of Vera from *The Mexican*: 'He has been through hell . . . no man could look like that who has not been through hell – and he is only a boy.'

The son of a gardener called Jose Guadalupe and a tradeswoman named Maria de Jesus, Lupe Pintor went through several layers of hell before he even made his teens. Stemming from the concept of machismo that has long permeated Mexican households, the old boxing adage that 'there ain't nothing tougher than a Mex' was planted in the seemingly bizarre need for Mexican men to show an exaggerated form of masculinity. This can be reflected in everything from reckless driving to extramarital affairs, but drinking is another outlet for the macho spirit and it is easy to appreciate the sobering hurt behind Pintor's words.

'My father was never a good friend to me,' he said. 'He was not like a father at all. We would argue and he was not nice to my mother. She left when I was very small and so I lived with my father. That was not a good time because he never cared for me. I lived and grew up in a house where fear paid us a daily, and sometimes hourly, visit. From that viewpoint, it's easy to say that this was the beginning of my fighting life. However, in the ring it's a one-on-one situation where your adversary weighs roughly the same amount and is probably about the same height, so I don't think it influenced my career choice. What I can say about the beatings handed out by my father to my brothers and myself is that I don't think a word exists to describe the level of terror we lived in. What he did to us was inhumane, ferocious and unforgivable.

'I looked after myself from the age of five and, when I was eight, I ran away from home. I lived on the street for about a year. I was looking for my mother and in some ways it was great. I would sleep in the market and had a little place of my own. I was given a blanket and I now look back at that as a really happy time. Nobody tried to attack me on the streets and I ate fantastically well, or at least it seemed that way at the time. When you have so little, every time you have a meal it is a feast fit for a king.'

Pintor was lucky. Scores of street children disappeared in Mexico City each year. Some were murdered, while others died from the plethora of diseases that festered on the filthy streets and in the makeshift homes in rancid drains and ventilation shafts. Yet the young Pintor was a resourceful boy who was merely happy to be free of his father's vacillating moods. 'I was totally independent and that was such a big thing for me.' One older man took him under his wing and gave him some money to buy shoe-shining equipment. 'I was cleaning shoes for men and I would carry ladies' shopping from the market. I would do anything to make money and they would give me tips. I had no parents telling me what to do and there was a freedom to it. To grow up without parents is a double-edged sword. Sometimes you need them there to say "go for it" and to give you that strength and courage. But if you don't have that, you learn from yourself. It means that, when life becomes difficult, you are prepared.'

One winter's day Pintor rose early, as usual. He joked with some of the other street boys. One of them was shivering and his lips were tinged with a blueness. They wrapped him in another blanket and trusted he would get better. Pintor had business to attend to as he had heard that his mother was living close by on the south side of the city, and so he continued on his search. Later that afternoon he found her, and the emotion of that reunion, and of having accomplished a journey so fraught with dangers, still causes his eyes to dull and dip.

'I was happy on the street. I would never have gone back, but my father tracked me down and came and got me. He found me and dragged me home. I didn't want to go, because he had never cared for me, but I had no choice. I didn't consider him my father. He used to beat me a lot after that. There were many, many beatings.'

The Pintors lived in Cuajimalpa, some twenty miles to the south-west of the District Federal. Now it is a built-up area, all rotting iron, scabrous brickwork and crumbling roads. Then it was a thinly populated village surrounded by forests and mountains. Like most boys his age, the young Pintor found himself selling something to make a crust. His father tended to his gardens and ran a tiny store, but that brought in little money and the frustration and failure polluted their home life.

In the stifling, smoked-throat heat, everyone needed ice. Sometimes Pintor's need differed from the norm and he would use it to soothe his own welts and bruises, but he did not like to waste it and would travel around the shops and homes selling.

'Everyone got to know me from my deliveries,' he said. 'It

was a good little business. But then people started to steal from me. The ice was all I had so I could not let that go on. That is why I started to fight.'

There were other reasons too. One night, when he was only eight, Pintor returned home from a day of selling. The winter nights were cold in Cuajimalpa and Pintor shivered. There was no electricity or drains and a putrid stench spread through the dark. Pintor checked the mayonnaise jar filled with marbles that was his prized possession. He climbed into bed and nuzzled close to his brother, Francisco. Tired by the day, he drifted off to sleep. He cannot remember seeing the door burst open, but he felt the temperature drop. And then the sheets were pulled off and he was dragged out of bed. His first thought was for Francisco, even as he felt a hand dig into the back of his neck.

'Why my brother?' Pintor said. 'He was only a child. We were picked up by our fingers. Can you believe that? And we were hit with the back of a machete.'

It was a terrifying assault and one that scarred his brother for years. His father would say the beating taught his children a lesson, but all it did was warp them. That night, for the young peddler already used to defending his wares against opportunist thieves, constituted his own initiation. He had already taken more punishment than anyone should, but now he fought back.

'I found out that, not only was I good at it, but I liked using my fists,' he said.

He did not know it, but he had started his journey along an inexorable road that would lead him to Johnny Owen.

The accident happened during the afternoon shift at the factory. Howard Winstone's job was to jab the button, and the huge press would thunder down on to the raw sheets of metal. Then he would remove the sheet and start again. But there was something wrong with the machine that day. Instead of staying in the safety position, it repeated and crashed down on to Howard's right hand. He cried out and the machine rumbled to a stop.

'Get me bloody out of here!' he yelled.

The fitters scurried around in panic as the colour drained from Howard's face.

'I was standing next to him when it happened,' Don James said. 'He was stuck in that machine for twenty minutes. Then an old man named Ieuan jumped on top of the machine. "Out of my way," he shouted and he undid the bolts and the press lifted back up. They had to cut the tips of his fingers off.

'He was out of the game for eight months. In between, a gang of us were still boxing at the gym and we became youth champions. Howard would spend his time up at the smallholding his father had. There were pigs and chickens there and a big bag of dirt hung from the roof as a makeshift punchbag.

'I'd become the kingpin of the gym while he was away, but then Howard came back. We never had to look for each other, us. When we boxed we fucking boxed. They used to come from the pubs to watch us spar.'

James and Winstone were close friends and showed promise. Eddie Thomas, the former British, European and Empire champion, began training them and let them know he had a strict code of ethics. He wanted his boys to be boxers not brawlers.

'Street-fighting was part of life,' James said. 'It was the culture. You had the gypsy environment – people coming from North Wales and Liverpool, the Italians, the Irish and the Poles. It was a right mix. In those old days in the 1930s, you'd see the boss of one street fighting the boss of the next, the boss of one town fighting the boss of the next. But Eddie didn't want us street-fighting.'

James tells the story of how he and Winstone became embroiled in a row with a man one day after he barged into their car. Winstone asked for an apology and the man refused. In an instant the man was lying on the ground with a bloody nose, whereupon there was a screech of burning tyres and a car came to a stop six inches from his head. Eddie Thomas emerged with a thunderous face and told the duo he did not want to see them in his gym again. 'He forgave us eventually,' James said.

At Thomas's gym, boys would turn up wearing trousers with patches and boots with nails stuck into the soles. This was their outlet. Thomas had an eye for talent and, though he was the sort of man who would call a spade a spade and then beat you over the head with it, he possessed a large heart.

'He loved singing and used to be in choirs,' James said. 'He was quite a guy. They were hard old days and that gym was our only education, but, by God, Eddie was one of the finest teachers in the world.'

He taught a lot of good boys, but Winstone was the best. He made a mockery of his three missing digits by going unbeaten in his first thirty-four professional fights. By that time, he had already won a gold medal at the 1958 Commonwealth Games. Seven years later Merthyr and Mexico clashed for the first time at Earls Court in London.

The depressed pocket of South Wales pulsed with expectation. Winstone was at the peak of his powers, but even the reason of those who loved him, the men who paid half-a-crown to watch his sparring sessions and drank in the fourteen pubs on the street where he grew up, suggested he might struggle to beat Vicente Saldivar, the world featherweight champion.

Winstone gave it his all and the bond was formed. The two men boxed, wrestled and sweated until they merged. At the end, though strangers, they knew each other intimately. Saldivar was the winner. Even the half-a-crown brigade, the jug-and-bottle crew and the journalists who willed him to defiance, knew. His wife soothed his hurt by telling him he had won, but Winstone arched an eyebrow and told the dressing room: 'That's women for you.'

It did not end there. Two years later, a rematch was set. Saldivar had only fought three times in the interim, all at home in Mexico City, but his reputation had been more active. He was a hero in his homeland and knew he had a long way to fall when he travelled to the Ninian Park football ground in Cardiff. The crowd bayed, not for blood, but for sense. 'Don't fight', they yelled at Winstone, imploring him to use his craft rather than his brawn. Saldivar was no 'banger', but he had a rugged artistry that suited toe-to-toe exchanges. For ten rounds Winstone boxed close to his peak, but then the rug was pulled from beneath his feet and the canvas rushed towards him. It was like being immersed in black water. His face contorted with effort, Saldivar pummelled Winstone against the ropes. They sagged with what was almost a dead weight. Yet still Winstone worked the jab, the rapier that had carved his name into every barroom in Wales. At the end Wally Thom, the referee, raised Saldivar's arm. He had given it to the champion by half a point. The stadium erupted. The disputed verdict meant a third fight was hastily arranged for four months later at the Aztec Stadium in Mexico.

Some who had witnessed the first two fights felt Winstone's chance had gone. His friend Heddwyn Taylor thought so.

'The one argument I always had with Eddie Thomas was why did he take Howard to Mexico for the third fight,' he said.

'If he couldn't get a decision here, he wasn't going to get one there. In the end Saldivar and Winstone finished each other off.'

Winstone was still in excellent condition, but the missing three fingertips ultimately blighted his prospects.

'People forget Howard fought his entire career with one hand,' James said.

He was still too good for most, but Saldivar stopped him with a cut eye in the twelfth round on 14 October 1967. The pair had brutalized each other for almost forty-two rounds of pulsating emotion. They were spent. Saldivar took the microphone and announced his retirement, while the Welsh Wizard went on to take the world title from Mitsunori Seki, a Japanese fighter who had once taken Saldivar the distance but who was never in the Mexican's class.

Following Winstone's retirement, boxing in the valleys struggled to find another hero.

'It went into the doldrums after Howard,' Taylor said. 'The sport went downhill. Although there were plenty of good fighters – people like Billy Vivian, Johnny Wall and Martyn Galleozzie – there was no one who captured the imagination like Howard. The place was crying out for someone. We needed another Winstone. And then along came Johnny.'

Winstone was sixty-one when he died in October 2000. Saldivar, who like so many fighters came out of retirement to sully his reputation and record, had a fatal heart attack in 1985. He was just forty-two. On his last fight night, some twelve years beforehand, he had been humiliated and knocked out by a man named Eder Jofre in a Brazilian backwater.

That was the end of one dream, and Mexico mourned the passing of an icon into ordinariness. Just as John Owens was silently forming a timeline to Winstone and Jimmy Wilde, a similar sort of alchemy was happening in Mexico City. Flushed with ambition and desire, Lupe Pintor pounded the streets and thought about emulating the great Vicente Saldivar.

ROUND TWO

At the first break there was only calm. Cuyo Hernandez, the gnarled manager of Pintor, leant through the ropes and offered some advice, but he had seen this in the past. Pintor was a self-confessed slow starter. It was as if Pintor, despite his record of thirty-two knockouts, relished the long haul, the sadomasochism of boxing. Johnny Owen was the same. He could run for ever. When Merthyr was still muted by the still of early morning, Owen would be out, pounding the streets, yard after yard, mile after mile, revitalizing his own innate reservoir with every uphill step, every breath blowing smoke rings amid the fiery furnaces. Willie Pastrano, the former light-heavyweight champion from the 1960s, said road work was hell on earth. He said he craved a pill that gave you the benefit of five miles without the agony. But five miles was nothing to Owen. He did nine miles a day even when he was not in training. Staying still was the bitterest pill and so he was always running.

There was quiet satisfaction in Owen's corner at their man's upbeat, grinding start. This was the way to beat Pintor, to box him until the sharpness had gone, the sum of the conflict more debilitating than the individual blows. Owen was relaxed, impassive. He did not think in those moments of Dilwyn, his kid brother, who was sleeping off the drinks he had downed to celebrate his nineteenth birthday. He did not pause to consider his mother, Edith, back home in Merthyr. This time she would find out the result early because they had installed a telephone in the hallway of their bulging council house. No longer would she have to don her coat, pull it tight around her and battle the wind, the hill and her chattering thoughts to make the public phone box. This time the call would come to her.

You're looking into the corner of the bantamweight champion, Lupe Pintor, from Mexico, a record of forty-one and seven, thirty-two knockouts, took the title away from Carlos Zarate in Las Vegas. There's Cuyo Hernandez, his manager, weighing in with the instructions.

The first exchange of blows in any round has an importance that goes beyond the physical. Hitting first is a statement of intent, to both your opponent and the judges. Boxing suffers from being a subjective sport, decided by ringside officials when the two men cannot deconstruct each other's skills to the point of semi-consciousness, but judges have different checklists and are governed by an often whimsical philosophy. They have also been corrupted by hype, showboating and backhanders, but they generally like their boxers to be aggressors. To take the initiative and show no fear. That is the way to flatten out the inconsistencies in the most wandering mind.

So Owen started with five unreturned jabs. Then they were locked together, Owen crouching and resting the right side of his head on Pintor's left. All the time he was throwing blows. Irritating short lefts followed by complementary rights.

Johnny Owen, the skeleton from Merthyr, Wales. That's a good right hand from Pintor, but Owen just keeps throwing leather. Two minutes remaining in round number two and Owen is right on top of Pintor, the champion. He's willing to mix it up inside and give Pintor all the action he wants.

Every time Pintor responded with showier, longer punches, the noise level grew. Pintor had power, no doubt, but Owen had been in with good men and had never been knocked down. Not once, not since the front room. And that had given rise to a sense of invincibility. This most devilish, crucifying sport is also the most psychological. If there was not much of him, as the Americans had so loved to joke over the last couple of weeks, every ounce was bursting with health.

Byron Board was happy. 'Get in close and they can't hurt you,' he said. 'That's the way, Johnny.' The landlord of the Ruperra Arms in

New Tredegar, he was Owen's greatest fan. He appreciated his talent, but loved his manner even more. It was rare to find someone so honest and pure. Everyone had a vice or an unkind word or a history, but Owen was extraordinary. Board had carried the skeleton standard into the ring and his pride overcame his shock at their treatment at the hands of 'the wetbacks'. He watched Owen tie up Pintor inside and smiled.

Allan Malamud had given the first round to Owen but wondered if he could truly hurt Pintor. *But if he keeps this up for ten rounds or so it could have a very telling effect*, Tom Kelly countered. He was right. Owen was not frightening Pintor with single scarlet explosions, but he was hurting him all right, as anyone at ringside witnessing the straight jab and the left-right combinations contorting the Mexican's face, morphing it into deformity before it slipped back into shape, could tell.

For all his slim stature, Owen keeps on top of his man and continues to throw leather. Pintor is trying to pick him off with something sharp and devastating inside, but Owen won't let him off the ropes. Johnny Owen stays right on top of him, in front of him, and it's a swarming, bruising type of fight. Owen looks like a stiff breeze would blow him straight into the English Channel but, boy, is he tough. Fourteen seconds remaining in round two.

Thirteen, twelve, eleven, ten, nine . . .

With eight seconds left on the huge digital scoreboard, way up in the gods, Pintor enjoyed his best moments so far. During an infinitessimal break in Owen's pursuit, Pintor rocked his weight on to his left instep. His right foot, stretched out behind him, sprung off the canvas until only his toes touched the floor. Then, at lightning speed, he drove a right hand against Owen's chin. The natural reaction for Owen was to hit back, to attack to defend, but as he waved a right hand, Pintor was already striking with a left against his jaw.

Seven . . .

Still the exchange was not over and another right cannoned into Owen's face. Right, left, right. Punches marching to the rhythm of the fight. The wild right that had seen Pintor stir the air with his glove moments before had been a range-finder.

Good right hand by Pintor and a left, and Owen didn't even flinch.

Six minutes is nothing. People waste hours every day of their lives. But in boxing the seconds count. The commentator could not help himself and again referred to Owen as the skeleton from Merthyr. He spat the words so that Merthyr became Meth-er. Owen was evidently 'not used to body shots' because he was from 'over there in the England area'. What would Owen, the proud Welshman, have made of that billing? Nobody seemed to know where Johnny Owen was from, but they knew what he was about after six minutes of a swarming, bruising type of fight.

4

THE MICE ARE IN

The boys walked through the haze of a smoking room that chimed with the sound of beer glasses. Men with flat caps and pockmarked ties placed dominoes on wet tables. There were no women. Outside the infant drama of another Friday night was winding its course through the blackened streets. Inside, John and Kelvin Owens made their way through the lounge of the Labour Club, their bags slung loosely over shoulders.

'It's Little John,' said a shammy-faced man with the head of his bitter clinging to his lip. 'Give 'em one from me, Little John.'

At the bottom of the stairs stood Charlie Rumble with his biscuit tin. He rattled it and other passing boys dug their hands into clammy pockets and threw in some coins. It cost sixpence a week to use the upstairs gym. Rumble smiled affectionately at Little John and his brother. He cast a cursory eye around the club, winked and nodded. The brothers passed through with their money safe in their pockets. Later, they would head to the Arcade Café and spend their subs on cream cakes. If they walked home and kept their bus fare they might even be able to afford a chocolate one.

Rumble smiled to himself. They were nice kids and so very small. Johnny was like Tiny Tim, as someone would write many years later. The skinniest limbs this side of an ostrich farm. The Bionic Bantam.

In the gym that evening, there was the usual hub of excitement. Boys were getting changed, issuing boasts, telling jokes. Danny Galleozzie was monitoring his minions when the Owens walked in with their duffle coats neatly fastened.

'The mice are in, boys. The mice are in.'

Already, the sounds of an amateur boxing gym were enlivening the scene. While the men drank and inhaled downstairs, health and hopes ringed the air in the attic, the purifying tap of the rope and the thud and sigh of the heavy bag echoing through the windows.

Those early years saw schoolboy boxers move clubs regularly as gyms closed or peers told them of greener grass. The Owens were no different. They had started in the hut before moving on to the old room above the smoke-addled Merthyr Labour Club. Because of the building's legal history, dating back to 1150, the gym was named Court House ABC. Alongside Galleozzie and Billy Davies, Dick Owens also started to take an active role in training.

Martyn Galleozzie does not remember John being outstanding in those early days.

'Everyone was small back then,' he said. 'When I started I was only eight and I weighed four and a half stone. I left school at six stone ten. There were no giants in the gym so John wasn't particularly unusual in that. He was different because of his features. We were all developed, but John never changed. He always looked like a boy.'

Fights were made and the Court House gym flourished. As well as John, Vivian, Kelvin and Dilwyn, the roster of fighters included Billy Vivian, an enduring friend. The new boxing ring, donated by the Guest Keen Ironworks on Ivor Street, sagged and sprung with optimism. The burgeoning reputation of Court House made it more difficult to get fights, and so a happy troupe of boys overloaded a minibus and spent seven hours being driven to Portsmouth one night.

'High Wycombe, Wolverhampton, Coventry, we'd go where the shows were,' Galleozzie said. 'Every week and every weight.'

The highlight of the year was the Welsh amateur championship.

'Every year you'd go to them and every year you had to be seven pounds heavier than the year before,' Galleozzie said. 'John never was. He was always more or less the same. We'd end up feeding him all the way down on the coach, plying him with biscuits and cakes, anything to try to boost his size. One year my mother actually sewed some lead into the lining of his shorts.'

In 1973 Galleozzie turned professional. One March night, he finished his shift on the building site and caught the train to London. He travelled across the sprawling metropolis until he came to the Royal Albert Hall. This was a different world from the ingrained grime of Court House. He changed, limbered up and waited. His hands were carefully bound and he slipped on the gloves, tapping them together. Vernon Sollas was a hard Scot from Edinburgh who would become a British champion. He was preparing himself in another room: another mindset, another epicentre. Sollas knocked Galleozzie out in the seventh round. The beating was chosen as fight of the week on *Grandstand*. Galleozzie collected his £120 purse and caught the late train home at 4 a.m. He bathed his face and did not go to bed. He couldn't afford another day off.

Around the same time, John Owens moved to Hoover's ABC, run by Don James and Idris Sutton.

Boxing had coursed through the blood of Sutton since he

was a nine-year-old ferrying seven pints of milk to the big house where Eddie and Hughie Thomas lived. It was a large order, but the boxers were thirsty men, in need of fuel to fire their own dreams. Eddie was to become a champion and a legend in Merthyr, immortalized in bronze on the road down to the town, loved for his generosity, idolized for his mercilessness. He needed his milk.

Sutton left his round to plunder the levels. The work was hard but the dangers were suppressed by pragmatic minds, and the wages were good. Toiling at the coalface for eight hours, the dust blackening fingers and daubing warpaint on faces, was a perilous way to live, but the conditions unearthed a camaraderie most people never experienced. Like boxing, the rewards made it a risk worth taking.

He was still a teenager when he had an accident while doing another job in the Star Supplies grocery store. Stationed on the cooked meat slicing machine, Sutton's hand got caught between the blade and the guard. It was pulled in and two fingers were severed. He was taken to the hospital, while the owner cleaned the machine with a cloth and soap, and had his mangled digits sewn back on. A week later gangrene had set in and he was forced to have one amputated. His interest in the job waned after that.

Maybe it was a subconscious anger at his misfortune or, more likely, it was down to boredom and necessity, but like so many boys in Merthyr, Sutton then began fighting in earnest. When he was a boy, the showgrounds were still dotted with boxing booths. You had to be able to take care of yourself to get the prize on offer and, if you showed any potential, somebody would say something and word would spread. This was the milk of Merthyr's kindness. Billy Evans was Sutton's first sagacious guide and his first bout was against Billy's son,

Georgie. The younger Evans was stronger and more skilled and knocked seven bells out of Sutton, but he was still standing at the end – beaten, but not humiliated. Billy Evans patted his son's back and looked at Sutton, his face despoiled by failure and his chest heaving with broken breaths.

'You'll be all right, kid.'

He got to know Howard Winstone at the gym and could empathize when his hand was also crumpled in a mechanical accident. Sutton knew how hard it must be for Winstone to close his fist properly. Sutton compensated by clenching his hand in a certain way to keep the stump protected.

After the Star Supplies, Sutton got another job, but he lost it when the foreman called him 'a bastard' and he responded by clouting him with the egg bucket. When the foreman got up, Sutton's father hit him again. 'My father never boxed because he only had one arm,' he recalled. 'But by God he could hit with the other.' Eight months of brawling followed before Sutton met his father one night and told him he was leaving the next morning to join the army.

The army was good to Sutton. Friends were made, respect instilled, the rough edges polished. Instead of fighting on the streets, he now boxed. He even got slung in jail for it when his refusal to play hockey because of its dangers irked the manicured army officer sitting behind the desk.

'But you box,' he muttered, his eyes remaining on his desk.

'Yes, sir,' Sutton said. 'But they don't have pucks in boxing.'

He got hurt in Hong Kong. The two sergeants in his corner assured him he was doing well, but the nausea and rib-ache told him otherwise. In the third round, Sutton took a big punch but survived. A second punch was too much, though, and 'the lights went out'. It was a bruising, bemusing game, but Sutton loved it and became the army champion in Hong Kong when he defied a broken hand to defeat a Gurkha. Sure, his hand throbbed in agony and his face was a dark balloon, but it was worth it.

He stopped when he broke his nose three times in six weeks, and was handed the task of coaching the regimental boxing team. It was that job that made him realize he could remain involved with the sport he loved by handing down his knowledge and experience. By 1970, Sutton had left the regular army and taken a job at the Hoover factory. James, the boyhood friend of Winstone and a former amateur champion, also worked there as a security fireman and they formed the Hoover ABC, with the financial backing of their bosses. Together with Owens's father, these two men played pivotal roles in honing John Owen's talents.

Sutton and James knew the people who trotted through the gym's doors and they were inevitably drawn to the odd-looking youth on the periphery. Sutton used to call him Mr Spock because of his protruding ears.

'There was more meat on a crisp than on Johnny,' he said.

James was just as quick with his tongue. 'He was never a big man, so imagine him as a schoolboy,' he said. 'He was like a sparrow.'

They set about growing their gym and used all their knowledge of boxing and life to do so.

'Johnny came to us from a gym where the only way to fight was to go forward,' James said. 'The people from that gym, Martyn Galleozzie, Les Pickett and the rest, were all the same. But the first thing Eddie Thomas always told us was to learn the corners. Marry the corners. Get in them and get to know them as much as you possibly can. When you get a man who is bigger than you, put your left leg in, turn him and walk away. You box and you keep your hands up at all times.

'I taught Johnny the Eddie Thomas style. Double left jab, left hook, right hand, one, two, three four. They were the basics. If you learnt them and mastered them, you were going to make one good fighter.'

Sutton was the self-styled master of the wind-up, and, inside the ring, he would abuse John.

'Is that all you've got?' he would grin. 'Powder-puff stuff. You can't punch. You can't hurt me. You're just pussy-footing around.'

It was basic psychology, a way of tapping into John's talent by stirring up his aggression. A naturally peaceful boy, he needed provoking into using the full range of his skills, and Sutton knew it.

'People would say he couldn't punch,' he said. 'But if you did four or five rounds' sparring with him, you knew he could punch all right. He hurt me and he hurt a lot of others.'

It was the hurting that meant Edith Owens could never be comfortable with her son's new passion. The mother who likes to see her son fight is rare, and she never watched John box. Once, during the early amateur days, she had agreed to do the food at a local boxing contest; as well as being thirsty, boxers were always hungry. John and Kelvin had long learnt how to take advantage of the situation, one boy having a meal and then passing his ticket to his brother, who would go back for more. 'Have you been boxing, son?' a man would say. 'Oh, yes, sir,' came the innocent reply.

As Edith handed out steaming plates, the boy whom John had recently beaten shuffled his way down the line. His nose was bleeding and his eyes had swelled up. Edith felt a natural pity and later rounded on her son for his actions.

'She gave John a right row for it,' his father recalled.

That incident settled things. As far as Edith was concerned, boxing was callous and cruel. She was similarly upset when John claimed he had a black eye.

'There was nothing there, but he kept looking in the mirror,' Dick explained.

Though she was proud of her son's achievements, nothing that happened after that day in the food queue would change her mind.

She was happier when Kelvin won a place at grammar school. It was a chance to gain a good education and win a safer way out of the underbelly, and also another sign that the family unit was growing and diverging. Now that they were older, the house seemed smaller, so Phillip went to live with Edith's parents while Vivian spent a lot of time with his paternal grandparents. John and Kelvin remained tight, though, a bond that was underscored when they were both selected to fight for Wales against the Midlands.

Dick had never seen John as nervous as he was on that night. He patrolled the arena 'like a cat on a tin roof' as he waited for his brother to make his bow. A light flyweight, Kelvin was due on before his brother and hoped the adrenaline would make up for a few nagging doubts.

'I knew I wasn't fit,' he said. 'He was a bit of a fighter and so I kept jabbing him, but I thought, "If he makes me work, I'm not going to last three rounds."'

At the back of the hall stood his brother, anxiously monitoring the fight and hollering instructions. For once, John's calm exterior was ruffled by a welter of conflicting emotions. John knew he should have been in the changing rooms, preparing for his own fight, and was spotted by Eddie Thomas.

'Stop screaming, son,' he told him. 'You're wasting your energy. You're on next and you shouldn't be out here. You should be thinking about your own fight.'

'That's my brother, sir,' John responded. 'I'm not missing this.'

Thomas considered the boy as he sauntered off to give more words of encouragement.

'Throw your right hand first, Kel!' he yelled, the veins on his neck forming a web of commitment. The younger brother heard the familiar voice and nodded inwardly. Normally, an orthodox boxer would not lead with his right for fear of being left wide open to the counter-attack, but trust won out and he did as he was told.

'I caught him a peach,' Kelvin remembered. 'I really hit him and he went flying back. John stayed there, despite what Eddie Thomas said, screaming his head off for the entire three rounds.'

Kelvin won his fight but John lost his. Afterwards, Thomas raised his eyebrows as if to say 'I told you so'.

John had no regrets. 'What did you expect?' he muttered. Loyalty was thicker than reason, blood was thicker than water. 'He's my brother.'

If Kelvin was the more gifted academically, his brother's dedication to boxing left him trailing. It was why John would not succumb to peer pressure and become embroiled in street fights on Saturday nights.

'I remember the Welsh and the Irish fighting every weekend down in Dowlais,' Sutton recalled. 'The next morning they'd be having a pint together and saying, "Good fight last night, eh, lads". They needed to let off steam. People used their hands and then took it up as a living. It's why boxing played such a major role in the life of that town.'

James claimed John was too clever to waste his talent for the fleeting fix of a street fight.

'He had too much savvy,' he said. 'He'd say, "If boys want to fight on the streets then let them do it," but he wanted none of it. He was so committed. I'd say, "Take it easy on the bags, you're sparring after," but he'd be hitting the bag as if there was no tomorrow. That's how he got so nimble and fit. It doesn't matter if you're the strongest guy in the world, if you can't hit a guy you aren't going to win.'

Kelvin also respected his brother's diplomacy. 'He would never get into fights,' he said. 'The only time anything happened like that was when I got into one with a boy at the end of our street. This boy had two brothers and one of them jumped on my back. John saw what was happening through a window and so he came tearing out and pulled him off. But then this boy's elder brother came out and started on John. There were five of us out there in the end. That was the only time John ever fought in the street.'

The image of a gentle, diffident figure, taunted for his angular features and scant physique, may seem at odds with his aggressive calling, but John Owens was a deeper figure than many journalists would later give him credit for. He never excelled at Georgetown Secondary Modern, quitting at sixteen to take a job as a machine operator at the Suko nuts and bolts factory, but he was clever enough to rise above the peer pressure. Against such a fermenting backdrop, where adolescent boasts and hastily hurled gauntlets were the harbingers of pumping fists, Owens dared to be different. It was a trait that should not be underestimated.

James believes he came of age one night in the gym at Hoover's. James loved to roll back the years and don the pads, and was teaching John to throw uppercuts under the watchful eye of his father. Nothing much was coming of the lesson. Then, as the last of his contemporaries made his way home and the gym echoed to James's voluble instructions, it clicked. John unsheathed a right uppercut that shot through James's guard and crashed against his jaw with a thud. His teeth cracked and his head pivoted.

'Dick!' James shouted when he recovered. 'Jesus, Dick! Did you see what the little bastard did to me?'

John's progression through the ranks was steady rather than spectacular. He fought a rising Charlie Magri in nearby Gurnos and lost. At that point the future was an impenetrable unknown and, plodding home from the moth-eaten club, John could not imagine that the Londoner would go on to become the world flyweight champion or that he, himself, would fight for the bantamweight crown.

'He never said, "I'm going to be the world champion" or anything like that,' his father said. There was no romantic pledge. 'I thought he'd do well, but I never thought he'd achieve what he did.'

In 1972 the Owens' chief concern was the present as the miners went on strike for the first time since 1926. For seven long weeks, coinciding with an Arctic winter, 135 pits closed in South Wales. A state of emergency was declared and Edward Heath's government was driven to reducing the working week to three days. During that perishing ordeal, John and Kelvin stood in the hallway of their home contemplating the three-foot snowdrift that barred their exit. 'Bloody hell,' Kelvin said, but they soon struggled over the ice hurdle and stuttered towards the road that had been reduced to a sea of slush. They grabbed a wooden cart and headed towards Winch Fawr in the direction of Swansea Road.

'We knew there was an open seam up there,' Kelvin recalled.

It was a long, cold trek in those conditions, but the two boys finally got to the seam and began gathering loose coal and putting it in their cart. They were not alone. Other boys, all looking for fuel and warmth, were shovelling coal into the baskets fastened to the fronts of their bicycles. And then a truck, its headlights wide and bright, hissed its way through the melting snow and ground to halt in front of them. Two men leapt out and began chasing the Owens, who fled with their cart.

'Keep out, you bloody little bastards!' they yelled.

Kelvin's eyes were saucers as he fled. His asthma was forgotten as the brothers ran to save themselves from a beating, the wind carrying the echoed threats after them. It was only when they reached the foot of Winch Fawr that they breathed easily and started laughing.

John trained in any weather and was improving. The Welsh amateur championships in 1973 planted another marker on the road to Los Angeles. Ready Roasted Chickens, suppliers of cooked poultry to the catering trade, sponsored the event at the Maerdy Workmen's hall in Rhondda one evening in May. John was the only boxer from Hoover's fighting that night, a seventeen-year-old entrant in the Junior 'C' 51 kilo class. Three two-minute rounds would decide the outcome.

It was just after 9 p.m. when he lined up in the blue corner against Brian Jones of Dyffryn ABC. His father stood in the corner and issued some basic instructions, nothing complicated, just a few words to anchor him to his ability. Two minutes later he cut an unhappy figure. As his son bounded back to the corner, Dick refused to offer him a drink or a stool and, instead, made his boy stand and listen.

'You're playing around,' he said. 'You haven't worked up enough sweat to sit down or have a drink. What's wrong with you? We've worked hard all year for this. Now you go out there and you stop him.'

It was one of the few occasions when Dick would question the work-rate of his son, but the lesson filtered through the startled eyes and Jones was stopped in the second round. 'A devastating display of controlled punching power', gushed the report in the local paper below a picture of John and a bench chock full of trophies.

By 1974, John, now eighteen was a fully-fledged senior and had the chance to become the champion when he took on Maurice O'Sullivan in Fairwater, Cardiff. It was a good bout for him. The double jab worked well and the hyperactive attrition that would become his signature bothered O'Sullivan. The Cardiff fighter, vastly more experienced than his opponent, tried to unleash some heavy bombs in the hope of restoring parity with a single blow, but John was both quick and durable. When his speed failed him and O'Sullivan connected, the younger man shrugged off the punches with barely a wince. It is a disheartening sight for any boxer to witness good blows being dismissed with insouciance, and O'Sullivan felt his face being torn with slashing blows, the whiff of leather merging with the smell of defeat.

In the corner, Dick glowed. This was a big win. More than that, it was a vindication of a way of life. It showed the sacrifice was worth it. He had known his time would come. That the road work would pay off, the strangulating, soul-sapping runs up the Glyn and by the sanatorium. He pictured John and Kelvin tearing up that savage incline, passing the bridge by the Blue Pool, the local suicide spot, and up beyond the old mental hospital. It was nine miles and, at one particular point, Kelvin would tear off over a crescent, leaving his brother behind. The competitive edge would drive John to new, lung-busting speeds. Then, one day, as he tore around the remainder of the well-worn route he spied a figure sitting on a stone wall. He slowed to an incredulous trot. 'Jesus, Kel, you were quick.' They did it two more times before Kelvin admitted he had shaved his route by taking an unseen short cut just over the tip of the hill. Thereafter, John was the king of the road, going backwards up the steepest runs to strengthen his calves and leaving his brother panting in his wake.

Dick smiled. Now it was payback. The Welsh senior amateur title. The punches had been thrown, the game plan executed. The bell had sounded and they were announcing the winner. But the first syllable was like a betrayal. O'Sullivan had the verdict. The nostalgia and delight segued into disgust. It was the night at Cymmer Afan revisited, only this time John was wiser and more experienced. As a fiercely patriotic teenager, he wanted the Welsh title badly, but he knew that when you looked beyond the inconsistencies of the judges, he had won. And boxing was about stripping yourself and showing what lay beneath. He knew it just like Dick did.

O'Sullivan appeared almost guilty. He knew he was the beneficiary of a fortunate verdict. When the boxers had changed, he approached the Owens's table.

'Look, John, I know this is your cup,' he said. 'You deserved it.'

It was a noble gesture, but John, despite being 'very pissed off', according to his father, insisted O'Sullivan keep his trophy.

Later, an official from the Welsh ABA confessed to Dick that his son had won the fight, but the powers that be had wanted O'Sullivan to go to the forthcoming Commonwealth Games in New Zealand. The candour did little to assuage the injustice, but it was not the first time that the politics of fighting and the muddled arbitrariness of its judges had gone against the Owens. Nor would it be the last.

ROUND THREE

In 360 seconds he had thrown 238 punches. Some had landed, some had missed, some were half-shots stopped by a counter-attack or a second thought, some merely slipped off the target. It was, however, a hellish concoction of blows and this was the round where they would take their toll. This was where Lupe Pintor, *El Indio*, began to experience the boxer's nemesis – not pain, but the shivering crescendo of pure, raw panic.

It started the same way as round two, Owen rifling off four unreturned jabs. The speed was awesome. A super-caffeinated metronome. Pintor parted his lips and his white gumshield dazzled against his olive skin. This was getting interesting. The Welsh on the Grand Avenue side of the Olympic were singing, temporarily drowning out the caterwauling from the Hispanic partisans. Whatever happened, the chorus of approval knew their man had put up the fight they had hoped he would.

Well, we knew the Welsh could sing, but we didn't know they could fight this good, Tom Kelly said. Danny Lopez then came up with his line of the night. *Owen reminds me of a praying mantis*, he said. That description reshaped Tom Kelly's face as dramatically as any leathered fist. He canted eyebrows, leaned forward and smiled. *Good call, Danny Lopez*, he gushed. *Good call*.

Danny had reason to be pleased. It was less than three months since he had retired after losing his WBC world featherweight title bout to Salvador Sanchez in Vegas. Twice he had fought Sanchez and twice he had lost. Twenty-seven hard-bleeding rounds. Now, at the age of twenty-eight, 'Little Red' Lopez needed to plan for the future and commentating was a start. He watched Johnny Owen and felt the boxer's natural respect. Boxing was a messy business of mesmerizing peaks and cold, black troughs. He had fought and won on the under-cards of Ali's two bouts with Leon Spinks and retained his own world title against Mike Ayala only the previous year. Then it had all looked so good, even when Ayala later admitted to being 'loaded' with drugs on the night of the fight. But there is always someone else. There is always a Saldivar, a Spinks or a Sanchez, products of fate's feeder system. Little Red was saddened by his defeat, but he would end up coaching kids and signing autographs at home in Utah. Sanchez, on his way to being one of the true greats, never realized his potential and would be killed when his Porsche ploughed into a tractor outside Mexico City a year on from the fight Little Red was now watching.

As Little Red watched Johnny Owen throw lefts and rights, upping the pace whenever he was hit, he might have pondered that he also knew what it was to be placed in a ring far away from home. After all, he had won the title in front of a hundred thousand Africans against David Kotey. When he got back to his dressing room, Little Red tried to call his family back home in the United States, but the phone lines were down across Ghana. He sent a telegram to the American embassy in Accra, but they were also gagged by the system failure and could not get his message through. It was not until he arrived home a week later and his family picked him up at the airport that Lopez could tell them that he was the new world champion. As he listened to Tom commentate, he thought that at least Johnny Owen's family would know the outcome quickly.

Dai Gardiner and his dad working in his corner. Owen in red, Pintor in white. Owen, this terribly thin challenger.

Would the body-blows slow him? They had heard Dick Owens and Dai Gardiner boast that their man could fight twenty-five rounds at the same breakneck pace, but Pintor had the staple weapon of every banging Mexican – the *gaucho*, a vicious left hook to the liver. It was the boxer's mace and Pintor was brandishing it with purpose.

Strangely enough, all the people who have seen Johnny Owen fight say the longer it goes, the tougher he gets. One forty-eight to go. Owen was warned a bit there by Marty Denkin.

The warning was for a perceived shove with his shoulder, but the contrast in height was the true culprit. And then, as they broke after Denkin's brief interlude, Owen threw a long left and a right. They connected and Pintor stuttered backwards until he was locked in Owen's corner. When they emerged, Owen raining blows to the body and the head, Pintor persevering with the uppercut, the damage was done.

Tom Kelly blinked. The crowd had bayed for blood and now they had it.

Pintor's cut! There's a cut on top of Pintor's eye! A pretty good-looking cut now as I see it on the eyebrow above his left eye. Marty Denkin, the third man, looking in. Owen is right on top of his man. Half a minute to go in round three.

Cuts are anathema to the boxer. The battle is all about heart. The boxer pushes himself to the limit and beyond, accepting welts and bruises and broken bones. The most unsatisfactory conclusion is to lose because of a cut face. Wounds heal, skin mends itself. However deep the cut, there are few boxers concerned enough by blood trickling into their eyes to acquiesce to conceding.

Denkin was neither concerned nor surprised by the cut. He had taken charge of Pintor's recent bout in Japan, a hard fifteen-rounder against Eijiro Murata. Hair-splittingly close. In the end the neutral American judge scored it a draw, the Japanese judge gave it to Murata by two points and the Mexican gave Pintor a five-round advantage. It was a winning draw for Pintor, who had been cut. That was only three months ago and Denkin was not shocked to see the work ethic of Johnny Owen reopen old wounds.

If the sensation of being cut is prone to scare the bleeder, it works like a steroid for his opponent. Owen saw the mark and, while it was only a blemish, it was evidence of a flaw in Pintor's armoury. So far the fight had been going to plan. He had attacked Pintor from the first jab and pressed him back. He had taken some of Pintor's best shots with a degree of comfort and had managed to step inside the wild swings to work at close quarters. Now Pintor was cut too. He could work on that, extend the bleeding, gouge deeper into the Mexican's self-doubt, deny him a tourniquet or a corner turned. That little fracture in the taut skin above the bushy black brow was a down payment on destiny.

Now using his longer reach, gentlemen, and that's a sharp left jab to keep Pintor away. Pintor, with a cut above his left eye, trying to get inside and Owen says welcome to the party. He's more than happy to have him come in there.

Stay busy, Owen was thinking. That was the way to win. His victory would be a gruelling affair, not the sudden revolution of the big banger. It was like he had written in the back of his little pocket diary. For friends, family and for Wales, Johnny Owen was doing it.

5

JESSE'S TALE

High in a vast, charcoal night, the young Jesse Harris had shaken a bag in the stable.

'There was nobody for me to bother with up the top of a bleeding mountain,' he recalled two decades on. 'It's black and wild so you stay at home. I had no idea what I was doing when I first walked into that gym with all those banshees. It was a real culture shock. I was only eleven and they were all older. The first night after training, when the trainers had gone, everybody was punching hell out of each other. It was a free-for-all. John looked after me.'

Harris lived at No. 9 Incline Side, Mountain Hare, known locally as 'Bogey Road'. He went to the same school as John, but was a few years younger. When he went down into the febrile pit of the gym he was happy to have a friend. His background, living on the mountain, where the lack of street-lights and even streets confined a boy's activities, had rendered him a quiet boy. He warmed to John's kindness and soon became familiar with the monastic masochism of his friend's routine. While other boys would try to skip training, John never did. Dick Owens remembered older fighters stopping off for pints of beer on their cross-country runs, and Kelvin was a self-confessed skiver. 'I just wanted to spar and fight,' he said. 'At the gym we had a different room for skipping. I'd sit on a chair and beat the rope on the floor. As soon as I heard someone reach the first step, I'd jump back up.'

Harris could sympathize. When James's gym suffered a compulsory purchase order and the boys returned to Court House, John would take training if his father failed to make it. Danny Galleozzie and Billy Davies were both suffering from bad health, and Dick had become the pivotal figure.

'I was gutted when Dick wasn't there, because John would go mad,' Harris said. 'When someone is doing twenty minutes' skipping by the side of you, it's hard to skive off. Some of the older boxers started to come back. It was a case of John did it so we did too. He was a leader in his own quiet way. So you didn't stop to tie your shoelaces because you knew he'd trained already that day. You knew he'd run to the gym and would be running home again afterwards.'

John ran for pleasure, Harris through necessity, down the mountain and back up its sheer, mud-softened paths. 'John always did that bit more,' Harris said. 'It didn't matter if it was snowing, raining or blowing a gale. You could tell he was going to get on because of the way he trained. We had a couple of good boys but they started with drink and girls and clubs. My old man would say, "You've got to be like John. Dick blunts an axe on concrete and then John goes and chops down trees." I thought, "Sod off. I'm not chopping down trees with a blunt hatchet. Get a bloody chainsaw, man!"'

John's commitment to training came from his father. The lingering deafness and darkness of being trapped in a miner's cage made Dick want to utilize his children's strengths in other ways. He took his boys to the ragged mountain tracks behind the Harp Inn and made them run sixty yards while he held a stopwatch in his hand. They had barely recovered their breath when Dick would increase the distance to eighty yards. By the end of a session, his boys would be red-cheeked and the air would be warmed by the breath of these steam trains.

One day, when John was showing plenty of promise in the amateurs, Dick sat his son down in the front room. He had picked his moment and the rest of the family was elsewhere.

'Look, John,' he said. 'Boxing is a tough sport. It's the hardest sport there is. If you are going to keep with it then you have got to be one hundred per cent dedicated. Ninety per cent is no good. It's all or nothing.'

His son followed his words but was nonplussed.

'I know that, Dad. And I'll do what it takes.'

'You have to give up everything,' Dick said. 'That means drink and sweets and girls. There will be plenty of time for that afterwards.'

'I'll do what it takes,' the boxer repeated. 'Whatever it takes.'

Vivian was a good boxer, a venomous counter-puncher, and though prone to bleeding from the nose he only gave up once he started being distracted by women and nicotine. Kelvin was never going to accept such a strict regime, and his interest began to wane in tandem with John's ascent, aided by his growing interest in an attractive blonde named Alison.

'It's too hard a game to pressure anyone into it,' their father said. 'They either want it or they don't. Kelvin would say, "I'm not doing that." He wanted to know the ins and outs of everything before he would do it. Then he'd say, "Bugger it." He was a lazy trainer. John, on the other hand, would run through a brick wall for me.'

Kelvin admitted as much.

'I hated the way Dick used to talk to me,' he said. 'He thought I boxed with my left hand held too low. He'd bawl at me all the time, I'd erupt and we'd get nowhere fast. We'd both end up rattled. John, though, might say, "Your left hand is bit low, Kel. Try this." And I'd listen.'

Dick had laughed when John suggested he train Kelvin for a night. 'Best of luck, John,' his father huffed, knowing how awkward Kelvin could be. After a torturous session, Kelvin found his father. 'Dad, if that's the training of the future then forget it, because he's going to kill us all off.'

John, by contrast, was happy to abstain from normal teenage pleasures and push himself through the pain – and prejudice – that came his way. Ahmed Younis, a cocksure boxer from the Midlands, was one of the first to belittle him for his physique after winning a fight in West Bromwich. Afterwards, he sought out his conquest. 'You were lucky I didn't knock you out,' he said.

John bristled with indignation but measured his words.

'I'll tell you this, if we ever meet again, you won't beat me.'

Younis laughed. 'Yeah, right,' he grinned. It was a slight he would quickly come to regret.

In the meantime, John was again selected for Wales, something that always provided a heightened motivation. In 1974 his performance against John Raeside in Pontypool helped Wales to a 7–4 triumph over Scotland, and, significantly, attracted the attention of the provincial press. Karl Woodward, a stalwart of the local boxing scene, picked John's win as the most impressive of the night.

'The 18-year-old flyweight from Merthyr, who gave ABA champion, Maurice O'Sullivan, such a hard contest in the Welsh final, reduced John Raeside to helplessness with a non-stop two-fisted assault that brought an abrupt halt after 30 seconds of the second round.'

A few months later came the chance for revenge against

Younis. John was picked for Wales to face a Wolverhampton team. Seven bouts were contested before John stood across the ring from the gifted English international. It was a good match. Younis's confidence was born of agile footwork and decent ringcraft, but John was strong and developing all the time. He had a marginal edge and got the decision after three breathless rounds. The shock on Younis's face was all the revenge John needed.

By the time they met again three months later, John had both the upper hand and the moral high ground. Younis's words had been exposed as vacuous, and defeat against the slight Welshman had cut deep. Now Younis felt bitter and vulnerable and butted John three times in the first round. Dick was furious, albeit he knew the attacks were evidence of Younis's desperation. 'Tommy Lawton would have been proud of him that night, and he got disqualified,' he said. First Younis had been beaten, now he had been reduced to petulance, his skills eroded by panic.

It was an early warning that only fools would rush to mock and form rash judgements on the evidence of the brittle-looking cover. Don James knew it and would feel a buzz of anticipation if he heard John slighted.

'We went to one show in Swansea,' he remembered. 'The other lad had beaten John in the past and told him he was going to get the same as last time. John didn't say a word as he walked up the steps. That was his way. But he turned to me and Dick just before the start and said softly, "We'll see who's going to get it this time." He went in and gave the boy one hell of a beating. He didn't gloat afterwards. He kept his dignity and didn't rise to the bait. He did his fighting where it mattered.'

People remained to be convinced, though. They laughed when he removed his gown while fighting for Wales against

Sweden in Stockholm. The sight of this tall, gangly fighter grated against stereotype and prompted ripples of mirth from the seats. The laughter faded when John stopped Ove Hallman in the second round.

It was a similar story in the flaking clubs and halls at home. On a Friday night in November 1975, a Welsh team travelled to Hanley for a match against the army. The programme for the night cost five pence and issued some quaint advice to the audience. 'Keep absolute silence during the progress of the rounds,' it suggested. 'Noise is apt to disturb the Referee and Judges and to distract the boxers' attention.' It went on: 'In order to ensure for everybody a clear view of the ring, don't smoke the whole of the time.'

Not that the Owens were worried about fags and boos. They had more serious matters to deal with. John was due to be the third bout on, but his pre-fight medical had caused a problem. Dick fidgeted and checked his watch. Then he saw John bobbing through the crowd.

'It's no good,' he said. 'The doctor says I'm too frail to box.'

Dick exhaled a tired groan. 'Of course you can box,' he said and started wrapping bandages around those bony paws. As he worked, a message arrived from the doctor, asking John to return. His father shook his head in bemusement as John departed again.

Eventually, Dick's patience snapped. He marched across the Victoria Hall and found the doctor's room. He knocked and entered and found the doctor holding a stethoscope to his son's chest.

'Is there a problem here?' Dick said bluntly.

Doctor Godfrey freed his ears. 'Well, nothing medical,' he said. 'It's just he's so frail that a puff of wind would knock him over.'

Dick had no time for this. The first bout was almost starting. 'Will you be at ringside?' he asked the doctor.

'Why, yes.'

'Well, I'd like your statement afterwards.'

The doctor shrugged. 'Okay.'

Passed fit to box, albeit by a doctor watching with a degree of scepticism, John beat Lance Corporal Phillip on points. His father was not about to let the matter pass and confronted the doctor at the after-show banquet.

'You're right,' Godfrey replied. 'He looks so frail but he is a very fit boy. I wouldn't have believed it if I hadn't seen it. I suppose . . . I suppose looks can deceive.' He took the boxer's pulse. It was a cool forty-two beats per minute. The point was proved again.

If looks could deceive doctors, it was no surprise they ensnared fighters too. Boxing has always paid more than lip service to braggadocio and it was little wonder fighters sought to play on John's physicality.

'He'd go in a ring in training and, if someone was taking liberties with him, he would get in a clinch and hold him close,' Kelvin said. 'Then he'd look around to see where the trainers were. When they had their backs to him, he would push the other guy off and paste him. Then you'd hear a voice flooding the place. "Owens!" You got what you deserved off John. You had to respect him.'

His amateur career was impressive but not stunning. He had won 106 bouts and lost eighteen. He had represented Wales seventeen times and lost only twice. There were ups and downs. It was tough, combining a working day at the factory with a gruelling regime in the gym and fights around the UK and even Europe. When he beat Chris Haggerty, Dick was unimpressed by his son's lugubrious efforts. He asked him what the problem was and hit the roof when he discovered his son had been tearing around playing football during his dinner break at Suko.

The job was causing another problem. Steel swarf was attacking his skin and turning it septic. It was a stealthy assault and a dangerous one. Dick implored him to pull out of the Welsh championships in 1975 because of a septic finger, knowing the pain must be far worse than he was letting on. But after his disappointment against O'Sullivan, John needed to fight. His father lanced the finger, but to no avail. The doctor then lanced it twice on the day of his bout with George Sutton, a highly promising puncher, whose path he would cross again. The championships took place in Cardiff where Sutton was a local hero. He tore after John, who battled as gamely as ever and tried to ignore the pain from his finger.

'Sutton hit him with everything but the corner stool,' Dick remembered. 'It was tough to watch. At the end of the second round we pleaded with him to retire.'

'No, I'm not hurt,' he replied.

'Well, you could have fooled me, boy,' his father countered.

John already had the same attitude that had governed his hero, Jimmy Wilde, who had beseeched his manager never to throw in the towel on his behalf. 'If any boxer can beat me, let him do it,' he wrote in *The Art of Boxing*. The towel would never be thrown in. Sutton won, but John retained his pride.

There were highs, such as beating John Bambrick, a Scot who had been to the Commonwealth Games and won a bronze medal at the European championships, and fighting on the same bill as Gerry Cooney in the Double Diamond Club in Caerphilly. Cooney went on to become America's great white hope, twice fighting for the world heavyweight title and twice losing. After retiring, following a defeat to George Foreman, Cooney would set up FIST, an organization to help boxers cope with the transition from sport to ordinary life, but in 1975, several months younger than John, he was still two years from turning professional and was delighted to give New York a 7–4 win over Wales with a left hook that landed squarely on the jaw of Terry Chard, the Welsh champion.

There were lows, too, the loss to a spoiling Jimmy Evans in his last shot at the Welsh senior amateur title among the most lingering and the defeat by Paul Chance in his final amateur bout the worst prelude to a pro career.

Nevertheless, few of those who had nurtured his talent doubted his readiness.

'The thing I remember about John is he was a real gentleman,' Idris Sutton said. 'I never saw him throw a foul punch or do anything dirty – no butting, no thumbs in the eyes. If he saw his opponent slipping, he would stand back and give him a chance to get up. He knew he had the ability to win so would never look to take advantage of an accident. And if you beat him fair and square he'd be the first to shake your hand.

'He was like Howard Winstone in a lot of respects. You never had to tell either of them to get on with it. They didn't shirk the graft. You didn't need to babysit them on road runs. They knew they needed it. Boxing is about sacrifice and some aren't ready for that sacrifice. Johnny and Howard were. Keep your elbows in and your chin down, you had to drum those things into other fighters, but not Johnny. The way he'd get out of trouble on the ropes, sliding out of trouble and standing back. He made every fight a classic.'

James, Sutton's friend and ally, knew it too.

'People looked at John and thought he was a skinny little runt. They thought he would be no trouble. They all got a surprise. Was there something driving him? Maybe. I know it sounds sentimental, but I think he had it in his head from a very early age that he could fight and make money for his family. He wanted to buy them a house, but, really, at the end of the day, the reason he boxed was because he had to.'

On the brink of the pro game, John Owens was all potential. Nobody knew for sure how far he could take his dream.

'Before he turned pro, he said he'd be happy if he won a British title and got a Lonsdale belt,' Kelvin said. 'He said he'd feel as if he'd achieved something if he got that. We knew he was good, but he was my brother, the kid whose shorts we split to add lead weights when he went running. To be honest, none of us ever thought he'd get as far as he did. Those sorts of things don't happen to people like us.'

Dick was confident. He knew his son from both a father's and a trainer's perspective and had seen enough. The skills were there, the record was good and the commitment unquestioned.

'It was about small steps rather than looking to this big goal,' he said. 'When he first boxed for Wales everybody was over the bloody moon. The thought of just turning pro was exciting.'

Jessie Harris had a different slant on his abilities. He was in a unique position because his friend had started to go into his corner and work as his trainer. Harris had got a bye through to the quarter-finals at the Welsh junior championships and the bout was to take place in Aberavon, where his opponent was a boy who had already beaten him two years earlier. Harris was nervous and John sensibly omitted to remind Harris of the earlier defeat. 'He doesn't look much,' he told Harris, who nodded hopefully. In the opposing corner, the boy's trainer was doing the opposite, inspiring his fighter with stories of his past triumph and inflating his confidence.

The bell sounded and Harris was immediately on the back foot.

'He was all over me like a rash,' he recalled. 'After the first round, I realized I'd better listen to John. And the thing is, you did listen because he was different. Most trainers would come out with exactly the same old thing – left, right, left. That's all they tell you. "Drink your water. Yeah, you're doing great." You sit there thinking, "My head's hurting. You keep saying left, right, left, but it's not bloody working."

'John would just sit there quietly and not bother with all that rubbish. He'd study the other guy and say, "He's dropping his right hand. Make him lead and then clip him." He'd look for weak points, anything to help you get through. But other trainers would have another boy in the ring after your fight and they'd say exactly the same thing to them.'

At the break after the opening round, Harris was dazed and confused. His opponent went back to his corner and was met by a grin. 'Keep it up son,' his trainer said. 'He's all yours.'

John let Harris catch his breath. 'He's holding his left arm up high,' he said slowly and methodically. 'Get down and get under it.' Harris nodded, the bell sounded and the fight changed.

'I stopped him in the third,' Harris said. 'It's soul-destroying when you hit someone with your best punches and they don't flinch. That was happening at the start of the fight, but John taught me body-punching. I slipped underneath, like John had said, and dropped him.'

As Harris bobbed out through the ropes, he was met by a beaming mentor.

'Well done, Jess,' he said. 'Good fight. Especially seeing as he'd already beaten you.'

Harris stopped in his tracks. 'What! Now you bloody tell me.'

The search for a chink in the armour was John's modus operandi. Shorn of the mighty punch, he had to search for

Top. Johnny, Susan and Kelvin on holiday
in Barry.

Above. Vivian, Johnny, Marilyn and Kelvin
at Bristol Zoo.

Right. Johnny on a motorcycle,
aged seven.

Johnny (front right) with his father, opposite, and Dai Gardiner, on his right. Note the orange juice.

The teenage Johnny (fourth from the right) and his Welsh teammates in Sweden.

Pintor and his father at his store.

Pintor and one of his many cars.

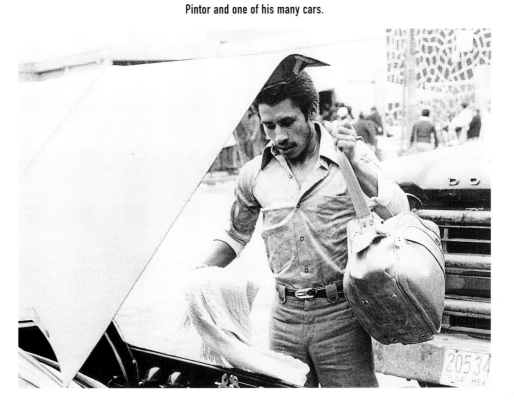

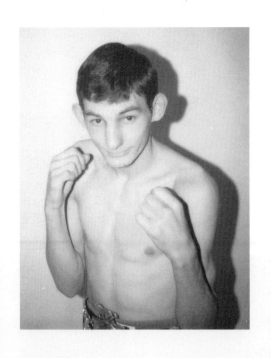

Training

Below. With Jeff Pritchard on the beach at Porthcawl.

Right. In the gym.

Above. Man of the people.

Right. Johnny and Edith
celebrate winning the British title.

Below. The family
celebrate another win.
From left: Dilwyn, Kelvin, Susan,
Les (Johnny's brother-in-law),
Johnny, Vivian, Phillip, Dick.

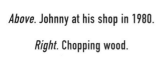

Above. Johnny at his shop in 1980.

Right. Chopping wood.

Johnny binds his hands at the gym in New Tredegar.

Dai Gardiner.   Johnny and a young fan.

other weapons. He did it with an intelligence that refuted later media reports of an introverted soul, slow and inarticulate. These reports were born of not knowing John at ease with himself, in the comfort of his Merthyr base, surrounded by the only people who mattered to him. He was certainly shy, but he was also warm and generous to a fault. He helped Harris for no other reason than he was his friend.

Of his brothers, Kelvin was the closest, and another beneficiary of his good nature. One night he threw an orange at John. The missile missed but splattered against John's winner's certificate from the Welsh junior championships, hanging on the wall in the front room. The juice smeared the felt-pen writing. Kelvin apologized profusely and his brother, though disappointed, accepted it. They removed the certificate from the frame and tried to clean it up, but their efforts only made the mess worse and they decided the best way forward was to replace it and hope their father would not notice. They got away with it for three weeks. It is a tale that hints at John's character. Instead of berating his younger brother, he tried to help Kelvin out of the mess he had created.

At home the prizes accumulated. In amateur circles, the awards were an arbitrary collection of old tat. Vivian won a mirror. John had his Romanian eggcups. Kelvin got some towels.

'It was anything they could get their hands on,' Kelvin said. 'We didn't know what a decanter was until we started boxing. What the hell they thought us working-class kids were going to do with one I don't know, but we ended up with loads.'

The prizes would be laid on a table before the bouts began and the boxers would peruse them as if it were a tombola stall.

Having avenged his earlier loss, Jesse Harris was now ready to fight for his big title. With John in his corner, he had made the finals of the 1976 Welsh schoolboy championships. Prior to the semis, he had been sent on an army assault course with his school class. A bunch of roughnecks and trouble-makers, the exercise was deemed a good way of attempting to stop them setting off fire alarms and wreaking all manner of havoc.

'I said I can't go over the assault course because I'm boxing in the semis of the Welsh championships,' Harris said. 'So they made me go over twice and said, if I didn't win, God help me when I came back.'

As he queued up to see the doctor at the finals, Harris recognized a few faces. They were good, big boxers and he felt anxious. Further up the line, he saw a boy turn and shout: 'Who's Jesse Harris?'

His mouth blanched. He gulped and said: 'I am.'

The boy looked Harris up and down. A slight figure who was just scraping into the weight limit at forty-nine kilos, Harris did not look an imposing threat to the heftier, taller boy.

'Well, you're fighting me, pal, and I'm going to batter you.'

Harris was riddled with doubts. ' "God, he's bleeding big," I thought. I went over to John and said, "Am I really fighting him?" '

John threw a knowing look at the loudmouth and shook his head. 'Can't be,' he mouthed. 'He's too big. I'll go and check.'

The news was bad.

'You *are* fighting him,' John said.

'You'll be a wreck by the time I've finished with you,' the boy glowered, his smile mocking the boy who was on his way to losing before he'd even had his medical.

But John came up with a plan that played on the fragile psychology of the boxer. Harris got into the ring, trying to banish the taunts and inches of his rival.

'Don't look at him,' John commanded. 'Look at me. When I

tell you, I want you to turn around, shake your fist and shout, "Come orrnn then" as loud as you can. Then turn back to me straightaway. It'll scare the life out of him.'

Harris's eyebrows almost shot through his curls. 'I couldn't stop my hand from shaking. I was absolutely shitting myself. This guy was huge. But I did it and turned back.'

John gave him a half-smile, but was not finished.

'Right, what you have to do is this,' he said. 'As soon as the bell goes and the referee says "Fight!", hammer across the ring as fast as you can. As soon as he sees you coming, he's going to stick out a left. It's the natural reaction. He's far too tall for you and has a far longer reach, so make him lead. As soon as he does, smack him with a right hand as hard as you can. You'll have no bother after that. He won't come near you.'

Harris was bemused and scared, but he trusted John like no other trainer. He tapped his gloves and sucked in a comforting breath. The tension in those last seconds made the air crackle.

'The bell went and I literally ran across the ring,' he said. 'And this guy did just what Johnny had said. I gave him a crack and he never came near me for three rounds. And once I hit him I wasn't stopping.'

The new Welsh schoolboy champion was ecstatic. He was presented with his vest and John showed a ruthless streak by making the defeated boy pay for his boasts. 'Go and show him the vest,' he said to Harris, who complied.

'The other boy was in tears but I wanted to get some back after all he'd been saying,' Harris said. 'His pride was battered more than he was, but he was sick as a pig. He must have been half a stone more than me, but at the time he looked two stone heavier. I owe John for that win. I owe him a lot.'

Harris did not fight much after his success. As a schoolboy champion, reputation now worked against him and other boys were loath to fight him, but Jesse knew his heart was not in it anyway.

'I didn't have the killer instinct,' he said. 'I could never have been like John in a million years. He'd plan a fight knowing he was going the distance. I wanted to go in and get out of the ring as fast as possible. We had five champions at Court House one year, but he was the only one going anywhere. None of us thought far ahead, but John was all about long-term goals. I'd think, "I've got a cold tonight so I don't need ten minutes' skipping." John would say, "I've got a cold so I'll train harder to sweat it out." Bugger off, John. Go home to bed. We thought, "You're a bloody nutter."'

'He did have focus,' Kelvin agreed. 'At home he'd have steaks and we'd have beans on toast, but we didn't mind because, even among the family, we all respected him. He was the only one we'd listen to.'

Harris also respected him. 'I looked up to him, oh yeah. My old man is seventy-eight and they've just stopped him going in the ring to spar. He loved it and he loved John. "Look at him," he'd say. "That's the way to be." John taught me how to skip because, when you start off, you're tripping all over the place. And you'd be sweating cobs while he would be hardly breathing.'

At sixteen Harris was all but finished with boxing. Sometimes, he thinks back to 1976. It was the year he was a champion, the year John Owens turned pro. Harris could not begin to imagine adopting John's style.

'We went in wanting to knock someone out,' he admitted. 'It's the easiest route, but John's way was to pick them off. In boxing you all know you're going to get hurt, so John's way was the hard way. He was fully prepared for what he was going to get.'

1976. Slade were in their pomp, Manchester United lost the

FA Cup Final to lowly Southampton and Muhammad Ali was the heavyweight champion. In Mexico, Carlos Zarate was nearing the summit, and in California, Alberto Davila was preparing for the first of two wars against Lupe Pintor. Nobody could know that Zarate, Davila and Pintor would all have roles to play in the story of the kid with lead shorts.

ROUND FOUR

In Jack London's *The Mexican*, there are groans when Felipe Rivera removes his sweater to reveal his bony body. They expect Danny Ward, their favourite, whose physique is alive with easy suppleness and health and strength, to massacre the fragment in the opposite corner. But they forget the power of the will. It was the same in the mythical story of a boy fighting for guns for the Mexican Revolution as it was in the Olympic Auditorium where a young man was also fighting for freedom.

London could have been writing about Johnny Owen's composed nature. 'He had gone through such vastly greater heats that this collective passion of ten thousand throats, rising surge on surge, was to his brain no more than the velvet cool of a twilight night.' And about the motivating force behind Lupe Pintor. The man with the snakelike eyes who was primitive like the wild wolf was pounding skin and bone for more than vanity or fleeting glory. 'He did not analyse,' wrote London. 'He merely knew that he must win this fight ... For behind him, nerving him to this belief, were profounder forces than any crowded house dreamed.'

By the fourth round the cadences and tone of the fight had been established. Owen was relentless. Knowing he lacked the knockout blow, he had worked hard and embraced pain to compensate. A natural athlete, he had toiled until hurt was a comfort.

In training Owen would run on seamless hills and the feather-down of a morning mist would shroud his routine. The Brecon Beacons were huge, impassive observers. Sometimes, Owen would get lost. He would deviate from the tarmac roads and, with the soft, dewy grass folding beneath his boots, he would let his mind and feet wander simultaneously. The mincing gait of sheep tottering from his path marked his climb, the blue dye labelling them. And here was Johnny Owen, the wet snare the accompaniment to his drift, the natural boy, marked invisibly and indelibly by time and place and ascent.

Johnny Owen, the challenger, from Meth-er, Wales, Pintor, from Mexico, trying to unload some heavy bombs. The minute Pintor tries to throw some big leather, Owen starts to swarm all over him with a rash of blows.

Byron Board was encouraged by what he was seeing. It was still early days but Owen was on top. Pintor was not hurting him, although Board had seen enough boxing to be wary of those roundhouse lefts and the quick, jolting uppercuts. He was also concerned about the canvas. When he had gone down to the Olympic for the weigh-in that morning, he had noticed how soft it seemed. Later he would say that it was a canvas that suited a puncher not a boxer. 'Home-town advantage,' he would gripe when the ring had cleared, the auditorium had emptied and the canvas had been locked away like a museum artefact.

Pintor began working the uppercut while Owen punched down at his head. It was a good fight between two men who wanted to prove themselves. It was about money but it was about other things too.

They went into a clinch and Pintor raised his right glove in protest. Marty Denkin stepped in and parted them with barely a word. In reality, Pintor was concerned by Owen's elbows. The height difference and Owen's extended reach conspired against Pintor. He caught an elbow in the face and, where once he might have winced it away, now he was cut and anxious.

Owen, tall and let's face it, very thin, to the point where he is preceded into the ring by a flag that uses a skeleton standard. But I tell you, he fights like a man possessed. Two minutes to go. Non-stop action with Johnny Owen.

Little Red Lopez was impressed. Like the rest of LA, he had thought Owen was going to be cannon fodder for a fighter who could be awesome. Pintor was as hard as nails. A testosterone drip. Yet he was in deep. He was also sometimes slow for a bantamweight and his habit of hanging low, his back bent, meant he could be relatively easy to hit. And Little Red knew that when you expected to win comfortably, a hard fight could gnaw away at your confidence.

Owen did not seem to be hurt by any of the those right hands, he said. The double-act with Tom was working well. Maybe retirement would not be so bad.

Tom held the microphone to his chest like a dagger. *He takes a good punch,* he said.

Sure does, Little Red said. *His attack is non-stop, relentless. And these punches he throws are slicing blows.*

Slicing enough to reveal Pintor's thinly-veiled scars. Having opened up one cut, Owen was now encouraged to see red specks forming above Pintor's other eye. The champion instinctively touched it with his glove, as if seeking confirmation. This was turning into an awful round. Boxing is a two-tiered art. It is about hitting and not being hit. When every blow is thrown, the boxer's defence is at its weakest, which is why punches are often exchanged together. The sensation of leather landing on something hard can neuter the firmer return blow and prove a bloody anaesthetic.

There is a smear of red over Pintor's right. There is blood on the trunks of Lupe Pintor. He was cut over the left in the second.

And then the commentators, the pressmen and the judges at ringside saw more. As blood seeped from Pintor's cut, Little Red pointed out there was a little red scratch under Owen's right eye. This was becoming a hard, vicious affair. Pintor's white trunks were now pink with the smeared spoils of Owen's success. But Owen was bleeding too. From his eye, from his nose and from his mouth.

Blood coming out of the nose of Owen and blood on the face of Pintor. These men have stood toe to toe from the opening bell, no quarter asked for and none given.

It was in the fourth round that the right-hand of Pintor began to strike home with more accuracy. With the golden numbers ticking down on the big clock, he bounced on to his left foot and planted it firmly in the canvas. His right leg was cocked to almost ninety degrees as his bodyweight was channelled into his right shoulder, down the arm and into the covered fist. The blow came from a distance, almost down on the floor, but it was fleet and firm. It caught Owen squarely on the side of the head, but the Welshman's anchor foot did not move an inch. Finally, Owen backed up to regain the centre of the ring and Pintor darted into the space to unleash more fire. Owen responded in the only way he knew how. Left, right, left, right. Body, liver, chin. Their heads rested side by side and they twirled around the ring like duelling stags. All the time, the tap, tap, tap, thud, thud, thud of red leather ground down the Mexican, ferreting away at the defensive foundations. But Pintor continued to throw the bigger blows. These were the punches that had protected his ice and denied his father. They were his life's story.

Five seconds to go and Owen continues to throw punches.

It was fight night in Los Angeles and the Olympic Auditorium was in uproar.

6

THE MAGUEY TREE

The maguey is known as the Tree of Wonders in Mexico. It has manifold uses, but, for a boy like Lupe Pintor, its primary attraction was in the pulpy sap where you could find *pulque*. From an early age, Pintor was drinking this alcoholic beverage, known as the 'nectar of the gods', which is quaffed as the opiate of the masses. His father would claim it was why he grew up so strong, perhaps believing in the mythical qualities of the plant or perhaps hoping to explain the fury that was now running wild inside his son's head. Either way, the drinking of this young boy was another handicap on the pitted path to his redemption in the boxing ring.

The machete incident would never leave Pintor, and he sought a form of twisted vengeance. He pleaded with his father to let him box, but the old man was embittered and refused. And so the fighting continued both within their walls and without. School became a battlefield, Pintor throwing up a misanthropic barrier against his peers, while home was psychological torment.

Pintor suspected everybody and there were days when he fell into a deep fog of melancholy. He was surrounded by thieves and brutes. In the boy's head, there was no mitigation and he only saw the machete and heard Francisco's screams. The vivid picture would ensure he was never taken by surprise again. His relationship with his father had flat-lined and a barely veiled mutual antipathy simmered.

'Friends?' his father said. 'He didn't have friends. Enemies more like. They were always expelling him from school for fighting. He was lost.'

But in this fractured family Pintor lived like a wild dog, scavenging for crumbs of comfort. One avenue for pleasure was sex. Pintor lost his virginity when he was just eleven and began a lifelong infatuation with women that lent credence to Mexican stereotypes. On the high trapeze, women would both catch and release him.

'I remember my first time very clearly,' he said. 'It was 2 February and she was twenty. She was dark and curvacious and extremely beautiful. I let three of them mature me and then, when I was sixteen, I told myself to stop. If I didn't then I never would have and, anyway, I was boxing then.'

The most peaceful times in the Pintor house came when Don Lupe would watch Saturday-night fights from the Coliseo Arena on television. The eleven-year-old Lupe and his brother, Francisco, would watch too and, perhaps without knowing it, became addicted to the calm that came from boxing. It took a year of nagging and repeated promises before his father relented and allowed Pintor to take up the sport.

'One day I was beaten by his desire and I said, "Okay, let's go find this gym you keep taking about," ' Don Lupe explained.

His son already knew where the gym was and they made the long journey from their home. His father was struck by the acridity of sweaty dreams in the Atlas, but his son was seduced by the sight of Ruben 'El Puas' Olivares training under the gaze of a multitude of eyes.

Olivares was the darling of the gym, a swarthy case of suppleness topped off with spiky hair and a gap-toothed grin. Even in his isolation on the Cuajimalpa plains, Pintor knew of El Puas. He was only twenty-one but he was the veteran of more than forty professional fights. He had fought at the Forum in Los Angeles and had a harem of writers fawning over him and proclaiming him as the next big thing. Their lyricism would be proved correct the following year when El Puas became the world bantamweight champion and they started to call him Rockabye. Pintor noted the admiration in the faces of those watching him dance a waltz with an invisible opponent. If John Owens's epiphany had come on a mountain top, Pintor's came when he stood on the viscous floor in that decrepit gym and sampled the primal thrill of stardom.

'I could hardly believe it,' Pintor recalled. 'I was so excited just being there and watching him. He was my idol. I haven't seen a boxer who uses his hands so freely and puts in the big punches. He wasn't what you'd call a stylish fighter, nor was he a big hitter; but his hands were incredible; he feinted, he tricked you and then suddenly, "Pam!", he gave you a smack; and when you gave him one back in reply, he'd already got there first, with the same hand and in the same spot. As time went on I decided to mimic his boxing technique.'

The gym stood on the corner of Camelia and Zarco in the Guerrero colony and was run by Arturo 'Cuyo' Hernandez. His wife, Hortensia, and stepdaughter, Elizabeth, ran a sports shop nearby. They sold boxing gloves made in a small factory owned by Atruro, Hernandez's son, and bearing the brand name 'Casanova', a homage to Rodolfo 'Chango' Casanova. Known as Baby, Casanova had won the world bantamweight title in 1933 in the Olympic Auditorium. Pintor could barely envisage those far-off days, but the names of the fighters – Speedy Dado, Sixto Escobar and Babyface Casanova – oozed romance. The shop, itself, Deportes Nancy, was named after Hernandez and Hortensia's daughter. It was not hard to see why the troubled tearaway should be won over by this close-knit family and its florid history.

'If you are going to do this then you have got to give it your all,' Don Lupe told his son that night. It was the same commitment Dick Owens had demanded of his son.

'Yes, boss, I promise. This is what I want and I'm going to do it.'

The father did not trust his son, however, and made him give his word a second time.

'Yes, boss,' he said, the flicker of something warming him, 'I promise.'

His father nodded, beaten by his son's desire and an inability to offer anything else.

For the first time in his life, Pintor had a purpose. At the time he was not thinking about money or titles, but the weapons with which he could wreak his vengeance. He could hear Francisco raging against his mangled fingers and could taste the dust as the bullies took his ice. He could also see Ruben Olivares dancing over a rope and the obsequious respect he instilled in all shapes of men.

Briefly, his father began to play a more positive role in his son's life. He woke him at 5 a.m. every day and told him to go running. He handed Pintor two rocks to take with him. 'Partly to use as weights and partly so that he could defend himself if he was ever attacked in the forest,' he said. 'In those days it wasn't like it is now. There were no houses around here and things happened. He used to run to the chapel, about an hour away. Then he'd come back to sleep for a while. Later, around midday, he'd get up again and head to the gym.'

It would be simplistic to suggest Pintor had found himself and was suddenly transformed from the angry loner to an equal in the Atlas. He still craved isolation and worked alone with his jumbled thoughts, absorbing the peccadilloes of others with a natural superiority. He was a boy in a gym of greats. Olivares was the daddy but there were others too. One of them was Carlos Zarate, a seventeen-year-old with a potent array of skills and an opinionated confidence. From the moment he met him, Pintor kept his distance, not through fear but because of a palpable dislike of his sureness. At the time, it seemed inconceivable that Zarate would play a significant role in Pintor's life. He was four years older and on the verge of the pro game, while Pintor was a raw novice.

'Zarate was there before me, but we were never good friends,' Pintor said with a degree of understatement. 'He was arrogant from the start and he did not live a good life or have a good heart. But I hardly had any friends in the gym. There were people I admired and looked up to because of the way they fought in the gym, but I never made friends with anybody.

'I had no interest in others. It was my own headstrong desire that was taking me along the road. I respected Olivares and liked his style, but I didn't want to be like anybody else. Hernandez was really strict and very harsh with us, but even at the start, I knew it was a good chance for all of us. He was right to be hard on us, but he was honest. Whoever showed dedication and spent most time in the gym had the chance to go somewhere with him.'

Pintor was a different breed from John Owens. Riddled with tinted passions he began the voyage that would merge their paths. Just as John was leaving damp footprints on the dewy fields in Wales, Pintor began running, kicking up dusty leg-warmers as he went.

'In Cuajimalpa you could not ask for more,' he said. 'To run through the middle of the forest, find your lunch in the mountains, run until you hit tiredness and pain, to freshen up in a brook of ice-cold water, that was enough to motivate me in those days. I had all the energy in the world. I was pumped up, ready for anything.'

Hernandez was a hard-boiled figure with a nest of lush greying hair. His yellow eyes, flecked with lines of blood, were clouded with experience and stared out from the depths of chiselled crevices. But beneath the ossified features was a warmth that sucked in his boys. He liked some better than others, but had a calculating mind that knew which could be polished into money-making career boxers and even champions. Olivares had it and, he thought, so did Zarate.

In those early days, though, Pintor was just another kid with a punch. So Hernandez handed him to Jorge Ugalde, a trainer who could get the best out of him, teach him basic ringcraft and see whether he was a listener. Ugalde was impressed. It was hard to get close to the boy and he knew there were problems elsewhere, but that was not unusual and it was good to have some anger.

'It wasn't easy in those days,' Pintor admitted. 'When I first started I sometimes went to the gym starving of hunger. In those days a bread roll only cost ten cents, but I was lucky if I had five. On those occasions when I had enough money, you've no idea how much I enjoyed it. Hunger is an awful thing. It saps your strength and affects your mind.'

The hunger would only last a year. When Pintor was four-teen, Ugalde was encouraged enough to send the boy to the

Mexican Olympic Sport Centre. Ugalde believed Pintor had enough promise to be groomed for the 1972 Olympics and his charge clung on to that belief. It was only a year since the Games had been held in Mexico City and Pintor knew it was a big deal, but he had more prosaic reasons for wanting to remain at the centre.

'They gave me a grant to fight and I was getting three meals a day,' he said. 'I started boxing to get out of the house and get away from my family. It was an escape route, but then I realized you could make money and I made up my mind that I would become the Olympic champion. It was a noble aim, but it got ruined by politics. It got nasty.'

Pintor discovered that some people at the centre did not want him to go to Munich and were blocking his efforts. He is not sure why, but was disgruntled enough to turn away from the grant and the cooked meals to return to Ugalde. Like John Owens, who had been denied a place at the Commonwealth Games by the politics of junior boxing, Pintor was kept back. He was only sixteen, and, having walked away from what he called his 'noble aim', he instead set about becoming a professional.

By the time he went back to the Atlas, Zarate had already begun his pro career and had a string of wins, all by knockout, behind him. Hernandez knew Zarate was in the revolving door. It only remained to be seen whether he would get through or be spat out on to the street. In his rumbling heart, Hernandez felt sure he would go all the way, another feather in his cap and another source of income. He would take more convincing about Pintor, whose dedication in the gym came couched with caveats about his waywardness out of it.

'I'd go back to the neighbourhood from the gym and start kicking off fights,' he admitted. 'I never told anybody I was training to be a boxer. I just kept my mouth shut and quietly went about beating them all up. You can't imagine what that was like because I had a lot of rage inside me, a lot of resentment for the world. I'd start dishing out punches for any slight reason. Sometimes, almost always, it was me who would provoke them. You know the kind of cocky idiot who looks at you and says, "What are you looking at?" The kind who doesn't care what you have to say. I was a real animal.'

Animal or not, Pintor was progressing. His amateur record was impressive and he had shown his independence by finally quitting his father's house for good at the age of sixteen. He had run away before, but this time it was different. Now, deep inside himself, Pintor maybe feared what he would do if his father kept up his ritual of violence. When he left home that day he knew it was for good. He travelled to his mother's house and was greeted by Francisco, who had already fled.

'Dude, what are you doing here?' Francisco said, surprise and pleasure tinting his face like ink on blotting paper.

Pintor explained and the pair hugged.

'It's great that you sent that lousy old arsehole to go fuck himself,' Francisco added. 'And don't worry about dough. You keep training and we'll see how we manage with the money I earn.'

One day at the Atlas, Hernandez took Ugalde to one side and engaged in a long discussion. It ended with him putting a hand on the trainer's shoulder and casting a cursory eye over to where Pintor was sounding out a rapid backbeat on the heavy bag. The look did not go unnoticed and Pintor knew what was coming. He was ready.

*

However, Hernandez found it hard to come up with a decent debut opponent for Pintor Who would want to see a novice pummelled in quick time? Sacrificial lambs were bad for business and the promoter, sitting by Hernandez in the Atlas, was not about to be browbeaten.

'He's just a kid, Cuyo,' he said. 'It's a mismatch.'

'Listen to me,' the manager said. 'Don't you worry about his age. He's a good kid.'

'Naah, I don't think so. He's never been in a ring. I can't do this.'

Hernandez fixed the promoter with a look that blurred the line between avuncular and threatening.

'I'll tell you what,' he said slowly. 'Take the fight and, if my boy loses, then I'll pay him myself.'

The promoter shrugged. He could afford a mismatch if it was free.

The fight was booked for 2 March 1974 in Tijuana. Pintor's opponent was Manuel Vasquez, a solid fighter who would end his career with as many losses as wins. He was never good enough to have a shot at any title, but he could make a living out of boxing. He was the career brawler, waging private wars for a steady income rather than gilt-edged ambitions, his face gradually flattening in compensation for the fattening wallet. He expected to beat Pintor, who was an unknown nineteen-year-old ripe for the humbling. And then the bell sounded and Pintor hit Vasquez and, from that first blow, the old pro realized all his preconceived ideas and the way he had massaged his ego with knee-jerk assumptions had been flawed. The fight did not go a single round.

'I knocked him out with a nice combination,' Pintor said. 'I had no nerves. I've never had nerves about fighting. The only time you feel like that is later in your career when you have trouble making the weight. Any wrong meal can mess it all up. That's a worry. But in 1974 I was carefree. It was easy and it was quick.'

The promoter paid Pintor and pulled Hernandez to one side.

'Hey, Cuyo, you've kept this kid well hidden. That was a lovely combination he put on Topo Gigio. What do you reckon we sign this form?'

Hernandez was never one to soften his fighters with fall guys and easy purses.

'I'll sign it,' he said 'but give me someone who'll go ten rounds.'

The promoter gave him Francisco Nunez, another rookie but one with a big punch and a strong record in the amateurs. Hernandez got his wish and the fight went ten rounds, with Pintor getting the decision.

'That was a really strange fight,' Pintor said. 'In fact I won it twice. I knocked him down in the fourth and we thought I'd won. I don't know what went on then and there was a lot of confusion and shouting, but the referee waved him back on. They kept this poor guy on his feet so I could hit him for ten rounds.'

Pintor was in a hurry in every area of his life. His boxing career was a rush of victories and, by the time of his second fight, he had moved out of his mother's house and got married to a sixteen-year-old girl named Coti. The daughter of a tortilleria owner, Coti had been infatuated with the muscular youth from the moment she'd met him.

'I'd just returned from a long trip and it was early in the morning, around six o'clock,' she remembered. 'He was already sweeping out the store and washing it down. I said, "This boy is mine."' The tortilleria was close to Don Lupe's store and Coti would be sent there to buy paper and matches. It was a task she enjoyed and, together, they learnt to dance rock and roll in the stockroom.

Despite his fiancée's age, Pintor had no qualms about telling his father he was getting married.

'You're only eighteen years of age,' he scoffed.

'I don't care,' Pintor replied. 'Coti is going to have a baby and I want it to grow up with me.'

Don Lupe looked barely interested. 'If you get married it's your problem and you'll have to sort it out.'

'I'm not asking you for anything,' Pintor said calmly. 'I've never counted on you for anything. I'm just letting you know so you can come with me to the wedding.'

'I don't have time for that,' Don Lupe snapped.

Pintor shrugged and left.

Nobody knows where Pintor's father was on his wedding day, but the groom was ambivalent about his absence. He used the five thousand pesos he had got for beating Vasquez to book a party and buy Coti a dress. He wore an old suit he had been given by the Olympic committee.

'The only thing I bought for myself was a tie, a really nice Hawaiian one, which I chose to clash with the colour of my suit and make me stand out,' he said.

Four months after his debut, Pintor was back in the ring. This time he did not have to make the trip to Tijuana and lined up opposite Manuel Casteneda in the Coliseo Arena.

'That place was a cock pit,' Eric Armit, an expert on Latin American boxing, said. 'Two guys would stand in the centre, toe to toe, and slug it out. If one of them moved towards the edge of the ring, to catch his breath for a moment, they were booed and abused. It was an incredibly macho environment.'

Olivares and Zarate had fought in the Coliseo, and Pintor

was happy not to have to travel. He did not tell his father, but Don Lupe found out anyway via a neighbour, who cajoled him into going along.

'We didn't even know where it was,' Pintor senior said. 'All we knew is that it was in the centre. Well, we got there and bought our tickets, but we were unlucky because they were right in the middle of the other guy's fans.'

Unaware that his father was watching, Pintor knocked Casteneda out in the fourth and impressed some of the seasoned boxing watchers. His father and his neighbour left in silence, not wanting to provoke Casteneda's supporters and sensing that Pintor would be just as unwelcoming.

Hernandez was now giving Pintor fights every two months. He craved more rounds for his latest charge because he knew nothing sustains a boxer like the knowledge that he can live with pain. Walkovers flattered egos. In September, Pintor returned to the Coliseo and got a points decision over Salvador Martinez. Hernandez was happy and Pintor was floating on air. He felt like a champion as Ugalde wrapped his hands in gauze and an elastic dressing a few weeks later, then attached the medical tape to hold them firm. Pintor flexed his hands. This was more than a ritual. He needed the gauze to protect more than twenty knuckle bones, but it had to be loose enough to allow his thumbs and fingers to be mobile. Already he trusted Ugalde. It was a partnership that was working and he felt like a world-beater. Zarate might be the star of the Atlas, but Pintor was the coming man. And then he sampled the other side of the coin. It was a windswept night at the Coliseo. The records say Magallo Lozada won after Pintor was disqualified in the fourth round, but he still disputes the verdict with righteous indignation.

'The fight was a fix,' Pintor said. 'I had it under control like you wouldn't believe. I was giving him a real beating and cut his eye. But his trainer claimed a headbutt and they fell for it. He was a smart guy. He knew what he was doing. It angered me for a while, but when I calmed down, I moved on. It didn't affect me because I knew in my heart I was right.'

Hernandez was irritated by the disqualification and the blip it put on the seamless record of victories, but he was not unduly concerned. Anyway, he had other fighters and bigger paydays to worry about. Zarate was edging towards a title shot and was now a Mexican hero, while Alfonso Zamora was just months away from becoming the WBA world champion on a heady night at the Forum. A bad decision for a rookie in a fight nobody would remember was no crisis, and he dismissed it by sending him back into battle just six weeks later. The lingering anger revealed itself in a second-round knockout. Pintor added seven more wins in 1975, all but one by knockout, and his reputation spread. For the first time he fought in America, knocking out Willie 'Birdlegs' Jensen, 'a tough and agile little negrito' at the Great Western Forum in Inglewood.

'I was outboxing him in the early rounds, but he put the pressure on after the fifth and started letting go with those low blows,' Jensen said. 'He caught me with a mean headbutt and they stopped it in the seventh. I didn't know if he'd go on to be a world champion at the time, but I knew he had to be good if they'd put him in a ring with me.' After twenty-two straight wins, Jensen had tasted the dark side of boxing for the first time.

Zarate also won that night, but Ruben 'El Puas' Olivares lost his world featherweight crown to David Kotey. That defeat saddened Pintor but he returned home from America armed with a mountain of furniture.

'We had no room and I said, "It's me or the furniture,"'

Coti recalled. 'He also had a top-of-the-range record player, which he attached to a pair of colourful speakers. He used to get home really excited and play his records at full volume. He really liked one about a red dress. He'd put it on every day and would look really happy and content, and that transferred to me.'

Back at the Atlas, his victory was heralded by a swarm of urchins buzzing around the entrance like flies, craving a sight of Pintor in action. Zarate, Olivares and many others who trained there also had their devoted flocks, but there was a new kid on the block, a new dream to test and a new hero to deify. 'CUYO'S LATEST JEWEL' cried the banner headline in the sports paper *Esto*. Jose Luis Gomez Camarillo was in his first year on the paper and found himself writing more and more about Hernandez's newest hope.

'He was eager to become one of the most known fighters on the team, but that was never going to be easy with the Z Men, Zamora and Zarate, and several other good prospects around,' he said. Pintor, though, had a bottomless pit of belief and his rugged aggression and punching power provided fixes for those who fed on the brutality of boxing. He was their man and his granitic violence inspired them.

Hernandez still felt Pintor was something of a loose cannon, but the Mexican backstreets and shanty towns were brimming with such volatility. He reasoned he could nurture him, but there were setbacks and gnawing doubts, fuelled in one instance by an ill-fated sparring session with a veteran named Lorenzo 'Halimi' Guiterrez. The old campaigner wanted to teach the young pup a lesson and used some wily tricks he had learnt during his long career to do so, holding Pintor by the arm while he swung a ·punch at his undefended side. He grinned. But Pintor shook himself loose, dropped his hands and kicked Guiterrez in the testicles. The fighter crumpled in a heap, his face plastered in pain and surprise. He caught a breath and launched himself at Pintor, sparking a brawl that spilled out on to the street.

'You're a fucking madman!' Guiterrez screamed. 'What the fuck's wrong with you?'

Pintor did not care.

Guiterrez wandered off, cursing his assailant, and complained to Hernandez. 'He's a, Cuyo. A crazy man.'

Hernandez nodded. Crazy, maybe, but he sure could punch.

Pintor enjoyed his new fame. He was twenty years old, full of resentment fused with vanity, and he liked the increasing attention of women. He was intoxicated by his ascent, disregarding the boxing code that casts the woman as a fatal seductress intent on shearing the fighter of his strength. Dick Owens told his son to forgo women until after his career ended. The advice was issued partly out of pity for the girlfriend who finds herself playing second fiddle to a road run or hanging around outside the gym on a Friday night, but also because romance and sex were seen as obstacles to dedication. Perhaps the sirens were partly responsible for luring Pintor on to the rocks when he met Alberto Davila for the first time on 25 February 1976.

Davila had spent his childhood in Texas but moved to Pomono, a short drive from Los Angeles, when he was twelve. It was a tough neighbourhood. Street gangs wore their allegiances with a restive pride and guns and drugs spewed a trail of carnage. Davila's father was a painter and carpenter and he sensed Alberto could do with something to encourage him to steer clear of the tempting ills. He told him to start boxing and so he joined the Sacred Heart Club, a gym attached to a local church.

Davila's heart really lay in LA. At the weekends he would say goodbye to his childhood sweetheart, Roberta, and drive over to the City of Angels. He would head for the famous Main Street Gym, an iconic sweatshop since it had opened in 1933, and ask if he could watch. If there was big title fight then the out-of-towners would train in there, and most of the greats had stood inside its tatty shell. 'World-rated boxers train here daily', the sign above the entrance read. Inside another said: 'Please don't bring children under 8 in the gym – we don't want anybody smarter than us here.' Davila knew the folklore and it thrilled him to stand where Rocky Marciano, Cassius Clay and Jack Dempsey had danced and slugged. Just as Pintor felt a rush of romance when he walked into the Atlas, so too Davila was hooked by his afternoons spent watching from the bench at the side of the gym.

'I'd drive over there and dream as I went,' he said.

The gym was owned and run by Howie Steindler. A feisty old crust with a soft spot for a sob story, Steindler had a lock on the phone in the office and a billy club on the wall. Occasionally, a down-and-out from the nearby Union Rescue Mission would wander in and need ejecting. Davila loved it. The place was a menagerie of exotic characters. There was big Duke Holloway with his green suit and derby hat. The mossy bear smoked a colossal cigar and had trained the almost mythical Joe Louis. There were the big names who might give him a wink or a smile, and then there was Steindler, the legend who had rebuilt the gym when it burnt down as the nightwatchman slept, and who would go on to be the model for the Burgess Meredith character in the *Rocky* films. Steindler only ever managed two boxers. One was Danny 'Little Red' Lopez. The other was Davila.

A glittering star of the amateur scene, Davila fought in

places like the East Side Boys Club and the Teamsters Gym, the Resurrection Gym and the Valley Gardens. He beat boys from Russia and Cuba and beyond. The move to the pro game came quickly, and he beat Carlos Villareal on his debut in LA in March 1973.

He won all but two of his next eighteen fights and became a regular at the Olympic Auditorium, that crumbling church of Hispanic angst. He was popular, and his slight frame, sleight of foot and tousled blond locks had earned him the nickname Tweedy, after the cartoon canary who always managed to evade trouble. Davila had also got married, to Roberta, and was receiving rave reviews.

'Pintor was the hardest man I ever faced,' he recalled. 'No question. He had a lot of technique to go with the power and was not a walk-in slugger by any means. He had a lot of KOs, but he had a lot of technique too. I did everything. I could avoid getting hit and I could be more aggressive when the time called for it. It was a good match.'

The fight with Pintor was a watershed for both men. Two rising stars, one Mexican, one American, bound up in a common aim, despite their differences. Davila was a clever man with a good brain and a decent code of ethics. He had never been involved with the street gangs back in Pomona and was faithful to his wife. A religious man, he saw no irony in tethering violence to a peaceful existence.

They met at the Great Western Forum at Inglewood. Danny 'Little Red' Lopez was on the undercard that night and won in four rounds. 'Good work, kid,' Howie Steindler spat. Now he would wait for the main event, the showdown between Davila, a manager's dream with his grace and looks, and another roughneck Mex from Cuyo Hernandez's gym.

'I was nothing out of this world in the gym,' Pintor said. 'I trained a lot of course, responsibly, and I put my back into it, but for some reason I looked a bit wiry and maybe a little bit weak. All that changed when I got in the ring. Perhaps that is just my way of acting in practically everything I do. I prefer to reserve my best, my ambition and my energy, for those things that are really important. But there's no room for being able to prepare better and ask for a rematch. I learnt all this quickly and the one who taught me was Alberto Davila.'

From the start Hernandez sensed something was not right. Davila was a virtuoso and was slipping Pintor's punches with some comfort, catching him with counter-attacks on the way out. The fluidity and pace of Davila exposed the more laboured toils of Pintor, who seemed intent on trying to knock his man to the canvas. But Davila was in a different class from anyone Pintor had faced and, although he was short and bony, he could hurt.

'He caught me real good,' Pintor said. 'It was my first fight at bantamweight and I got beat up. I didn't get a sniff and, from the first to the tenth round, he won the lot. If I finished on my feet at the end it was only because he didn't quite have the power of the great champions. It was a key point in my career because you know what it is like when you are young and arrogant. I thought I was the best. I was believing in myself too much.'

Davila outboxed Pintor and took an obvious decision. He embraced Roberta and had a meal with his delighted wife, but as he sunk into a hot bath he could feel his back stiffen and his stomach cramp in protest.

'I got hit by him once and I felt my entire body shake,' he said. 'I could feel that blow tingling in my toes. In those situations you don't let him see that you're hurt. You bluff. You come on and hit, try and make him miss. You just need to recover but inside you're hurting like hell.'

Pintor did not speak to Davila afterwards, something the smaller man would remember with a mixture of amusement and curiosity. Pintor was hurting, not so much from the accurate blows, the educated jab and the sweet right, but from embarrassment and regret.

'Every boxer comes to a crossroads and that was mine,' he said. 'You can go down one of two paths. You either work harder and improve or you are finished. I wasn't looking after myself properly at that point and I opened my mind to the fact I still had a lot to learn. From the night I lost to Davila I discovered something new from every fight. I paid attention to how my opponent boxed and gathered more experience. My style didn't change but my approach did. Losing motivated me to go on with a lot of courage. I got disciplined. I trained so hard I could have fought twenty rounds. The distance never bothered me. The longer the better. You learn so much as you mature, about techniques, styles and defence, but the most important thing is to stay in good shape. Any fighter, it does not matter who he is or how talented he is, has to be in great shape or, sooner or later, he will find himself in serious trouble. Boxing is a beautiful career because it is about discipline. The person who is most dedicated will get his reward.

'After Davila, life was hard for a bit. Everybody started getting on my back. The press criticized me and they made fun of me in the neighbourhood. It started to get me down because I still felt like a champion, even though I wasn't one and had got a hiding. Wherever I went, they would say, "Hey, *cabrón*, this time you took a good beating, huh?"'

Ugalde removed the bandages from Pintor's hands and spoke

about next time. The words drifted into the rotten air, unheard and unwelcome. In another changing room Davila got down on one knee, crossed himself and prayed for God to protect himself and his opponent. He knew their fight was not over.

ROUND FIVE

The impervious will of this ordinary man was stunning to behold that night in the Olympic. The innocence painted on those alabaster features would leave many observers pondering unanswerable questions. Guilt, pity, admiration and love would flood together in a maddening rush. It was fight night in Los Angeles and Merthyr was proud again.

Lupe Pintor, in white and blood-splattered trunks, most of it from cuts over his eyes. One over each now. Pintor with a right, just grazing the point of the chin, Owen comes back with a couple of his own, swarming on top of Pintor, throwing a lot of leather, another left, forcing the action.

Johnny Owen threw 148 punches in the fifth. Many were not true shots so much as the chugging, relentless breaths of the indefatigable, but they were thrown nevertheless. To put this in perspective, the all-time record for a single round is the 207 thrown by Zack Padilla in a WBO light-welterweight contest. Padilla's record was set in the last, when everything is on the line, the most brutal, desperate round of all. Yet Johnny Owen threw 148 punches in the fifth. *It makes you wonder if they are going to go another ten at this pace*, said Little Red. *It's definitely blistering.*

Tom Kelly was also absorbed by the action. Deep down, he suspected Pintor would come good. Owen did not look to have the power to stop Pintor and it would be hard to get a verdict in the Mexican's adopted home. And Pintor did have a habit of getting better as fights progressed. Owen might have been ahead but it was marginal. A lot could happen and this was only the fifth. *A good left-hand upper-*

cut from Pintor. It's obvious that Pintor hits harder but Owen hits more frequently.

Both men were being caught by punches. Pintor's crouching style meant Owen was often punching downwards. Left, right to the body, left, right to the head.

'I cannot understand the inclination of so many boxers to adopt an exaggerated crouch,' Jimmy Wilde wrote years ago in *The Art of Boxing.* 'It is not pretty and, what is more important, it is not effective.'

As the round drifted on, Pintor switched to a southpaw stance, boxing temporarily as a left-handed fighter. Again, Wilde would have been unimpressed. 'Presumably, the boxer who affects this stance is really left-handed, for that can be his only excuse – other than trying to perplex an adversary – for this attitude.'

Of course, boxing had changed enormously since Wilde's day, when fighters were more upright and less mobile, and Pintor, from his crouched southpaw stance, unleashed three uppercuts. The most vicious blow in the boxer's arsenal, they sprung Owen's head backwards. The uppercut is effectively designed to damage the brain and induce dizziness, but Owen shrugged them off. The effect appeared to last for only a fraction of a second as he came back harder, just as he had done when fighting against Marilyn back in the front room of their Merthyr council house. And there was always the sight of Pintor's blood, growing from blobs to streams, to act as his cheerleaders.

It's a pretty good gash. Opened in second round and it has grown. And Pintor has a cut over the right eye as well. The champion is marked and bloody, trunks more red than white. One minute to go in round five. They've been like this, toe to toe, since the bell started this fight. Johnny Owen is really showing us some kind of fighter.

It was another good round for Owen. He was bearing up well against by far the toughest man he had ever faced. As Pintor clasped his left with a cocked arm, Owen tapped him hard on the side of the face with his right. There was no respite for Pintor.

When the bell sounded, Pintor bounced to his corner. From the corner of a blood-drenched eye, he could see the people leaping up and down in the ringside seats and Johnny Owen walking back to his corner, slowly and methodically, hands hanging by his side. He knew he would be back for more. Just a natural-born fighter and tough beyond belief, as Jack London had once written. Just a mirror image of himself.

7

ASCENT

Vivian Owens never saw the boy. He was driving in the dark when the blur of colour dragged him into the present. He hit the brakes hard, pressing his right foot almost through the floor and instinctively wrenching the wheel in the opposite direction. It was too late. The bumper struck the child a glancing blow. The car screeched to a belated halt and, for an instant, there was a moment of calm as heavy breaths vied with the guiltless buzz of the radio. Then Vivian got out and he could hear the mother screaming and someone shouting for an ambulance.

Vivian tried to apologize but it was hard, and the woman scrunched up her face and pounded her palms into his chest.

'I'm sorry,' he spluttered. 'I didn't see him. He just ran out from behind the parked car.'

'You were going too fast,' she yelled as she bent to cradle her son. 'Too fast.'

Vivian's face was stretched. 'Is he okay?' he asked.

From the rear of a group that materialized like smoke from the drains, someone shouted: 'Ambulance is on its way.'

Vivian repeated: 'Is he okay?' The emotion cracked his voice.

Ten minutes later the boy was placed on a stretcher. Vivian could see that he was crying and felt a morsel of relief that he was well enough to do so. The mother waved a damning hand at him and mouthed something, but the words drifted off into the void. He realized the engine of his car was still humming. The blue lights flashed and the siren trumpeted his despair. He watched the ambulance disappear from sight and rubbed his forehead. It felt like the whole world was looking at him, twitching the nets and tutting judgement. A policeman arose from nowhere and said he needed to know what happened. The mother's words ebbed back into his mind and he remembered the threats.

'Better get a good solicitor, son,' the policeman said. Vivian nodded.

Somehow he drove to his parents' house. He was dazed and confused. He knocked on the door and the events tumbled out of him. Later that evening he and Dick visited the hospital and felt a leaden weight lift from their shoulders when they discovered the boy was shocked and bruised but not badly hurt. The mother, though, was still smarting and again shouted at Vivian.

'You could have killed him, you bloody idiot!' A nurse asked her to calm down, but the mother wanted a sounding board.

'I'm going to sue you for everything you've got,' she added.

'Now hang on,' Dick said. 'The police said it wasn't Vivian's fault. He ran out in the road. The main thing is he's okay.'

The mother refused to be placated. 'Yeah, you would say that. Well, I'm going to sue. I promise you that. I'll sue you for what you've done.'

Father and son left mother and son, grateful that the boy was not seriously hurt, but worried by the threat of legal action. They went home and sat in the front room, trying to reassure themselves that the mother would calm down. Their eyes ached from thought, the skin around their brows stretched tight. The latch opened and they instantly felt the cold. John stood there in his factory clothes and was surprised to see his brother. He scanned the drained faces.

'What's up?' he said.

'There's been an accident,' his father began and quickly recounted the story. 'How the hell are we going to afford a solicitor?' he pondered, the defeatism sinking in, Vivian wrestling with his head.

John sat down. 'Don't worry,' he said softly. 'I'll turn pro.'

Dai Gardiner was there. He had a thick nest of curly hair and matching beard. He had taken thirteen professional fights himself before a detached retina put paid to his own wars. After boxing, he worked down the pit, dug holes and laid pipes for the gas board, moonlighting as an amateur trainer.

'I started in a gym next to the old Empire,' he said. 'It used to be an old snooker hall and we stripped off the slates to make the first ring. There was a tin miner's bath and it was freezing cold. The only warm place was the dressing room.'

He had taken out his manager's licence in 1973, when he realized he was going to lose his best amateurs if he did not, and now held the registration number 92268 in his big, clammy hands.

Also sitting around the table at the New Inn in Tredegar on 1 September 1976 was Heddwyn Taylor. One of five children, he had been raised in a squat terrace and had skived off school once a month to follow the coal lorries, shovelling up the waste from the deliveries and selling it to the power stations. The teenage Taylor wanted to be a singer and passed his audition to train at the College of Music and Drama in Cardiff. A decade on he did a summer season in Jersey and came home to open a mine with his brother.

'It was a disaster,' he said. 'We owed the bank a lot of money, but we persevered because we knew there was coal up there.'

That was ten years ago and the coal had indeed run deep. It was black gold for Taylor and he was now a wealthy man with contacts. The previous winter he had been sitting in the Grosvenor House Hotel in Park Lane when Stanley Baker, the actor, asked him to sing. Taylor got up and belted out 'Bonny Mary Of Argyle', whereupon Stewart Granger, the Hollywood star, began applauding. 'He said, "That was lovely. It's my grandfather's favourite song. Look me up sometime."' Never one to let a chance go by, Taylor did.

Boxing was his other love. As a boy, he had travelled to London to watch Dai Dower fight and had been mesmerized by Winstone's talents when he sat in on his sparring sessions. So, bankrolled by his mine, he had decided to move into promoting and was now offering John £60 to buy some equipment.

Billy Vivian was also there. A big-hearted man with a dense Merthyr accent, he had started training with Gardiner when he was seven. He had won the Welsh senior featherweight title as an amateur when he had just turned seventeen and the future was bright. The he went off the rails.

'I got in with the wrong crowd at the wrong time and worked out a little borstal,' he said.

Four months later he was released and spent eighteen months working as a steel erector. Then he 'got caught' again and was sent back to borstal. When he re-emerged that April, he knew he was at his crossroads.

'It was only teenage stuff, but I had to make a decision. So I came home and the first thing I did was ask my dad where my boots were. I hadn't boxed for three years, but I had to do it to stop myself.'

He felt strong. He was not worried about the time he had spent out of the game or about his talent dimming. Married, with his young son, Lee, at home, he was turning pro and turning his back on his past.

Danny Galleozzie, John's old trainer, was there to pass on the flame, and Dick and Vivian Owens completed the septet. Vivian wanted to give his brother some moral support. He was supping from a pint and was feeling happy. The mother had not turned up to the court and the case against Vivian had been dismissed. Nevertheless, he was full of gratitude that his brother had accelerated his decision to make a living from boxing. It proved the ties of blood, and his brother's unfathomable good-ness. He was the skinny little kid who, as Dick had predicted, was looking after them all.

Dick felt a surge of pride and was glad he and Kelvin had persuaded the boxer to ditch his favoured *nom de guerre*. The registration forms allowed a moniker of the boxer's choice, but everyone baulked against John's suggestion of Sion Rhisiart Owain, which they believed, wrongly as it turned out, to be the Welsh translation of his name. They were all proud patriots, but they knew such a cumbersome banner would be a burden. And so they argued and bickered and eventually Sion Rhisiart Owain became plain and simple Johnny Owen.

In Merthyr's pubs and gyms, opinions are offered with disarming candour. There is no time for niceties. Different people have different angles. For Jeff Pritchard, who would become Johnny's principal sparring partner, Dai Gardiner was a fantastic trainer. To Billy Vivian, who became soured by his treatment and the paltry purses, he was anything but. To those

119

whom he had helped via his charity work, he was a legend, while Dick Owens would for years refuse to even shake the hand of the man he once partnered. But in the New Inn on that evening there was only excitement. Johnny and Billy Vivian signed the forms and turned pro. If they thought that would mark the end of their problems they would be disappointed.

The first came with the first fight. After just a few days' training in Gardiner's gym in New Tredegar, nestled into a cliff-face on a steep sweep down a valleyside, the manager had come up with an opponent, George Sutton, the same boxer who had beaten Johnny as an amateur when he had been suffering with a septic finger. He was rated the no. 3 challenger for the British title and it presented a daunting initiation for a fighter taking his first steps into the real hurting business.

Martyn Galleozzie knew both men well. He had already been a professional for three years and was managed by Mac Williams, whose stable also included Sutton. Galleozzie had been there when the match was made at the National Sporting Club in London. The matchmaker, Les Roberts, had been sceptical.

'I can't believe they think they can put this Owen fella in with Georgie,' he'd scoffed. 'He won't have a prayer.'

It was what Williams wanted to hear. Some people were already labelling Sutton as the best prospect to come out of Wales since Winstone. It was an outlandish claim, born of the instant gratification that came from a big punch and one that overlooked Sutton's habit of smoking a cigarette just before his fights. Nevertheless, Williams could envisage a long and lucrative career, with all its accompanying titles and trappings. Georgie had a chance and he did not need the bubble bursting.

'What do you think, Martyn?' he asked.

Galleozzie shrugged his eyebrows and, in his soft velvet voice, said: 'I know Johnny Owen.'

'So what do you think?'

Galleozzie sniffed. 'Get him fit.'

'Oh, come on,' Williams said. 'Georgie's a banger.'

'I know he's a banger, Mac,' Galleozzie replied. 'But get him fit. Very fit.'

And so, on 30 September 1976, the dance began. The leisure centre in Pontypool rocked with Sutton's growing support. Marion Evans, Wales's only woman promoter, and her husband, Jack, were busy telling everyone Owen deserved his place on the top of the bill.

'Sutton hasn't had much experience either,' Jack Evans said. 'And I'm sure Owen could have beaten everyone Sutton's met.'

Sutton was confident and Gardiner had some festering doubts. He had already clashed with Dick by suggesting they should pull Johnny out and look for a smoother baptism.

'You should have thought of that before you took the fight,' Dick had said. 'Leave the match on. John will beat Sutton.'

Gardiner was nervous. He had faith in Johnny, but had a mounting sense of regret. 'I'll get hauled over the coals if something goes wrong,' he groused.

When Johnny made his way to the ring there were guffaws and catcalls. A fat man in a cap and muffler stood up and shouted: 'I thought we were having boxing tonight – not a bloody greyhound meeting.' In the balcony Johnny's sister Susan grimaced. Her heart beat a drum roll. She fidgeted in her seat and grabbed a pint of lager off Vivian. 'My need is greater than yours,' she said and took a long swig.

When the bell sounded, both men seemed wary, edging their way into the fight, a double-fisted flurry from Sutton evincing his power, Johnny tapping away with a relentless rhythm. And then, to the delight of his sister in the balcony, it was as if the mists of negativity cleared and he was standing in naked defiance in the centre of that ring. Suddenly, he had the measure of Sutton. He began to dictate the pace of the bout and frustrated Sutton by soaking up his heavier shots. In the sixth round, Johnny's endeavours opened a cut above the more experienced man's left eye and the crowd, witnessing Pontypool's first full professional fight night for a quarter of a century, groaned for their man.

At the break before the eighth and last round, Williams doused his man in water and told him it was all or nothing. That is boxing – fight or flight, win or lose, there is no middle ground.

Sutton tried. He tore after Johnny and rained down the clubbing fists, but his opponent slipped some and was unhurt by the others. He returned the fury and took the decision. Susan and Vivian hugged, while Dick wiped away the sweat with the towel that had hung unused over his shoulder. The official verdict was a half-point triumph, but the local pressmen agreed that the margin flattered Sutton.

'It's back to the drawing board,' Williams told them. 'George's greater experience should have carried him through, but Owen fought really well.'

Gardiner was jubilant and also relieved.

'I would have been in trouble with the boxing authorities if he had been a flop,' he told the local hacks as he celebrated. It was Gardiner shooting from the hip, a trait that was endearing to some but which would help sever his alliance with Dick in the years ahead. Johnny himself was generous as he conducted his first interview.

'Sparring with excellent boxers like Billy Vivian and Jeff Pritchard really sharpened me,' he said.

In the background, his father sloped away to the payphone and queued impatiently to ring the call box at the agreed time so that he could tell Edith the news.

Johnny's sparring partners also toasted the triumph. Their relationship with him would be the bedrock of his success. They all shared in the hardship of pro boxing. Johnny got a net £125 for his win over Sutton. Pritchard, meanwhile, was embroiled in a wrangle with his old manager, Benny Jacobs, claiming he had not had enough bouts to cover the loss of £200 he had suffered by taking his advice and switching from a job down the Britannia Pit to one on the surface.

Pritchard had a bit of the devil in him and knew how to handle himself. When he had been at mining school, one braggart from another mine had mocked him.

'He said we were all wankers at Britannia,' he recalled. 'He fancied himself and wanted to have a go because he knew I did a bit of boxing. I told him to shut up, but he said "Put your money where your mouth is." I didn't want to do it but I had to. By the time we were called into the manager's office, the other boy had two black eyes. Johnny wasn't like the rest of us. He was a gentleman.'

Johnny would pick up Billy Vivian and drive him to training.

'When you sparred with him he was a pest,' Billy said. 'He was always in your face. It was just continuous. He'd bore you to death. But he had a wicked sense of humour. We'd have a great laugh and always take the piss out of each other. And the women were all over him. They wanted to mother him.'

Pritchard has similar memories.

'I probably sparred with Johnny as much as anyone. Literally thousands upon thousands of rounds. We'd do eight every night and Johnny would have done twenty if you'd let him. I was nearly a stone heavier than him and hit him with some cracking right hands. I'm not being big-headed, but I was good and he took it all. He didn't have a good jab and he didn't have a good right hand, but it was poom, poom, poom. He would fight all day. I'd say, "Fuck off, Johnny, get out of my face." Then I'd say, "For God's sake, Johnny, go back a bit," but he couldn't take a backwards step – it wasn't his nature.'

Vivian was unconvinced by Gardiner's methods.

'All Dai Gardiner ever did was call time and spar. We had no weights and there was another problem. I never fought a bum but I wasn't getting any money. My first fight was against someone who had already had eight bouts. Then I fought a former all-Ireland champion. Dai said it was hard getting fights because of my reputation, but I hadn't boxed for three years. I didn't have a fucking reputation.

'I was due to fight Tommy Dunn from Reading, but one Sunday at training, Dai told me he'd pulled out. "They want you to fight Colin Power instead," he said. Now Colin Power was very tasty. "And they want you to take a cut in wages," he added. I'm stupid so I said okay. I went from £400 to £250 and got beaten up in two rounds. I didn't know any better at the time.'

There was another incident that further tested Vivian's impression of his trainer. One night at the gym the boxers were surprised to see a man dressed in his karate whites, barefoot and tying his black belt around his waist. Gardiner explained that he was a guest and he felt he could teach the boxers some new skills. Quite how the posturing and kicks would translate to the ring was unclear.

'Right, I want you to hit him, John,' Gardiner said.

'Are you sure?' the boxer replied.

'Go on, it'll be okay.'

The smallest of the boxers, Johnny raised his eyebrows, clenched his fist and punched the black belt's padded hand. He went flying backwards.

'Now fuck off out of here,' Vivian said before turning on Gardiner. 'What are you doing, man?' The karate experiment was never repeated.

The bond between the gym-mates grew with each day and fight. Johnny and Vivian were both on the bill on a bizarre night in Londonderry for what were their second fights as professionals. Given a police escort, the party, including Vivian's father, Billy senior, Byron Board and Vivian Owens, were amused and concerned as they made their way to their hotel by the southern border with the Republic on the eve of the bout. They were warned not to wear poppies and were given a guided tour of the Troubles' bombsites by their taxi driver.

Fight night was be no less eventful. Billy Vivian was the first of the Merthyr men to take his place and suffered the indignity of being sent sprawling to the canvas.

'It was the end of the first round and the first time I'd ever been on my arse,' he said. 'It was my first knockdown and it was more of a shock thing than anything else. You don't worry about being knocked out as a boxer, because you don't feel it. I got up and boxed like a dream.'

His points win would prove one of the least eventful aspects of the night's action. During the boxing, a phalanx of soldiers trotted into the Templemore Sports Complex to a cacophony of boos. People held chairs aloft and waved them angrily at the troops. Word quickly spread that a phone call had been received and there was a bomb in the building. Unused to such twists, Billy Vivian senior twitched in his seat and suggested they all leave, whereupon a pink-faced local stopped him.

'Don't you worry, Taff,' he said. 'They aren't going to bomb this place. The top boys are all in here.'

The bouts continued and finally the top-of-the-bill clash between Johnny Owen and Neil McLaughlin, a former Ireland international, was called. It was a one-sided affair as Johnny pursued an evasive opponent around every inch of the canvas. He was totting up a comfortable points win when the lights went out and plunged the arena into pitch darkness. The Welsh party was frustrated and panicked, naturally linking the black-out to the bomb scare. Voices permeated the fog and tempers frayed in the blindness. Two minutes passed as slowly as two hours before light was restored.

'Clever buggers,' Vivian senior said. 'You've switched your man with his twin because he was losing.'

Those close to him laughed and the tension washed away. Vivian's son, however, noticed something telling in the ring.

'When the lights came back on, the thing I remember is Johnny was still holding his position, standing just off centre, looking to where McLaughlin was. He didn't go back to his corner. He just stood there, not moving, ready and waiting. He won the fight but they scored it a draw.'

It was not mere bias that governed Vivian's appraisal. At an after-show party, where the Olympian Mary Peters met the Owens, the promoter, Charlie 'Ming' Harkin, sought out the novice fighter and shook his hand.

'I've had a very good night but I feel sorry for you, John,' he said. 'But that's pro boxing. You'll find that you are going to have to accept bad decisions.'

In his next contest Johnny clubbed Ian Murray to the floor of the Rhondda Sports Centre twice to remove any iota of doubt. The bout was promoted by Eddie Thomas and was a union between different generations of Merthyr's finest.

By Christmas 1976, Johnny had been a professional for three months and had taken three fights. It had been a decent start. As the wintry drizzle blurred Merthyr, he drove over to the gym. He opened the car boot and took out bundles of brightly wrapped presents. Inside, the strained lighting swathed Pritchard and Vivian in a dirty yellow. Then they saw Johnny and stopped. The ball and bag swung to stillness.

'I've got Christmas presents for the kids,' he said.

Neither man has forgotten the generosity.

'He knew who your children were,' Vivian said. 'They weren't just any old presents. He really thought about what they'd like. There were a few of us in the gym then. Stuart Taylor had a little baby so he got a soft toy. My son, Lee, got a toy rifle. Jeff had two kids and they got something. Little things like that tell you a lot about a man.

'When Lee was five he went to one of Johnny's fights and all you could hear was this little kid shouting, "Stick him, Johnny, stick him." He loved John. Now he's thirty-one and a martial artist. He has still got Johnny's gloves and there's two photos on his mantelpiece – one of me and one of Johnny.'

Pritchard was also touched.

'When John won titles he would always come to the house at Christmas and bring presents for us,' he remembered. 'I had two boys and he'd get them things like a rocking horse. Not little things. He had a heart of gold.'

Pritchard appreciated the gesture in the Christmas of '76 as his career had taken a knock a few weeks earlier when he had been given a shot at Les Pickett, the Welsh featherweight champion. The title bout filled the gym with a sense of anticipation, but the fight in Solihull was a brutal affair for Pritchard.

'I underestimated Les Pickett,' he said. 'I'd sparred with him two years before when fighting in the Welsh ABA finals. Bang, bang, bang. He cut all his lip and had a bleeding nose, so I thought Les Pickett won't hurt me. I didn't train as hard as I could and he put me down in the second. I was down again in the fifth and Dai said, "You're not going out for the eighth." I said I was. I went out for the ninth too, but came back and said, "Dai, that's it." Les was five foot five inches and a built like a bulldog. That's what he was. A dog of a man.'

Les and his brother, Mike, came from Merthyr too and would become friends of the Owens. They were all linked by their scars, waging personal assaults on the world. There was Pritchard, Vivian, the Pickett boys and Martyn Galleozzie, the son of Owen's old kind-hearted trainer. That December Galleozzie had won the vacant Welsh lightweight title and was in the midst of a two-bout epic against Johnny Wall. He won one and lost one, the vagaries of boxing summed up in those two brutal contests.

'We'd grown up together and I won the first one on points,' Galleozzie said. 'There wasn't much in it, but I never thought I could lose. Without being big-headed, and I really don't want to be big-headed, I was always a better boxer and bigger puncher. That was my downfall in the rematch. I went in thinking I couldn't be beaten. I wanted to hurt him and that meant it wasn't easy. It was all-out war but it wasn't like a brawl. It was a quality fight. Good toe-to-toe punches. Johnny Wall was a good combination puncher and a good body-puncher. I got a cut and lost. I was gutted for a long time. The he lost the title to Kelvin Webber and I took it back. I offered Johnny a third fight but he wouldn't have it. Two years later I fought an eliminator for the British title, but by then I was gone.'

Jim Brimmel, the experienced referee who had taken charge of European title bouts, described the second all-Merthyr affair between Galleozzie and Wall as 'the greatest fight I have ever refereed'. Wall told the local press that a punch from Pritchard, his sparring partner, had opened up a one-inch gash on his bottom lip and had put the fight in jeopardy. He added that he was going to buy a new car with his £1,000 cheque. 'I only passed my test last week.'

On the undercard that night was Billy Vivian, fighting and winning after 10 p.m. to avoid infringing the rule that prohibits a fighter who has been knocked out from returning to the ring within three weeks. And there was Johnny Owen too, out-pointing Neil McLaughlin for the second time in a month to push himself towards a Welsh title bout against his old adversary, George Sutton. It had been a modest performance, however, which convinced his brother Kelvin that he was a jinx. In future, he told himself, he would stay away.

For a patriot like Johnny, the prospect of a Welsh championship made him salivate. Sutton had sworn to avenge his earlier defeat and had even taken to growing a beard as a reminder he had a score to settle. 'I'll shave it off when I beat him,' he said, although the rule barring beards did the job first. Heddwyn Taylor had pulled off a coup by securing the rights for what would be his first promotion. He had also convinced the Welsh Area Council to sanction the fight as a Welsh championship bout. Doubts about Owen's lack of experience had been a barrier, but now the council relented. Indeed, the bout was slated as an eliminator for the British title and Taylor, blessed with the bottomless blarney of the boxing suits, was already talking of bringing Paddy Maguire, the champion, to Ebbw

Vale. Never mind the fact that Maguire's silver-tongued manager was Mickey Duff. 'Oh, I'll offer him enough money,' Taylor boasted perkily.

In the build-up Johnny did his usual preparation. Frank Martin, the foreman at the factory where he worked, had come up with an idea to help his strength. He said he knew a spot of land by the old canal that had once shipped coal to Cardiff. There was an old miner's cottage down there and the place was owned by a man named Darren Hill. Martin knew Hill and suggested Johnny go there and chop down trees. Hill was happy to agree, and his four daughters would sit on a wall and watch the boxer go through his paces.

'They used to have a good old natter,' Dick Owens said. 'He loved being with children.'

Johnny loved the work, too, and the pain it induced in his shoulders as he held the axe and scythed down the rambling trees. He knew it was doing him good. So he cut and ran. Up the hills and the Glyn and by the Blue Pool and the sanatorium. Down the streets in his grey sweats topped off with his red and white bobble hat, oblivious to the lorries spraying him with mud, acknowledging the cries of those growing familiar with his daily routine.

Taylor had booked the fight for 29 March 1977 at the Ebbw Vale Leisure Centre. Johnny would fight in the compact arena another six times. 'It was his home turf,' Taylor said.

Sutton could not cope. A right hook sent him spinning in the fifth, by which time he was bleeding and tiring. Johnny came back to the corner and looked surprised.

'He's cursing me,' he said. 'You should hear it. Terrible language.'

The power that had posed a lurking danger in the early exchanges filtered away from Sutton. He tried to revitalize himself with a warm-up routine between rounds, but he was an ailing force and the body-shots from Johnny sapped him of his will.

'George was the blue-eyed boy of Welsh boxing, but John was convinced he could beat him over the longer distance,' Kelvin said.

At the final bell Sutton tapped Johnny on the back of his head, a small but noble gesture and an acknowledgement that he had won. The referee, Joe Morgan, scored the fight 99–97½.

Gardiner remembered: 'Georgie said to me, "Dai, he's like a bleeding octopus. Hands come out of nowhere." But Sutton always admired Johnny. He was a lovely boy, George, but he was a bit of a drinker. It was a shame because he could have gone a long way.'

The title achieved, the celebrations began.

'We met up with Byron Board's wife, Esther, and we went to a Greek café in Cardiff to celebrate,' Dick said. 'We had a party until about three in the morning. Byron and Esther went home and me and the family went back to Merthyr, but we were so excited that we drove up to the Brecon Beacons. It was a great night. There was John, his mother, Susan, Vivian, Kelvin, Dilwyn and myself. We were all running about for hours, happy and laughing. We were lucky nobody saw us or they would have thought we were a bunch of loonies.'

The boxer and his family danced on the Beacons until the hush of twilight was replaced by the rising sun. The family drifted home at 6.30 a.m. and the first knock on the door from a reporter came an hour later. When they picked up the local paper they realized Johnny was no longer routinely referred to as the machine-setter from Merthyr.

'Sutton came from a family of boxers and was a clear favourite,' Gareth Jones, then working for the *Western Mail*, explained. 'But Johnny had this incredible work-rate. He had big ears and was skinny, but it was his energy that surprised me. He never stopped, like a Duracell bunny. These were the days when *The Six Million Dollar Man* was on TV, so I started calling him the 'bionic bantam' and he liked it. The next thing I knew he was wearing a T-shirt with it printed on.'

Gardiner was delighted too. Pritchard and Vivian had also won that night, but Gardiner sensed Johnny was special and had a unique pulling power, an extra dimension. His appeal went way beyond the Labour Club, the fourteen pubs and the station café which used to be a drop-in centre for the fight fraternity.

Gardiner remembered: 'When people bought a ticket for Johnny's fight, they'd say, "I want one for my wife, one for my daughter and one for my mother-in-law." Everybody wanted to nurse him. I took some terrible abuse off women telling me I shouldn't let him box. It got very bad. They said I was starving him.

'When he won the titles, all he wanted was a gateau and a curry. Nothing else. He lived like that for three days and then he was back on the road. But though he was very thin, Johnny was big-boned. We had to be very careful keeping him on the weight. I always brought him on the scales smack on. He would train four pounds overweight, but it wasn't hard to take that off. In title fights everyone had to be under the eight-stone, six-pound limit.'

To escape the press, who were clamouring to get a word with the new Welsh champion, Johnny and his father crept out and walked up the mountain. It was their time to reflect. Dick contemplated his son and the yawn of Merthyr.

'Did you see the way they threw nobbins into the ring after the Noel Evans and Jimmy Bott fight?' he asked.

Johnny's breath turned to smoke. He felt like a Welsh dragon, inviolable and defiant. Nothing could stop him. He had seen the nobbins, the coins thrown by the crowd in appreciation of a particularly savage war, but failed to see what it had to do with him.

'I don't want to see that in any of your fights,' his father continued. 'They only throw nobbins when you've been in a tough, gruelling fight. I don't want that for you.'

His son gave him a sly, almost imperceptible, half-smile but said nothing. They both realized that tougher fights lay ahead.

ROUND SIX

Colin Hart knew Merthyr. He had been at the Garden the night Ken Buchanan beat Ismael Laguna and Eddie Thomas slit his man's eye with a razor blade. 'Cut him, Eddie, for God's sake, cut him!' Peter Wilson, the doyen of British sports writers, had screamed from the ringside in New York. Wilson, who carried a sword inside a walking stick in case anyone decided to seek revenge for something he had written, grew increasingly animated. Sitting next to Hart that night had been David Gray, the tennis writer for the *Guardian*, who had been told to cover the fight while attending the US Open at Forest Hills. 'What does he mean?' he had asked as he listened to Wilson's strenuous pleas. 'He wants Eddie to cut his eye,' Hart explained.

'You're not serious,' Gray replied. The doctor looked in at the corner. That was when Eddie had taken out the blade and slit the bloated skin, unleashing a geyser of blood. 'It was like a fountain,' Hart would recall. 'And Gray's face went as grey as his name. He nearly fainted.' That had been a wonderful night. It had been one of those occasions when the smarting anguish of this sport meshed with Runyonesque romance. Thomas had had doubts about whether Owen should have taken the Pintor fight, but the proof was on that roped stage. Hart, meanwhile, would have to write his report for the *Sun* and record a piece for BBC Radio, and he hoped he would be the messenger of glad tidings. At one-third distance he had Owen ahead on his card.

I'm Tom Kelly and I'm here with former featherweight champion, Danny Lopez, and sports editor of the LA Herald-Examiner, *Allan Malamud. It's the start of round six and Johnny Owen has simply been a marvel.*

If there was one thing that set Owen apart from the hundreds of boys who clenched fists on colourless streets at home, it was his dedication. The dedication had spawned a resilience which blossomed into heart. Owen could not punch as hard as Pintor, but he could mitigate his opponent's blows. He locked his head with Pintor's and they pushed at each other. Pintor's cuts and the apparent ineffectiveness of his punches pricked at the champion's cavernous belief in himself. He never doubted his ability to last the course, but the soft sensation of blood on his lids and the air in the torn flesh confused him. There were no breathers. This was not a fight where the boxers strutted as peacocks. There were few long-range jabs, a paucity of classical exchanges. Both men were thinking, plotting courses to the higher ground, but it manifested itself in a little war.

The sixth was another good round for Owen. Pintor threw a long left that missed by a good six inches as Owen ducked. It was a ragged blow that smacked of desperation. Some of those at ringside wondered if Pintor's cuts were provoking him into a careless quest for a quick knockout. Owen kept stabbing away, a left and right through Pintor's defence propelling him into the Mexican's greying face. Owen was trying to put as much glove into those cuts as he could.

Danny, if you were throwing as much leather as Pintor and hitting your man with as much leather as Pintor is, you'd have to be a little bit discouraged that the guy is still there throwing punches at you.

Little Red agreed. Pintor had landed with some of his best shots. The lefts to the body were heinous blows, while the right hook had careered on to Owen's head in almost every round. But Owen was incredible, an untainted spirit and a man who clearly felt he could win this fight. They had written him off and they had mocked him, but Johnny Owen was putting up a hell of a fight.

Kelly was just as impressed. *Pintor must wonder whether Owen has a connecting rod between jaw and brain because he does not seem to mind a thing. One and a half to go in round six.*

Malamud was as surprised as his fellow commentators. Pintor was a fairly typical Mexican fighter. Hugely popular for his unsubtle style, it had seemed inconceivable that Pintor would lose to this rake. But it was hard to pick a winner at this point. As well as being freakishly thin, Owen was also oddly tall for a bantamweight. At five foot eight inches, he had four inches on Pintor, which was a definite plus for him. Pintor tried to unleash uppercuts to undermine those inches, to chop Owen down and cut the bark. There was blood on their faces, but both men looked as strong as ever. This one might even go the distance.

Halfway through the round, Pintor stood back to make room and fired off a series of slow and deliberate punches. It was as if his arms were attached to a pulley system and for a fleeting moment it rendered him an almost pathetic figure. It was measured stuff that again made some consider whether Pintor was fighting from memory. Boxing is full of drama. The combatants are masters of disguise, masking their inadequacies with tricks. They are high-stakes poker players, pulling the skin tight over whitened knuckles but never showing their hands. They bluff and smile and drop their guards to impress their strength on an opponent, while secretly feeling like strangled cadavers.

On the balcony above the Welsh, the most virulent of the Mexican fans urinated in the beer cups they had drained and threw them into the blackness. And the Welsh kept on singing. Hart could hear them at ringside. He had seen them when they walked in, brandishing their banners and in happy voice. 'They know not what they do,' he had thought. And the power of the bear pit seduced them all.

Cuyo Hernandez had seen it all before. He knew Pintor was good, but he was still disconcerted by the blood. Hernandez ruled his fighters with tough love, but he was also a man steeped in the whims and traditions of this noblest and seediest of games. There had been rumours that he had invented some of Zarate's early fights to cover a spell when he had been in prison. How else could Zarate have come from absolutely nowhere to top the rankings? Hernandez denied any such wrongdoing, though he loved his fighters enough to stretch the boundaries.

Now he looked at Pintor and was worried. Between the rounds he would offer a few words of advice and try to pick up his boxer. He would hold a swab-stick against the cuts and absorb the blood. He flicked one between his teeth like a toothpick. Then he would apply a blob of Vaseline. In the past there had been lots of stories of bizarre concoctions, magic potions and something called Elephant Shit. Some were true, some were urban myths. Hernandez had seen fighters' careers wrecked because of cuts, but he knew any one of those drunks out there would trade a shredded face to be the world champion. Lupe was the same. If his skin was damaged for ever, thinned to parchment around the eyes, then it was worth it to stay at the top. Surely he could not lose, but hell, this Owen kid was tough.

Johnny Owen looks to me like the sort of guy you would want on your side when the fight started in the pub. Pintor with a flurry, Owen right back with a flurry of his own. Half a minute to go in the sixth round. Pintor with mouth open and mouthpiece showing. Twenty seconds to go and Johnny Owen has been doing what he's doing now, throwing leather, almost non-stop, for six solid rounds.

As the end of another round neared, some of those at ringside noticed something ominous for the first time. Marty Denkin had seen it long ago. Dick Owens and Dai Gardiner knew about it and were monitoring it. Now it was bad enough for the ringsiders to see. Black-red blood was seeping from the corner of Johnny Owen's mouth. The bottom lip was severed. Up close Denkin could see that the skin was flapping loose and Owen was having to swallow his own blood.

Owen tried to ignore it and, in those last few seconds of the sixth, struck with a combination that rocked Pintor. It was a good, accurate assault. The right landed on Pintor's nose and slipped into the cut right eye. The left was not as powerful, but kept Pintor thinking. *He's backed Pintor up again and the bell will bring us to the end of round number six.*

Little Red saw the blood and puffed out his cheeks. This was a gruelling, wrenching, fight. All around men were singing and screaming. It was entertainment, but it was being provided at a cost. Few of these people realized just what a boxer gives under the pseudonym of sport, but their blood-lust could not be sated. They had been sucked down into the maelstrom.

8

THE NAKED BOXER

The cruelty of boxing is that the better you get the harder it becomes. Overcome an obstacle and there will always be another, bigger, more perilous one in the distance. Like the desert traveller reaching for the horizon, tantalizingly close but forever out of grasp, it is a never-ending journey. The best that you can hope for is to find an oasis of calm along the way and bask in its reviving sting.

George Sutton would fight Johnny Owen again in September 1977 and would lose for a third time. No longer did anyone suggest he was the new Winstone. Now his lobbyists would be mocked for claiming he had an iota of Winstone's skill or charisma. Sutton would win just five of his last eighteen bouts before he disappeared into the sands of time, just another brave man who never made it. But for the hundreds struggling to confront their limitations, there are those who continue to rise. If they fall, they haul themselves to their feet, rather than seeking solace in drink and nicotine. They are the concentrated fighters, the pure spirits, the naked flames. When Sutton was beaten to the Welsh title, it was only a matter of time before Johnny Owen would stand in a ring with the British title at stake, burning with ambition, singeing the corners with his incandescence, ready to scald unblemished skin with his fire.

His father bought him a statuette to mark his triumph, as the Welsh title only came with a certificate, and talk quickly turned to a possible bout with Paddy Maguire, the reigning British champion. Dick was intent on keeping his son focussed rather than have him trip on scampering dreams, and so they worked harder than ever. The father and sons – Vivian and Kelvin – bundled into a van and followed the boxer up steep, knee-knocking roads. At one point Vivian would jump out and race his brother for two hundred yards. Exhausted, he would get back into the car and Kelvin would take a turn. When they came to the house where the clanking chain signified a charging dog, Johnny would run on the other side of the van. He kept chopping trees too, sometimes too many.

'Bloody hell,' one landowner said as he approached him, shaking his arms aloft. 'Don't chop any more down here. There's an order on them. You'll land us all in jail.'

His time was coming, but boxing is a lurching ride with problems never more than a rogue punch away. Things went off course on a bitter night at the gym. It was one of the few sessions Dick did not attend and, back at home, he checked his watch and frowned.

'Where's John?' he asked his wife.

Edith was clearing up the plates.

'I don't know. He hasn't been home yet.'

That was odd, Dick thought. Time was getting on and the boxer was punctual. When the latch finally clicked and the door was edged open, they heard a voice.

'Don't panic,' it said. Why should they panic? And then he walked into the front room with a huge white pad clutched over one eye.

'What happened?' Dick said solemnly.

'It was an accident,' his son began. 'I was sparring and the strap of my headguard broke. Dai said it would be all right to carry on.'

'He said what!' Dick exploded. 'I've told you not to spar without the guard. Jesus.'

'The punch missed me, but the elbow didn't,' Johnny continued. 'I've been up Prince Charles Hospital.'

It was a horrible gash, the skin seared and black-red.

'You should have listened to me,' Dick said. 'If that cut keeps opening, your future as a boxer is non-existent.'

In the following weeks, Dick drew on all his knowledge. He spent weeks working on the cut with his rough magic. The cut men are not surgeons or nurses, but they have the knack. They are the tribal chiefs, concocting potions and listening to their muse, from bar to street to bookie. Like Eddie Thomas slitting Buchanan's eye and Cuyo Hernandez and his Elephant Shit. When the cut had healed, Dick began the hardening process.

'I had to be careful,' he said. 'One mistake and he might lose his eye. I rubbed in oil so that the skin wouldn't crack.'

Gardiner said the eye had healed and that Johnny could recommence sparring, but Dick disagreed.

'It'll take weeks before the inside of the cut is healed,' he told him.

'If he spars tonight and a punch opens it up, then I'll tell him that he should finish boxing.' Gardiner shook his head and left him to it. This was all they needed.

Dick used the recipe he had been given by an old mountain man. He took his son into the toilets, applied liquid plastic to the wound and waited for it to solidify. Then he added make-up to the eyebrow.

'I did it for five or six fights,' he said. 'The cut never opened.'

The next fight was in Scotland against John Kellie, the Scottish champion, but the preamble was again marked by the different approaches of Dick and Gardiner. At the weigh-in, Dick told his son to remove only his shoes and coat, but Gardiner ordered: 'Strip to your underpants.' Dick's theory was that it was self-defeating to let an opponent know your true weight. The officials and Kellie all looked at each other as the Welshman's weight was clocked at eight stone, two and a half pounds. 'I knew they would be saying he's too light,' Dick said.

Kellie, though, was out of his depth against the younger man – 'a gangling bag of bones with dynamite in his fists' as one Scottish report put it. He clung on to the corners of that bag in the hope of brief respite and was aided by the referee, Wally Thom, who turned a blind eye to such tactics.

'Next time he holds you, throw him off,' Gardiner spat at the break.

Johnny took Gardiner literally and hurled Kellie to the floor, provoking a stern lecture from Thom. Dick wondered whether this would be another of those nights when a bad decision was made against them. A lost gumshield added to his pessimism. Thom insisted Johnny carry on without it, but the fighter knew that was dangerous. One well-placed blow could break his teeth, split his lips and spill blood. Invigorated by concern, Johnny tore into his opponent, felled him twice and was declared the winner in the sixth round.

Everything was now geared towards keeping him fit for the prospect of a shot at Maguire, but wrapping a boxer in cotton wool is a parlous task, given that the essence of the sport is violence. To break the routine, Gardiner took Johnny over to the Rhondda to train with Bryn Griffiths. The session passed off without note until Gardiner put Johnny in with a middleweight. For some reason, whether it was the wounded pride of being in with a lighter man or inter-gym rivalry, the boxer kept holding Johnny firmly below the elbows and picking him up. Dick was concerned and had a word with his son after another round of malicious hugs.

'John, you've got to be careful, man,' he said. 'This guy could break your arms if he keeps doing that.' The grail of a British title glistened in the distance and the father and son duo were damned if they were going to let some middleweight bully erase it.

The middleweight grabbed him again and wrapped his gloves around the crooks of the waif's elbows, but as he prepared to lift him and exercise his brute strength, he felt the boxer's foot shoot down and stamp hard on his foot. He released his grip and bounded around on one foot. Dick fell about laughing, while his son threw up a screen of leather as the middleweight sought revenge.

Heddwyn Taylor declared he had agreed terms for the Maguire fight to take place in Ebbw Vale in October. It would be only Johnny's tenth professional fight. If his amateur career had been a slow-burning affair, his professional one was proving a powder keg.

In June 1977, there was a chance for Billy Vivian to provide a good-luck omen. Vivian had suffered a mixed bag of results since being demolished by Colin Power, winning two bouts but being flattened by Cornelius Boza-Edwards within a single round on his last outing. Boza-Edwards would become a world champion, but it was still a crushing defeat. Nevertheless, Vivian was given a chance to take on Johnny Wall for the Welsh lightweight title in Ebbw Vale, top of a bill that would also see Johnny Owen fight Ulster's Terry Hanna.

For several weeks, Vivian asked Gardiner how much he would be getting for the fight and was told to leave it to the manager. But money mattered. It was why people boxed – the need to pay the bills and put food on the table. One day, Dick pulled Vivian aside in the gym.

'I've got to tell you, Bill, this is eating me up,' he said.

He immediately had Vivian's attention.

'I've had a word from the horse's mouth.'

Dick told him that Georgie Evans, Johnny Wall's manager, had admitted his fighter was getting £1,000. For Vivian, boxing for a modest £250, it was a bolt from the blue.

'Without me there wouldn't have been bums on seats,' he said. 'People from Merthyr wouldn't have gone to watch Johnny Wall. I was furious.'

On the undercard that night, Johnny Owen's meeting with Hanna proved a one-sided affair. Johnny bewildered Hanna with his hyperactive style, pummelled his numbed head in the second and then forced a premature end in the fourth as the Irishman's body sagged into the ropes like a snared tuna. Johnny showered, changed and then watched his friend vie for the title and something to hang all the pain on. It would prove another rugged, debilitating fight, with Vivian sacrificing his greater skills to engage in a slug-fest with the big hitter. The seventh round proved the zenith, both men ransacking their pasts and futures to blaze away with wrought-iron gloves. The crowd was on its feet and so was Johnny Owen. The last round was the hardest round, spent spirits giving more still. And then the decision. Pandemonium. Johnny hung his head and sighed.

'I lost on points, and the only one who thought I lost was the one who mattered,' Vivian said. 'The fight ended and Johnny Wall turned his back. The referee had to turn him round to grab his hand. I looked into their corner and Georgie Evans was mopping him up. I'd made a mess of him, his eyes, lip, nose. I had a bruise where we'd clashed heads, but that was it. There was no celebration in their corner. Boxing. It can be a fucking disaster.'

Martyn Galleozzie was in the midst of a year's sabbatical following his own loss to Wall and has a similar opinion of his sport.

'In those days you'd have a dozen fighters turn pro every year,' he said. 'It was hard. There were no easy fights. You'd get up off the floor to beat someone. I was a champion but I don't think I did well. Boxing was a waste of time for me.'

But in 1977 it still mattered. They were still young men, unencumbered by the wisdom of hindsight and free to carry on down that blinkered path. Flushed with his latest triumph, Johnny enjoyed the thick cream cake his mother had made for him, smeared in lush chocolate.

One Friday night in September, Gardiner arrived at the gym in New Tredegar and told Johnny and his father that he had a fight booked for the following Monday.

'I know it's short notice, but it'll be good for you.'

This was the third fight against his old adversary, George Sutton, who, though he lost for a third time, did have the satisfaction of some transient success on this occasion. In the sixth round of the contest in Solihull, Sutton connected with a left hook. Johnny's knees dropped a couple of inches and he fell back on to the ropes. In the corner Dick's heart sank.

'George clipped John on the jaw and his legs wobbled,' he remembered. 'But George looked surprised and was slow to capitalize. It was only a few seconds and John was all right. He came straight back on the attack. George had his chance but he didn't take it. John won on points.'

The passage was carved. Wayne Evans, the official challenger, said he needed more warm-up fights before he took on

Maguire for the British title, so Johnny had his chance. Now they were verging on the big time, as Heddwyn Taylor found out when he had the bout taken from him and Wales. When purse offers closed, the highest bid came from Les Roberts, which meant the fight would take place in the refined environment of the National Sporting Club at the Café Royal in London. Gardiner was ecstatic. This was what they had waited for, and he made short work of telling the media what he thought.

'Maguire is there to be taken,' he said. 'He's getting on and he's taken a couple of beatings in recent fights.'

Boxing News enthusiastically reported that the purse topped £7,000, but that was hopelessly optimistic. In fact, when expenses, the manager's cut and the promoter's slice were deducted, Johnny would make just £800 from the bout. Yet that was significantly more than he was used to. In his nine previous bouts Johnny had earned a net total of £1,563. His biggest pay day had been the £288 he had pocketed from taking on Kellie in Glasgow. This was small beer, even in 1977, but never mind – Johnny had his heart set on the British title. Then, who knew?

By now he was a popular figure. The fans had taken to the man who looked so unlike the usual image of a boxer and who behaved with such dignity out of the ring.

'When people got to know Johnny, he was packing out places,' Gardiner said. 'Mums were curious and, I'll tell you this, when parents saw Johnny, they started putting their boys into boxing. We had so many coming to the gym wanting to train like him and be like him. He was quiet, but he loved boxing, the adrenaline, the atmosphere. He never went looking for the cameras, but he liked it.'

The media attention was growing in a modest fashion. British title fights were routinely covered by the BBC, and national newspapers now started to show interest as well as the local South Wales press. Harry Carpenter, the esteemed BBC commentator, was already familiar with the Bionic Bantam.

'I first came across Johnny Owen when he was a Welsh amateur international,' he said. 'It was strange that he didn't win a Welsh (senior) ABA title because he was obviously good enough. When he turned pro, there were always comments about his looks – he was terribly thin and had these rather prominent ears – but he didn't mind. That was the nice thing. He was a rather shy boy and never said much, but he had a sense of humour. The skeleton banner was a little joke against himself. But the thing about Johnny Owen was he had an extraordinary build for his weight. Bantamweight is less than eight stone, seven pounds and he was five feet, eight inches. That made him a difficult man to box. Difficult to get at. He made fairly easy work of his early pro fights.'

Colin Hart, the boxing writer for the *Sun*, had also started to take notice of the unusual-looking kid.

'I remember a fighter being told one night up at NSC that he was going to fight Johnny Owen soon. He looked over and said, "Jesus, he looks like the fucking FA Cup."

'He was skeletal. He looked like a xylophone, but he was immensely strong. He lived for boxing, nothing else, didn't have a girlfriend, never had a drink, such a sweetheart.'

In the *Sun* on 29 November, Hart wrote his prediction of the Owen–Maguire fight. 'If Owen can withstand Maguire's early onslaught, he will go on to a points victory.' Gareth Jones was less conservative and predicted a Welsh win in 11 or 12 rounds.

Others just hoped for the best. Idris Sutton, Johnny's old amateur trainer, remembered the build-up well.

'Paddy Maguire had an awesome reputation compared with

John,' he said. 'This was a bloke who'd fought for the European title while John was a kid off the street who had lost a Welsh ABA title against George Sutton. People thought Dai was mad for making the match.'

At home in Merthyr, Susan Owens was sulking. When it had become clear that the title bout would take place in London rather than Ebbw Vale, she had expected to join the party travelling up on the Monday before the fight. But then she was told that the NSC was a men-only arena. She had bickered and complained and vowed to go to town and get her hair cut short, buy a dinner suit and disguise herself as a man. Dick tried to placate her and told her he would ring her as soon as he could afterwards. The Owens still had no phone and, given the abuse Gardiner was now receiving from those who felt he was cruel for 'forcing' Johnny to box, had no intention of getting one. Susan could go to the payphone at an allotted time or make a call to the sports desk of the *Western Mail*. This would become a familiar routine, although on that night, still disgruntled, she went to the Gellideg Social Club with her mother instead.

Billy Vivian and Jeff Pritchard bought new suits for the trip. The NSC was now a bastion of decency in boxing. This was a world away from its more seamy beginnings, when shouts of 'more gore' would permeate the raucous aura and corruption, bribery and ringside brawls were part and parcel of its daily life. By the time Johnny Owen took on Maguire, it had been reformed and revived. Lord Lonsdale had cleaned up boxing and in 1955 the club had moved to the Café Royal, leaving the great and the good to tuck into smoked trout in the Napoleon Room, shrouded by green satin walls and lush gold drapes.

'I fought up there and it was a strange old place,' Pritchard said. 'You can't shout out and you just get polite applause at the end of each round.'

Martyn Galleozzie had also sampled the curious atmosphere. 'Every boxer loved it there,' he said. 'It was a beautiful place to box because there was total silence.'

Galleozzie was determined to see the fight, but he did not have one of the £25 tickets. 'It's a private club and you couldn't get in for love or money,' he said. Les Roberts, the promoter, knew Galleozzie from his dates at the NSC and pulled some strings. 'I couldn't get in the main hall, but I watched it from through an open door in the kitchens,' he said. 'It wasn't a very big place so we still had a decent view. My uncle and brother were with me.'

In the dressing room, Dick and Dai were anxious but confident. Maguire was a good fighter, a heavy-punching Belfast veteran who doubled as a Lambeth roofer, but he had suffered a depressing loss in his recent bid for the European crown. There were those who felt Maguire, at the age of twenty-nine, was nearing the end of the long and winding road, but he had vast experience, bottomless pride and well-honed power.

Maguire's camp, led by Mickey Duff, did their best to upset the Welsh. Having settled into their corner, the Owens were told they would have to go to the opposite one. They passed Duff and his cornermen on the way. 'We've beaten one Welsh bastard tonight already and we'll beat another,' one said.

'Bugger off,' Dick replied.

Gareth Jones jotted down the beginnings of his report. 'In the corner before the start, Owen looked like a young lad sent down to the corner shop by his mother who had turned in at the wrong door.' Jones knew looks counted for nothing with Johnny and that many had been tricked by his frame.

A butter mountain of a man in the front row turned to Dick and asked: 'Will your boy win?'

Dick nodded. 'He'll win. Don't you worry.'

The butter-mountain smiled.

The confidence was well placed. Maguire never looked likely to retain his title. Thinning on top and four inches shorter, he was reduced to a powerless has-been as he tried unsuccessfully to duck under Johnny's jabs and was warned by Syd Nathan, the veteran referee, for a series of low blows. He was also warned in the third for illegal use of the heel of the glove, but got away with some deliberate headbutting. The assortment of shady tactics earned their reward when a cut opened above Johnny's right eye in the sixth round, but he responded with a right uppercut that left Maguire splay-legged.

'Come on, John, use the left hand,' Pritchard shouted from his seat.

'Sshhhh,' came the response, and Pritchard stifled his natural inclination to roar advice and suffered in silence.

He need not have worried. The cut was not severe, and Maguire was bleeding himself by the seventh. His left eye puffed up. Another butt, another low blow. Maguire began to look older than his twenty-nine years. The bell sounded for the end of the ninth. Both men tapped each other on the chin.

Nathan warned Maguire for hitting low and the outcome was now pregnant with inevitability. A raft of applause, a dash of jelly on the brow, a towel on the face. The bell. Left, left, right, left. Body, head, body. Jab, jab, hook. The referee stepped in. They were in no-man's-land. Ninety seconds gone. Maguire had too far to go to reach his trench. Nathan thumbed the cut. His eyes narrowed. His hands crossed and Maguire's last energy slumped from his battered frame. It was over.

Pritchard and Vivian leapt into the air and shouted. Nothing could stop them this time. In the kitchens, Galleozzie smiled.

Duff hugged Maguire and whispered something. The watching Henry Cooper applauded. 'He makes Jimmy Wilde look like Charles Atlas,' one wag shouted.

The butter mountain tapped Dick on the shoulder. 'You should get in there.'

Dick shook his head. 'That's my son,' he said, the tears rolling quickly down his cheeks. 'It's his win. There's no need for me to take any glamour off him.' The butter mountain smiled.

The Duke of Gloucester, tall and bespectacled, made his way into the ring and presented Johnny with his Lonsdale belt. Maguire took the microphone and announced his retirement. Later, after having four stitches in his wound, he said: 'I've had a good run and got no regrets. I've earned some money, paid off the house and will probably go home to Belfast next year.' His red and white skin contrasted with the green silk robe. He was getting out at the right time.

The phone rang at the Gellideg Social Club and Edith made her way through the tables. She took the receiver and breathed a huge sigh of satisfaction. It was the sigh of the reprieved.

'I felt just great when I heard,' she said. 'But it was always awful hard waiting to see how he had gone on.'

Edith found that even she could not escape the press and was asked how she felt about her son boxing.

'I hate to see anybody hurt,' she said, 'but boys will be boys. I would never try to stop him.'

In London the boxer celebrated with a meal in a Chinese restaurant.

'After the fight we were walking out, me, Jeff and Johnny,' Billy Vivian recalled. 'Byron Board, Dick and my old man were ahead of us. Suddenly these two birds and a fella come up to us. One of the women says to John, "Do you want some fun?" He said, "No, love, you're all right." He was embarrassed, but she seemed taken aback and said, "For a tenner you can suck my tits." I looked at her and said, "This is the new British champion." My old man and Dick were killing themselves.'

Heddwyn Taylor took the group on to the Grosvenor Hotel. It was St Andrew's night and a party was in full swing.

'Jeff could hear bagpipes and so we went off to see what it was,' Vivian explained. 'Before you knew it we were in this huge room and Johnny was getting introduced to the crowd. It was a great night. We were hitting the drink, but Johnny stuck with his orange juice.'

It was a riotous night for Dick, his brother Jim, and his sons, Vivian and Dilwyn. The rest was a blur. Ken Bryant, the cornerman, drove home with Eddie Thomas. It was just after 3 a.m. when the patrol car pulled his Jaguar over.

'Where have you been?' the constable asked.

'I've been to London to see the new British bantamweight champion,' Bryant replied. He got off with a warning.

Dick rose early the next morning, the excitement still enlivening him. He went across to Gardiner's room at the Regent's Palace and knocked on the door. He pushed it open and laughed at what he saw. Billy Vivian and Pritchard had crashed out on the double bed, leaving the new British champion asleep on the floor, still wearing his Lonsdale belt.

Later that morning, as the photographers took their pictures in the hotel foyer, Dick noticed that his son no longer had the famous old belt. He shuffled through the throng surrounding the first Welshman to win the British bantamweight crown for sixty-four years. 'John, where's the belt?' he whispered.

His son smiled. 'It's by the counter,' he said.

Dick upped his pace and found it lying under yesterday's newspaper. He held it tight and kept it in his grasp. They had only had it a few hours but, somehow, the boxer looked naked without it. At the age of twenty-one his boy had become a man.

ROUND SEVEN

John Beyrooty knew Mexico. As the boxing correspondent for the *LA Herald-Examiner*, he had got to know Zarate and Pintor and the rest, and he had seen fights in Vegas where it had been easy to be seduced by the glitz, the kitsch and the chintz. He particularly liked Pintor as a quiet, respectful man, free of brash-talking egotism. Later, Pintor would favour Beyrooty with a simple act of kindness that never left the writer. Having knocked out an opponent at the Olympic in 1984, Pintor returned to the anodyne dullness of the dressing room. Beyrooty was the only journalist there. 'Those rooms were awful, dingy things,' he said. 'I went in like I'd always do. I must have been back eight or nine times in all and he must have recognized me because he said "*Uno minuto*" in that soft voice. Then he got up and walked out. At first, I thought he'd gone for a piss. When he came back he was carrying the shorts he'd worn. He handed them to me as a present. It was like he appreciated my interest in him. Imagine that. It was a classy act. No other fighter has ever done anything like that for me. It created a bond and I was glad, because I'd always liked the guy.'

That was in the future, though. In the reality of the present, there were no gifts. This was boxing without the trimmings. Beyrooty had been as surprised as the rest when he saw Owen take off his gown.

'He was like a ghost,' he said.

But he also knew Pintor could not underestimate him.

'Pintor was not a one-punch man,' he said. 'And he was not that quick. He wasn't flashy. He wasn't a typical Mexican brawler. Sure, he had the trademark left hook to the body, but his policy was to grind and grind. There were never any easy fights with Pintor. He was not the sort of guy who was going to go out there and blow you away and he couldn't afford to take anyone lightly. This was not a mismatch. Owen had credentials.'

The bookies at ringside had made Owen a 4–1 long shot, but now the cuts on Pintor's brow were widening from pinpricks to dangerous wounds. Owen was suffering too with his cut lip, but the fight was progressing well for him. It was always going to be his hardest fight, but he was winning. Not just in his own mind or the hearts of the devoted legion with their beery songs. Not just in the hopes of Dick Owens and Dai Gardiner, watching with pride and unblinking tension over in the corner. Johnny Owen was doing what he had done for his entire life. From the boys who called him Flappy to the fighters who laughed and then fell, Owen was a hero in puny clothing. Nowhere in that taper-like body was the merest hint of the warrior. Yet in those first six rounds, the seeds of doubt had been sown and the mendacity of his physique forced many to gulp on careless words. In the commentary booth, Tom Kelly and Little Red Lopez had given four of the opening six rounds to Owen. It had been a dream start.

Although Owen is not a devastating puncher, he throws slashing blows that cut the face very easily, Lopez pointed out. *I think that's what happened to Pintor's eyes. It's those slashing blows he's throwing.* Not every fighter can pick up the nuances of a bout, but Little Red was proving an astute observer.

Pintor began the round with a couple of heavy misses. Owen fired off four left jabs and, having breached his opponent's defence with his sheer bloody will, powered forward. 'Poom, poom, poom, poom,' was how Pintor would describe that attack.

Yet the seventh was the round where the tide turned. The endless waves of assault drained away as the momentum veered towards a new course, not savagely, not drastically, but softly, quickly and almost invisibly to the vast bulk of the 10,000 spectators. Suddenly, there was daylight between the two men. Their heads were not locked and Pintor began to find a solid destination for his punches. A right landed and shook Owen briefly before he retaliated in the only way he knew, by stepping on to the front foot. It was the Jimmy Wilde way. Attacking to erase a passing moment of concern.

These two fighters at long range, I think, for the first time in the this fight. A good right hand from Pintor and all it did was just kind of set Owen's motor on, he came right back at him. Pintor having the best of it in the early going in round seven. Owen has a cut lip, Pintor cuts over both eyes, a minute twenty-five to go in round seven. 'MEXICO!' the partisan crowd scream.

Who knows whether Owen heard that peal of bias? In the concentrated blur of the ring, it was possible to ignore everything. In this most naked of places, exposed to thousands of thrill-seekers, it was still possible to feel alone. The two men were putting on a private show of fortitude. This was their stage, and they had entered that netherworld where boxers marry pain and pleasure – but the cry of 'Mexico, Mexico, Mexico' was a portent of change. At least four out of six rounds had been Owen's, but in those opening ninety seconds of the seventh, Pintor had fashioned the beginnings of a comeback.

Mickey Duff, the British promoter, could see it. He leaned over Little Red and waved his arms at Owen. *He wants Owen to come on and keep the pressure on,* Lopez reported. He could see it too. If Johnny Owen was going to win this fight, he needed to get inside. Despite having a reach advantage, Owen needed to make this a close-quarters affair. If he stood back, one of those torpedoes from Pintor might strike its target.

Colin Hart also had Owen ahead. He was producing a canny fight. This kid deserved to be the champion. A few days before, Hart had visited Owen in his room at the fraying hotel in the Hispanic area of LA. He had wondered why they had chosen the hotel, even if Pintor was staying there too, and noted the bars on the windows of the ground-floor headquarters. Owen was sitting on his bed, his eyes as wide as saucers.

'Mr Hart,' he had said, ignoring repeated instructions to call the *Sun*'s boxing man by his Christian name, 'Mr Hart.'

There had been sirens and squad cars and guns. It had all taken place right outside the segmented window of Owen's musty hotel room. The police had leapt out of a car and grabbed a Mexican. They had wrestled him to the floor, while others fixed their pistols on the man's prone frame. Owen never found out what the Mexican had done, but the consensus was it was probably drugs. And Colin Hart never forgot the innocence on Johnny Owen's face as he recounted the escapade.

'Mr Hart,' he said. 'It was just like watching *Kojak*.'

This Mexican refused to be wrestled to the ground. He had stood almost on Owen's feet for six rounds and slugged away like a sadistic lumberjack. The gumshield was still visible as an indicator of the effort he was putting in, but Pintor had decided to take a step back and was landing blows with greater regularity. None stopped Owen for more than a millisecond, but boxing is a sport of broad scope and narrow margins. On tiny details, lucky blows and sudden frangibility fights are turned.

Strangely enough, this is the best round Pintor has had and it's been at long range. He's kept Owen from doing any real damage and now they're back inside, which is where Owen seems to fight the best. Forty-seven seconds remaining in round seven.

Allan Malamud then remarked on the novelty of seeing a British fighter doing the cutting rather than the bleeding. *Henry Cooper once got cut shadow-boxing*, he quipped and Tom Kelly laughed. If America could not condescend to Britain then who else could? And big, brave Cooper had been more red than white when Cassius Clay had finished with him. How the Brits loved Cooper for flooring Clay and how they overlooked the carnage wrought on those noble features by the fastest heavyweight hands of them all. But now here was Johnny Owen. He had looked every inch the archetypal British fall guy until he had thrown a punch and everybody in the Olympic, from Beyrooty to Hart, from Dick Owens to Cuyo Hernandez and, most knowingly, from Johnny to Lupe, realized this was a real fight.

When Kelly stopped smiling, he noticed the cut above Pintor's right eye had opened again.

It's a good-size cut and shows a bright slash of red. And the bell brings us to the close of our quietest round.

It was a quiet riot for El Indio. By taking a step backwards he had moved forward and shifted the direction of the fight. By the end of the seventh, Lupe Pintor was not a professional athlete seeking a rich payday, but a boy fighting for survival.

9

THE Z MAN SLEEPS

Coti Pintor was feeding the birds at her home in Cuajimalpa. The sun was making the earth outside ache and she heard the old woman opposite scold her husband for some crime committed or job undone. She cast anxious glances at the large television in the corner of the room and felt her chest tighten. It was her birthday but the presents lay unopened on the kitchen table. Then she got down on her knees and put her palms together. 'Lord protect him with your blessed cloak,' she whispered. It was a familiar routine when her husband was fighting, but she was battling new emotions on this occasion.

'I always prayed because, in the end, it's a sport, and sometimes you win and sometimes you lose,' she recalled. 'As long as nothing bad happens to anybody, that's all that mattered. But this time it was different. I was asking Him to help in any way he could, even if it was just with a single point or something.'

It was 3 June 1979, and far away, in Las Vegas, her husband was staring across the ring at Carlos Zarate with the WBC world bantamweight championship at stake.

It had been a winding road for Pintor. Since losing to Davila in 1976, he had taken twenty-eight fights in little over three years. Some had been easy, a spate of one-round knockouts confirming his potency, but others had seen him stumble towards the precipice. The humiliation of his first Davila fight had not humbled him instantly, and he had arrived ill prepared for his bout with Samuel Machorro, a game and skilled fighter, in Mexico City four months later.

'I don't know what happened but I arrived at the Coliseo Arena feeling very dehydrated,' he remembered. 'In the morning I weighed fifty-four kilos, but, in the evening, when I walked into the place, I was almost sixty.'

Dr Ramirez Mercado was not going to let Pintor fight. He grabbed him by the arm and said: 'Hey, what did you eat?'

Pintor shrugged.

'I can't let you fight like this,' Mercado continued. 'You're very heavy and I can't let you take the risk. You'll get a good beating and you might get killed.'

Cuyo Hernandez then weighed into the argument and the fight went ahead because of the consensus that Machorro was not a big puncher. It was a response that underscored the cavalier approach to the boxer's welfare in the second-rate halls and flea pits.

'I decided I had to try and hammer him in the first few rounds,' Pintor said. 'I did that but then got tired. He started to get on top and landed some nice shots. We went ten rounds and, in truth, I was lucky to get the decision.'

Hernandez was furious. He had trained champions, legends even, and it sapped his patience to see an up-and-coming fighter succumb to ruinous influences.

'What the hell was wrong with you?' he scolded.

Pintor grinned. 'Hey, I ate a chido,' he said. He laughed, but Hernandez frowned. Where was the dedication he had been promised in the post-Davila depression?

Several months later Pintor returned to the ring to take on Babe San Martin, a relative novice, but a boxer inspired by the same goals as his opponent.

'We hit each other for seven beautiful rounds,' Pintor said. 'There was no holding, no fouls, nothing underhand. It was a pure exchange of blows and a contest to see who could hit the other the hardest. I remember him knocking me down near the start, but I got up and gave it to him. Until the seventh, when he went down.'

Even then, as a third-year pro, Pintor was casting his eyes towards a world title bout. His memories of his tarnished Olympic dream meant he did not take it as a given, but he was filling up his innate reservoir with strength and hurt. When San Martin floored him in front of a drunken crowd in Reynosa, he took the blow and the lesson simultaneously.

'The worst thing that can happen to you in a ring, like life itself, is not to take a hit and fall to the canvas,' he said. 'Nor is it being caught on the wrong end of a flurry of punches and being unable to dodge them. It is not even losing, with everything that the word "defeat" brings. The worst thing is not having the opportunity to reach the level of success everyone feels they are capable of; to not find the key which opens the door.'

Pintor was still a hair-trigger malcontent, but he knew he was being given a chance. And so he picked himself up off the floor and worked on enhancing his reputation. He hit the canvas again on 12 April 1977 in San Antonio – the pace slowed and the sound became badly dubbed. Two hours later Pintor opened his eyes and recognized the familiar surroundings of the changing rooms. He felt the water jolt his mind and saw Hernandez and Ugalde laughing. They were talking about Pintor's recovery and how he was not hit by a single blow after dragging himself away from disaster. The shower pounded like a speedball, and Pintor remembered the last thing he saw – his right hand connecting with the jaw of Gabe Cantera.

Hernandez had reason to be happy. In 1977, he was the manager of the WBC world bantamweight champion. Carlos Zarate had taken the crown when he had dismantled Rodolofo Martinez in nine rounds the previous year. It was the beginning of the era of the Z Men, as they were being called by the media, who were now the toast of Mexico and Hispanic Los Angeles. Zarate was the WBC champion and had never been beaten. Few boxers maintain a superhuman aura when they risk it by taking fights so regularly. Every fight night is a chance for the ego to be shredded, but Zarate seemed immune to danger. He had the technical dexterity of Davila and the raw power of Pintor, sugar-coated with a self-belief that defeated many even before the gauze had been wrapped around their knuckles.

Alfonso Zamora was just as popular. He was the WBA champion but his relationship with Hernandez had soured. In 1976 Hernandez had sold Zamora's contract to the fighter's father, Alfonso senior, in a move that was seen as a disrespectful snub. That is precisely what it was: Hernandez was drawing a line in the sand and siding with Zarate. In March 1977 the pair had met at the Olympic Auditorium. It should have been a fight to unify the bantamweight division, but the enmity and politicizing ensured it was merely the most eagerly awaited non-title bout Los Angeles had seen for years. Insults were traded in the papers by Hernandez and Zamora senior, and, a week after Pintor had suffered his blackout against Gabe Cantera, the Z men descended into the Fabulous Forum.

It was one of those bone-jarring, jaw-dropping, breath-bating boxing nights. Someone had to lose and, when that meant someone shedding their omnipotence, the bloodsuckers were going to be more than sated. It was a crazy fight. Fifty-two seconds had elapsed when a drunk, wearing only a white T-shirt and grey shorts, jumped into the ring. Five policemen clad in full riot gear quickly followed and ejected him with a few blows to the head for good measure.

The Z men ignored the incident and resumed hostilities. By the time Zamora's father threw in the towel in the fourth round, his son had been floored repeatedly. He cradled his son and then, venting all the passion and anger that had been fuelled by the pettiness of the past few weeks, tore across the ring and attacked Hernandez from behind. Fifteen minutes after beating a drunk, the five riot policemen returned to drag a despairing father from the ring.

Zamora never recovered from having intimations of his mortality delivered to him in such bloody fashion. In his next fight he was knocked out in ten rounds to lose his WBA title. He retired at the age of twenty-six, his last fight a sad three-round loss on an undercard at the Olympic, a fight that was overshadowed by the top-of-the-bill contest between Lupe Pintor and Johnny Owen.

Zarate, though, was on the crest of a wave. He took two more quick defences, including one against Juan Francisco Rodriguez, the European champion, in Madrid, and then came up against Alberto Davila.

In the aftermath of beating Pintor in 1976, Davila had experienced the rough side of boxing. He had lost two of his next three fights and he and Roberta had wondered whether he was as good as they thought. It got worse. At around 7 p.m. on 9 March 1977, someone saw Howie Steindler, Davila's irascible manager, on the corner of Lindley Avenue and Killion Street only a block from his LA home. Steindler was involved in a heated discussion with two black men, tempers escalated out of control and they began manhandling him. Punches were thrown. The witness would tell police that the men forced the 72-year-old into his car and drove away at high speed. An hour later Steindler's vehicle was discovered abandoned on the Ventura Freeway. Steindler was dead on the back seat. He had been robbed and smothered.

One month later Davila climbed through the ropes to win a decision. Slowly he mended his record until he got his shot at Zarate, but the champion was too good and the referee called a halt after two minutes and sixteen seconds of the eighth round. Davila quickly got another chance at the title, the WBA version, on the undercard of Muhammad Ali's rematch with Leon Spinks in New Orleans, but he lost on points.

Davila was at his lowest ebb in 1978, but Pintor was on the way up and was installed as the number-one challenger to Zarate. It was his dream to take on the arrogant Z Man as part of the civil war between Atlas rivals, but Pintor was concerned by the way Hernandez was dragging his heels. Having the two top bantamweights under one roof was a mixed blessing, a goldmine tempered by the jealousies and suspicions of the two fighters.

Pintor's mounting disgruntlement was intensified by problems at home. The birds he had bought had become a symbol of marital discord. When they died or escaped he blamed his wife for not caring for them enough. She, in turn, told him that he was not caring for her. The marriage existed on a plateau. 'I think that he loved me and wanted me, but I can't say I was the love of his life,' Coti said. 'He saw me as an escape route, to have somebody who would tend to him and help him. As soon as we married, he abandoned me and left me to take control of the house. All I wanted was a crumb of his love, but I didn't get it. I thought I could keep sacrificing myself so that my husband would love me, but I was just being ignorant and my self-esteem was very low.'

The backdrop of an unhappy domestic life and dissatisfaction with Hernandez may explain why Pintor, for the first time in his life, lost fights back-to-back. His opponents were nothing special, but after twenty-one straight victories, he lost on points in Puerto Rico and then Culiacan in Mexico. To make matters worse, Jorge Ugalde, his trusted trainer, left. 'He was the best I ever had,' Pintor admitted. 'But he got a more lucrative offer from elsewhere and so that was that.' His replacement was the colourful Antonio Torres Bombela, a likeable member of Hernandez's team. Known to all as plain Tony Torres, he quickly became inseparable from Pintor.

The meeting between Zarate and Pintor was inevitable and split loyalties even more than the battle of the Z Men had. Some hacks were understandably in thrall to Zarate's bountiful talent. It gave them their fix of magic. Others favoured Pintor, a quieter man less prone to bragging but versed in suffering. Hernandez had taken to calling Pintor 'Indio', and the challenger quickly became known as *El Indio de Cuajimalpa*. Another moniker he liked was 'Grillo', a reference to the brown crickets that chirruped on the plains of home. On his trunks, however, the name was always Indio.

Eventually, the match was made. The date was set – Sunday, 3 June 1979. The venue was to be Caesar's Palace, one of the great boxing venues on the strip. This was the opportunity Pintor had craved, but had begun to doubt would happen. His record was good, but he had suffered four defeats. Zarate's record was one of the talking points of professional boxing. Officially, it stood at fifty-four wins with only one defeat, and the loss had come when he had tried to punch above his weight and take the WBC Super Bantamweight title from Wilfredo Gomez.

Zarate, to most, was considered unbeatable at bantamweight, but Pintor was using his hatred to carry him to untold heights. Both men came from troubled backgrounds. Like Pintor, Zarate was often expelled from school in Ramos Millan on the edge of Mexico City. He was brought up without a father and only found a direction when his mother dragged him to Hernandez's gym where, like Pintor, he breathed in the happy family environment.

'When I found out I was finally going to fight Zarate I was really excited,' Pintor remembered. 'Journalists would come to the gym and ask me what I thought, and I'd tell them that he was a great champion and it was going to be a tough fight. Inside, I was thinking, "I'm either going to beat this buey or die." I knew it was a really important point in my career because if you want to make money in boxing there was no other way. I knew that my life would change if I beat him.

'In the gym it wasn't a problem. Zarate had his own trainer and I had Tony. He had his space and I had mine. For Cuyo, it was the perfect situation. He couldn't lose, but I think he had more faith in me at that time. He knew that it was the right time for me and that I'd have a good chance of beating him.

'Zarate was the star of the gym and I was just a prospect. We never spoke to each other. We were totally different personalities and didn't have any sort of a relationship. But I have never wanted to beat anyone as badly in my life. It was the challenge, the rivalry, the chance.'

Where Pintor used a little diplomacy in his dealings with the press, who flocked to the Atlas on a daily basis to run the rule over the two duellists and pick over their strengths and faults, Zarate was dismissive of his opponent.

'He was saying he was going to hurt me badly,' Pintor said. 'He was saying how he was going to do this to me and that. That angered me. Professional sportspeople should have respect and admiration for their rivals. It's an unwritten agreement that exists, even if one is of an inferior standard. Inside the ring, we all want to be the best, but outside you should be like brothers. Zarate, though, was never a good friend. He did not understand that, while one person can be a better boxer, when the day ends we are all human beings.'

The training was hard but comforting. Pintor allowed himself no distractions this time. The enormity of what lay ahead was there in the other corner of the gym. Old fight posters faded on the rough stone walls. Pintor and Zarate would take turns to watch themselves in the huge mirror. Journalists scribbled and guessed at who was stronger. And then there were the boys, crowding to get a glimpse of these two warriors, begging to get in and start living dreams of their own.

Eventually, after this seemingly interminable imprisonment, the men found themselves transplanted to Las Vegas. The referee for the night was Mills Lane, a balding attorney from Reno who would go on to become a judge and host his own TV show. It was a big payday. The glamour was everywhere and the promise of all manner of worldly delights, some carnal, some monetary, flickered in the fountains outside. Tony Torres dressed Pintor's hands in the dressing room. He knew his man was in the best shape of his life, but could not know for sure whether it would be enough to dethrone a champion like Zarate.

The same thoughts went through the heads of those at home. Francisco and Pintor's other brothers, Benjamin, Efrain and

Manuel, hoped for the best. His sister, Rosario, and his mother wrung their hands, and even Don Lupe toasted his son as he drank in a bar. Jorge Ugalde sent a good-luck message. Cuyo Hernandez was not working either corner that night, to avoid any accusation of bias. He offered some simple words of encouragement. He knew that the important thing now was to remain calm, but without stubbing out the internal fires of hate and rage and desire. And there was Coti, feeding Pintor's beloved birds and listening to their song before she turned on the television set and waited.

After so long the actual event was a blur, like finally taking your seat on a seaside roller-coaster ride and hearing the chain tighten and pull you taut with excitement. Now Pintor was in the ring, the crowd roaring, the lights dimming, feet bouncing on the edge of a chasm.

'This was my chance to change my life,' he said. 'You must fight for a cause. There was no doubt that Zarate was a fantastic world champion and an outstanding boxer, but I never respected him as a person. Yet, contrary to what some people might think, I never once set out to hurt an opponent out of malice. I know that as a youngster I tried to seek revenge for some of the suffering I had undergone and I am not proud of the fact. I have made mistakes and, in some cases, was unable or unaware of how to repair the damage. I am sorry and thank God that He straightened me up in time. But Zarate was the turning point. Beating him would spark the change.'

At ringside a man in a yellow polo shirt and blue baseball cap looked on. This was Joe Louis, the Brown Bomber and one of the most resilient of boxing's fables. A trim figure whose ruffled locks hung down to sit on his fawn shirt put on his headphones. A camera caught him and he waved. Ryan O'Neal was a Hollywood star and knew how to work the lens.

The bell sounded. It was a clash of contrasts. Zarate, tall and slim in white trunks, was accurate and stylish; Pintor, short and stocky in yellow, aggressive and powerful. From the start, it was clear Zarate's huge reach would cause Pintor the same problems as for all who had gone before him. Zarate shaded a patient first round. His lubricated combinations were smooth and eye-catching. Pintor, by contrast, looked awkward as he bounced twice on his left instep and lunged forward in an attempt to bridge the gap. By coming inside he left himself open to the venom of Zarate, and his cheeks were bruised and hurting by the end of the second.

At the break Pintor swigged water from a two-litre milk carton and spat it on the canvas. In the opposite corner, Zarate sipped his refreshment from an old wine bottle wrapped in white linen. Even that choice hinted at the culture clash.

By the third round the slow opening, marked by respect and fear as both tried to work out their opponent, evolved into the viciousness the fans had wanted. Pintor continued to press forward and get picked off by Zarate's dead-eye blows, but he had trapped the champion's ego and was provoking him into standing toe to toe in the centre of the ring. Pintor wanted to make this a war rather than a textbook display of boxing artistry, and Zarate was too proud to ignore the challenge.

At home Coti shuddered. She had never watched her husband box in the flesh and she winced at every blow that slewed into his face. Little Lupe, their son, also watched and began to cry at seeing his father hurt. Coti was happy when the voices of the couple arguing next door drowned out the commentary, but could do nothing to banish her anxiety when her husband hit the floor in the fourth round. There were thirty seconds left in the round as the men circled each other in the centre of the deep-blue ring. Pintor continued to try to slow Zarate and lock his sights before he could unleash his missiles, but the champion was skilled in the art of evasion. 'Cultivate speed,' Jimmy Wilde wrote in *The Art of Boxing*. 'I have never seen a real champion who lacked it. Also maintain a good balance and poise.' At his best, Zarate had the balance of a ballerina and the speed of a spitting cobra. Coti shepherded Lupe away and told him it would be all right. The boy was transfixed and traumatized by the picture of his father sitting on the floor on the television screen.

The left-right combination from Zarate had worked so well because of his timing as well as the raw power. Pintor had felt his backside bounce on the canvas. He spat out his gumshield to draw in some desperate breaths and rose. Now he was in no-man's-land, exposed and fragile. The blows he threw in those next seconds would be among the most important of his life.

Zarate was searching for the finish and, for the first time, backed his man into the snare of the red, white and blue ropes. He unleashed all of his ammunition and Pintor responded with desperate attacks of his own. When the bell sounded, he was still standing, but he was hanging on to the jaws of the chasm.

However, surviving everything he'd faced had sharpened Pintor's senses. He was in pain, his face already contorted, and he was losing the fight, but he was still there.

'He could hit, of that there's no doubt,' he said. 'Hard and precise, like the great champion he was. But I got the impression that it was as if they had forgotten to tell him that I could hit too, and that if I knocked him out then it wouldn't be due to witchcraft or divine intervention.

'Afterwards they said you could tell who won by just looking at our faces – he was virtually clean while my face was completely disfigured. That was just idle talk and angry bitterness. I'm not denying that one or two of his punches hurt me, but if my face was swollen it was because in the third round he broke my nose. It was a jab and a bit of a fluke. After the fourth the fracture was causing me breathing problems, so I went back to my corner, sat down and, in an amateurish error, blew my nose. A huge clot flew out and the air rushed into the space behind it, not just into my lungs, but also through to my skin. That was why I looked like I did.'

Yet by the sixth round Pintor was beginning to enjoy parity with Zarate. It was in that round that he connected for the first time with a big right hand. He was heaving his entire body into blows, targeting Zarate's head as if it were part of a coconut shy. At the end of the round both touched each other gently on the arms, acknowledging that they were pushing each other to new heights. Jorge Zarate stood over his son in his white shirt and blue slacks and waved a towel. Tony Torres grimaced inwardly at the sunken face before him, but made sure he looked confident and did not transfer his concern to his man. He iced the swelling and Pintor remembered the same cold heat that had burned him when he had dressed his bruises as a boy. Who knows whether that fleeting memory inspired him to turn the course of the fight in the next round?

It was a great left, followed swiftly by a right, that shook Zarate. Two more lefts followed as Pintor saw an opportunity. Suddenly, Zarate's grace was gone and he stumbled as the challenger hurled him round. In the following round, Mills Lane warned Zarate for putting a sharp elbow into Pintor's face. It was an ugly blow, out of character and evidence of a faltering conviction. Zarate still felt he was too good for Pintor, but he now knew that he was embroiled in a bloody battle of wills as well as boxing skills. He launched one of his trademark counters, but it was stopped at birth by another straight left from Pintor, and they ended the ninth with their feet almost touching, slugging each other as if fighting on some Mexican street corner. Man and man, shoulder to shoulder, in savage solidarity.

Pintor did not speak at the break before the tenth, but Torres could see in those bloated eyes that the desire was flaming again. No bantamweight had been able to do this to Zarate and, while it was close, the momentum was swinging their way. Torres did his job and offered a few token words of praise. In one corner of Cuajimalpa, Coti Pintor watched the birds on their perches; in another Francisco and his brothers punched the air and shouted.

The tenth was Pintor's best round yet. Zarate's impeccable poise had gone and he was sacrificing his superior reach for the sake of proving he could beat his man in any way he saw fit. So the gap between them diminished and Pintor's shorter blows began connecting with frightening intensity. A left over the top of a tepid Zarate blow cracked against the jawbone. Instantly, Pintor hit him again. Zarate's legs wavered and he staggered for a few brief steps. Just as Zarate had done in the fourth, little more than twenty minutes earlier, now Pintor went in manic search of the knockout blow. Zarate cushioned himself in the ropes and covered his face. Pintor waved his red gloves in front of him like maracas and then struck. The uppercut, the hook, the *gaucho*, everything he had learnt from watching Olivares, Marciano and Louis, who touched the brim of his baseball cap at ringside.

But Zarate was a legend. The memory of the Gomez fight meant he knew what it was to be in trouble, and he used that. Sometimes he sailed close to the rules, putting another cocked elbow in Pintor's disfigured face and then getting a warning for hitting with his right while holding his rival's head, but he was still dancing. He did all he could to convince the judges. He shuffled his feet and bounced on them after the bell for the end of the eleventh, as if to highlight his boundless energy. Pintor marched solemnly back to his corner. He had no time for whims and deceits. As he went, he did not notice Zarate glaring at him.

Torres picked up another chunk of ice and pressed it into Pintor's sagging flesh. There was blood coming from his mouth and a scar on his left brow. The bell called the boxers forward like Pavlov's dogs. They scowled and tore and scratched. Pintor was now pressing forward all the time, as Zarate picked his punches and tried to dismantle the onslaught with one carefully conceived combination. He had some success and pounced on the moment with all the expediency of a seasoned veteran. Those at ringside yelled, but few appreciated the scale of the bravery and the delicacy of the situation.

In those last rounds the arguments, the enmity and the disparate styles ebbed away to leave two naked boxers surviving on rehearsed strength and heart. They dragged their innate reservoirs and fought to the inner clock.

They touched gloves at the start of the fifteenth and final round. This was the epilogue, a chance to add some perspective to all that had gone before, to reiterate what had happened and influence the myopic judges.

It was Pintor's round. A packed crowd rose to their feet. Joe Louis and Ryan O'Neal applauded, Torres told his man he was the champion and Coti Pintor cowered behind her cupped hands, thankful that Little Lupe had gone off to sleep. Pintor stood in his corner as Torres tried to sooth his face. The olive glow was now grey shadows, the protruding bones almost turning his face inside out. Torres held a sponge to the bleeding mouth and blocked the view of the judges with his back.

Zarate had put one arm around Pintor at the end and raised his other to the roof. He smiled at the crowd, fisted the air and let nobody doubt that he should be the winner. Mills Lane stood with his hands on his hips, chewing calmly and awaiting the verdict. In those few moments, Coti prayed again. So did Francisco. Don Lupe downed another glass of *pulque* and raised his eyebrows. Who could tell?

The man in the brown suit, frilly shirt and oversized lapels, accepted a card and pulled down a microphone from the sky. Pintor did not seem to recognize the words 'new WBC bantam-weight champion', but then broke into a gummy red smile. His first instinct was to shake Zarate's hand, but the dethroned champion would not look at him. Torres waved dismissively at Zarate. Amid the cheers, there was a volley of boos. It was a decision that has been much disputed ever since – and one that changed Pintor's life.

In the aftermath, Zarate was a graceless loser, and his supporters claimed the fight had been fixed. Some said Zarate had told Hernandez beforehand that this was going to be his last fight, regardless of the outcome, and that the old trainer had used his influence to ensure the title stayed in the 'family'. Others said Hernandez had paid off Zarate, but the brutality of the fight proved the idiocy of such claims.

A poll taken after the fight found plenty of journalists who disagreed with the verdict, but others sided with Pintor, and a review of the tape suggests objective accounts have been lost in the passage of time.

'I thought he did more in the fight and I had him a narrow winner,' John Beyrooty said.

The judges' scorecards added to the confusion. Art Lurie and Harold Buck answered Coti's prayers by giving the nod to Pintor by a single point, but the third judge, Bob Martin, gave it to Zarate by an incredible twelve points.

'I wrote that Martin should never be allowed to score

another fight in Vegas,' Beyrooty said. 'He'd forgot the fight was scored on the ten-point system and instead used the old five-point system. So he had Zarate winning a close fight with a lot of 5–4 rounds. When he discovered his mistake, his way of sorting out the problem was to double the scores for every round – so suddenly Zarate was winning all these rounds 10–8.

'It was my first world title fight but I didn't think it was a bad decision. Hernandez did not go in either corner. No way was it tainted. I didn't think anything about it afterwards. Nobody did. It's only been in recent times that people have started to question it.'

Pintor returned a hero, although the reception he received from Coti was mixed. Any hope that his new status might mend the fault-lines in their relationship was soon quashed. She loved him but she knew she had lost him. 'He was young, rich and famous and there came a time where he lost stability within himself and let loose,' she said. 'We started to have arguments and, on one occasion, I left to go and live with my mother.'

On 14 July 1979, things degenerated further. Pintor was involved in a minor car accident, but was angered by the attitude of the policemen. In the aftermath he was accused of hitting one of them, although he claimed the policemen had stolen his camera and money. He spent almost twenty-four hours locked in a dirty cell in Mexico City before being released without charge. Nevertheless, the rush of beating Zarate stayed with him for weeks, despite the attempts by his rival's camp to diminish the triumph. He bought himself a car and, despite all that had happened, set up his father in a new house.

'Zarate was a really hard fight and it was the first time in my career that I had cuts over both eyes,' Pintor said. 'That was because Zarate fought dirty with his elbows and shoulders and lost all dignity. By doing that he gave me a chance. Zarate never normally fought like that but he changed his style because he was scared of me.'

Zarate retired after the fight and continued to gripe about the way he had been cheated. Pintor is adamant that he would have been happy to give Zarate a rematch, but the shattered champion showed no interest. It was easier to live with his contempt beneath a cloak of suspicion, rather than drive himself to the edge of his existence in the search of restitution.

'There are nights when I get nostalgic,' Pintor said. 'Memories come trickling back at first and then it's a flood. The one thing that still makes me feel dissatisfied is that Zarate retired before giving me the chance for revenge. It sounds curious to talk about revenge when I won the fight, but so much has been said, that the referee helped me and that the judges handed it to me on a plate, that it would have been nice to demonstrate who was the best and end the rumours that his cronies have repeated ever since.'

Zarate spent seven years away from boxing before he returned for the money in 1986. His pulling power meant he got another shot at the title, the WBC Super Bantamweight crown, but he was knocked out in four rounds by Jeff Fenech in Sydney. Four months later he got another shot, but lost to Daniel Zaragoza at the Forum. Afterwards, it was reported that he had been seen trying to cash his cheque in the crowd. He was thirty-six and washed up.

'I've heard that Zarate is on the street now,' Pintor said. 'He is into alcohol and drugs and that will finish anyone. Being a world champion opens many doors, some good, many more bad. People talk about you all over the world and it brings money, but you have to know how to deal with it. It is a starting point, but it depends on you as to where you go from there.

'I heard Zarate is dying of hunger. It is sad but he got what was coming to him. Carlos Zarate was a nasty person. There are many sayings in Mexico and one of them is that everyone is the architect of their own destiny. Do I have any sympathy? None whatsoever. If you live badly you end up badly. If he came here and said, "I'm hungry," then I would say, "Take whatever you want." If he asks me for a peso I will give it. But I am not going to go out and find him and give him help. I don't owe him anything. When he was the world champion he had everything. The world was at the tips of his fingers but he threw it all away.'

In 1979, the new champion made sure that he would not make the same mistakes. He played his records, fed his birds and went to the beach. He wore dark glasses and tried to avoid the cloying cameras. He breathed in the air. It was a familiar landscape, but he knew his place in it would never be the same again.

ROUND EIGHT

Lupe Pintor was worried about his cuts. At the start of the eighth, Marty Denkin held a thumb to the top of his brow and examined them briefly. He also held a hand out to the jaw of Johnny Owen. The lip was bad.

At the break, Dick Owens, Dai Gardiner and Ken Bryant, the other member of their corner team, formed a protective phalanx around their man.

'Don't let him see me,' Owen said. 'I don't want the ref seeing me.'

They cast a cursory glance at Denkin. To have come so far, to be winning the world title fight against a great champion in his adopted backyard, and to risk having that taken away because of a cut, would be too much to bear.

'The lip was done in the third round,' Dick Owens said. 'It was bad, a bloody gash, right across the corner of his mouth. But John was winning. Pintor was creeping up, but John was ahead on points. The crowd had gone very quiet because John was getting on top. They'd thought it was going to be easy when they saw how thin he was. I'd told John, "He'll go to your body." I didn't worry about that. We knew how much training he'd done.'

Bryant felt a buzz of excitement as the fight passed the halfway point. Owen's strength was in his stamina and, as far as Bryant was concerned, the longer the fight went on, the better their prospects.

'When you first saw him, you thought he's not a boxer,' he recalled. 'Young lads coming up against him thought it would be a walkover. It was the same out in America. They called him the Elephant Boy and took the piss. He was frail-looking, but he had the stamina of ten men. He was so strong.'

Pintor knew that. Strength manifests itself in different ways. Zarate had punched far harder than Owen, but he had not been in his face like this. Davila did not have the knee-buckling knockout blow in his arsenal. He might be a lithe artist who wrapped his sledgehammers in silk, but even he did not have this work-rate. And Pintor could feel the freezing hurt of the cuts undermining his efforts. The self-centredness and bottomless belief that every champion needs was slipping away as the blood ran into his eyes. The fight was moving towards the perimeters of his control.

Mickey Duff giving more advice. Get on him, swarm all over him. Vaseline wiped away by Marty Denkin and Owen continues the festivities in round eight. Moves in on Pintor, the champion. I have been very impressed with Johnny Owen. Win, lose or draw, he has put up a tremendous show of ability against Lupe Pintor.

Owen threw fourteen punches in the opening eight seconds of the round, sensing that there had been a subtle shift of power in the seventh. Throughout his career, Owen had been blessed with the ability to judge a fight as if he were watching from the ringside rather than in the mixer. He knew when he was on top and when he had lost. After seven rounds, it was close but he was in front. Parity for the rest of the bout and he would be the champion.

Pintor, though, was throwing better punches now. Owen's work-rate still pressed him back, the number of punches forming a red blur in front of his damaged eyes, but he too was landing. By giving himself a little more room, he was wielding more power and not relying on the uppercut. His timing had also improved. Owen jabbed Pintor with a straight left hand, almost perfectly horizontal, but Pintor saw the attack as his chance. His opponent had a good guard, peering carefully from behind the red globes, but when a blow was dispatched, half the defence went with it. It was a case of taking a punch to land one, a terrible deal struck with your own spirit. Owen's glove slipped off the side of Pintor's burning cheek and the champion's own right flew over the dropping arm of his assailant and into bone.

Tom Kelly and Little Red had been won over by Owen's courage, but Allan Malumud, the third member of their commentary team, was still obsessing about his physique. *The only time Owen had any trouble making the weight was as a ten-year-old in an amateur fight when he had to put a lead weight under his trunks*, he said. *I guess that is literally making the weight.*

Kelly did not respond to the comment and carried on calling the blows. *Pintor has been bloodied and cut and this tall, thin challenger takes the play away from him.* The pace of the game meant the next time Kelly spoke, he was lauding Pintor. *Pintor, now winning the eighth round, trying to put the fight back where the odds-makers expected it to be. But that's a mean-looking cut above his eye.*

Little Red also felt Pintor was growing as the minutes ticked by. *Pintor staying out where he wants to be now and turning the whole tide of the fight around. Johnny Owen is not keeping the pressure on like he was.*

Owen's individual blows were not as hurtful as Pintor's, but he was taking the initiative and had not yet been rocked by a single punch, whether they were harder or not. But who could know, for sure, whether the total of Owen's incredible assault had caused more damage than the heavier, more sporadic salvos of Pintor? Midway through the round, two unerring lefts crashed into the right side of Pintor's jaw. The second was harder, the backswing more pronounced and the angle of delivery wider as Owen's cocked gun sprang from his side. Pintor winced. Johnny Owen could punch all right.

In the last ten seconds of the eighth round a total of twenty punches were thrown. Ten: Owen put his gloves on Pintor's shoulders and shoved him away. Nine: a downward right scraped the back of Pintor's head as the champion crouched. Eight: A left tested the elasticity of Pintor's nose. Seven: Pintor emerged from his crouch with his left arm trailing behind him. Six: The arm was swung as a golf club and thudded into Owen's midriff. Five: a left-right combination forced Pintor to gasp for air. Four: Their heads locked. Three: Owen ducked under Pintor's sweeping left. Two: Pintor's mouth was pressed into Owen's shoulder. One. His jaw ached from another left. A bell sounded somewhere in the distance.

10

BROTHERS (1)

Lupe Pintor spent heavily on cars as he celebrated his status as world champion. His collection grew quickly until he had a Mercedes, a Corvette, a Mercury, a Super Bee and, finally, a Porsche. The last purchase was particularly sweet for Pintor. To his mind, a Porsche was a symbol that undid the poverty of his past and raised him to vertiginous heights.

Johnny Owen marked his own ascent by buying a second-hand Austin Allegro. He drove his brothers up into the Brecon Beacons, along grey roads snaking a course through the greenery, until they came to the strip, a long undulating stretch by a reservoir with trees forming an arc above it. Kelvin and Vivian would then get out and watch their brother drive off to the far end of the road. One of them would raise a hand, prompting the engine roar, wheel-spin and stench of burning rubber. The Allegro would thunder towards them, straining for a higher gear, until one of the watchers would click the stopwatch as it passed by and shrieked to a halt. Then Vivian would have a go and then Kelvin. Not surprisingly, it was not long before steam rose in protest from the sizzling engine.

'I'm not going near that, bud,' Kelvin said. 'It might blow.'

Johnny smiled. 'Don't be soft.'

179

They took it back to the garage, played hell and got a Cortina estate as a courtesy car. It was not long before they were back on the strip, murdering the replacement with their games. 'It was rally country up there and we hammered it,' Kelvin recalled.

The dangers of those nights revealed a wild streak that seemed out of kilter with Johnny's general personality. He was modest, dedicated and honest, yet willing to take grave risks on blind corners and hidden dips along a bending road. However, while boxers come in all shapes and forms, to a degree, all are adrenaline-junkies.

Johnny, in fact, prized cars as highly as Pintor did. Whether this was down to the need for status symbols or a reflection of the fighter's subconscious knowledge that fame is ephemeral we can't know, but Kelvin recalled that the only time he ever saw his brother explode into a foul temper was because of a car.

'As he got more successful, he got a Datsun,' he said. 'The registration was JBO 62N, and he thought that was great because it was Johnny Bionic Owen. I'd smashed my car up. I was a nutter in a car in those days. I was engaged to a girl called Alison at the time and I borrowed his car to take her up in the forest. I was bombing down the hill, came to a ninety-degree angle in the road and went straight off. I remember flying through the air and seeing a tree coming towards us. We smashed into it. The car was a mess. The windscreen was smashed, the bonnet crumpled, but thankfully we were all right. Somehow the engine was still running, so we put the mats under wheels and managed to pull it out.

'I wanted to make sure we got the insurance money, so I took it to the police station and made up a story of how someone had forced me off a certain road. I can't believe how stupid I was because the road I'd named has no trees on it and the policeman went outside and started pulling twigs and bark out of the bonnet. He said he was going to book me for wasting police time, but he could see Alison was very embarrassed because we'd been up to the forest and so he let us off.'

When Kelvin told his brother what he had done, he went outside to look at the damage. That was when he erupted in a way Kelvin had never seen. 'He was screaming and shouting and threatening me,' he said. 'They wouldn't let him near me because they wondered what he might do. It was very rare to see John mad and that night was the worst. I made sure I kept out of his way. It cost £500 to fix it and I paid him about £250. He let me off the rest as an engagement present. That was generous because it was a lot of money in those days. Eventually, he calmed down and forgave me, but he never let me borrow his car again.'

Kelvin's surprise at what, to many, would be a normal reaction to such flagrant abuse of a favour was testament to Johnny's unnatural calm. He was a champion boxer who avoided conflict. His father remembers a night spent at a restaurant in Middlesbrough before his bout with Antonio Medina. A passing waiter inadvertently tipped a plate of salad over the British champion. The waiter apologized and tried to brush Johnny down. 'He just kept on eating,' Dick said. 'John was shy and knew people were looking at him because of the commotion. He didn't like the attention and didn't want any fuss.'

At the weigh-in for the Medina bout, concerns about Johnny's physique again surfaced. 'I could hold you up against a lightbulb to examine you,' the doctor said beforehand. The Owens had grown inured to such remarks, despite the abusive phone calls Gardiner still received, and despite their frustration that critics ignored his record.

The Medina fight was significant for other reasons. One was the fact that Gardiner had not wanted to take the bout, reasoning that Medina was too experienced. He had been outvoted by Johnny and his father and his doubts were dismissed by a comfortable eight-round decision. The other reason was an incident that Dick remembers clearly. One of the archaic traditions of boxing is to have an attractive woman parade around the ring at each break, usually in flimsy attire, with a card indicating the number of the next round. As Gardiner spoke to Johnny during one such hiatus that the boxer said; 'Get out of the way, Dai, you're blocking my view.'

'What?' the manager said, glancing over his shoulder.

Johnny grinned. 'Blimey, I wouldn't mind going a few rounds with her.'

It was an apparently inconsequential exchange, but one that showed that Johnny, contrary to the whisper and innuendo fuelled by the media fascination with his celibacy, did have a healthy regard for the opposite sex.

'The discourteous comments about John not having a girlfriend used to bother me,' Kelvin said. It is why he bristled at the description of his brother as 'the virgin soldier' in an article in the *Observer* by Hugh McIlvanney, but the lack of girlfriends inevitably intrigued the press and Gardiner was happy to give a few sound bites and grab whatever headlines he could. 'I've known him since he was a baby and he's never been out with a girl in his life,' he told *Boxing News*. 'He is totally dedicated and just devours everything he can about Jimmy Wilde, his hero.'

Jeff Pritchard is proud to recall that his wife, Yvonne, was the first woman Johnny danced with, one night at the Double Diamond Club in Caerphilly, while Billy Vivian remembers taking a Polaroid of his wife, Linda, in Johnny's Lonsdale belt.

Kelvin says there was a girl his brother liked at school, but there were no love affairs, romances or clandestine meetings in a Beacons-bound Datsun. For the main part, Johnny Owen was a boxer – plain, certainly, but not as simple as some have suggested.

'He noticed women even if he didn't do much about it,' Gareth Jones, the journalist who befriended the Owens, said. 'He was pretty exceptional to be able to turn away the groupies, because there were a lot of women around. Johnny wasn't articulate, but he certainly wasn't stupid either. It was just that there wasn't so much media involved in those days. Now you're on Sky every week and he'd have got used to it.'

Graham Walters, the man who would carry the Welsh flag into the Olympic Auditorium the following year, said: 'He didn't say much, but his brain was razor-sharp. I remember watching him do a TV interview and suddenly realizing that he was actually playing with the reporter.'

Ironically, the shyness endeared him to both public and media and they wanted more of him as a result, but that was not his way. At 10.30 p.m. on 27 February 1978, the phone rang on the sports desk at the *Western Mail*. Jones picked up the receiver and heard a familiar, nervous voice. 'It's Johnny Owen calling,' it said. 'I won on points.' It was the first telephone call the British champion had ever made. He was twenty-two.

After fourteen months as a professional, Johnny was named the Welsh Boxer of the Year and came third in the Welsh Sports Personality of the Year, behind David Broome, the showjumper, leaving Johnny to reflect: 'Bloody hell, I was beaten by a horse.' He was on the up, his common-sense approach extending from his teetotalism to his scepticism over Gardiner's claim that, now he was the British champion, he could be a millionaire within twelve months. It was an extravagant claim that cast doubts in the boxer's mind. 'Dai must be bonkers,' he told his father. 'A millionaire? When I retire, I should have about £100,000, I reckon.'

His father nodded. 'That's more realistic, son.'

It was indeed. Still working as a machine-setter, Johnny dreamed of owning a hotel or a shop. He took home a net £535 for beating Alan Oag in his first fight since becoming the British champion and £600 for out-pointing Medina. 'The relationship between a manager, promoter and boxer is cast in stone,' Kelvin said. 'You can take it as read that the promoter is in it for himself and is out to make money. Most promoters don't give a damn about who his boxer fights. Occasionally, you will get a manager who will try and make matches correctly, but there are plenty of others who will let you fight anyone as long as they get their twenty-five per cent.' Now, though, Johnny was about to earn £1,708, after expenses (double his best previous purse), for his first title defence against Wayne Evans.

It was a bold choice by the Owen camp. First defences are often one-sided affairs as a manager and promoter seek to protect their asset, but Evans had won all his eleven fights and was regarded as a ferocious puncher. The prospect of fighting in Ebbw Vale would scarcely bother him either, since he had been born in the Rhondda Valley before his family uprooted and moved to Hampshire. His manager and father, Gwyn, had even been a National Collieries champion and expressed his gratitude to Heddwyn Taylor for allowing them to fight in their home-land. Mickey Duff, the promoter, was another part of the Evans camp and wanted to avenge the loss to Maguire. Everyone in the gym at New Tredegar knew this was a major test for their man, but they had been altering their own goalposts in the wake of Johnny's dramatic rise. 'My first ambition was to be British champion,' he said. 'Now it's to win the Lonsdale belt for good. Then the European championship. After that, who knows?'

Gardiner, too, was changing his mind.

'I never thought he'd get as far as he did,' he said. 'I'd never been that far in my life so how could I know? But I'd sparred with Winstone at his best and I'd seen Johnny at his best. Johnny didn't have Winstone's class, nobody did, but his dedication, work-rate and stamina were unbelievable. I'd known he was at least a British champion, but now I was thinking maybe European and maybe more.'

On the morning of the fight Johnny tucked into his normal breakfast of boiled cod, with the water pressed out between two plates, a poached egg, half a slice of toast and a cup of sweet tea. Then, as usual, he walked around town and popped into the railway station to see Bill Lucas, who weighed him on the parcel scale. He was right on the limit, yet by the time of the official weigh-in at the Royal Oak pub in Ystrad, he was two ounces overweight. Evans laughed at his rival's predicament and offered him a glass of orange juice. It was a slight that Johnny would remember and use against him. He lost the weight quickly at Gardiner's house and returned to the Royal Oak for his pre-bout meal of a tuna sandwich, yoghurt and honey, washed down with some vitamin tablets.

'Wayne will pay for trying to make a fool out of me,' he told his father.

If they needed more ammunition it came from Evans's father, who had been stoking the pot with some bullish words.

'Wayne will win,' he told journalists. 'No doubt about it, without any argument. Only this morning my trainer told me that Wayne had knocked out a middleweight. Owen has not met anybody in Wayne's class. I cannot see it going ten rounds.'

It was an intoxicating night at the Ebbw Vale Leisure Centre.

'Bursting with atmosphere', as Harry Carpenter put it on his BBC commentary. 'Owen has an extraordinary physique and looks as if a puff of wind would blow him over, but he is in fact a hard-bitten, tough, cagey and stylish little man.'

The fight would support that appraisal as Johnny dismantled Evans.

'Owen has the look of a man totally confident that he can hold on to this championship,' Carpenter said in the fourth. It continued in the same vein. Evans reverted to his bad habit of jumping into punches against taller opponents and looked awkward. 'It's gone by like a flash, it's been so interesting,' Carpenter chimed in his prim, authoritative tone. 'Jimmy Wilde was his hero and he is a bit like Wilde. He was a frail-looking man who they used to call the Ghost with the Hammer in his Hand. You could easily plant that nickname on Owen.'

Evans could punch, though, and a right hand punctured Johnny's left eardrum. He came back to the corner complaining that he could not hear as his father wiped away the seeping blood. It is testament to the boxer's innate reservoir that such a horrible injury was dismissed as an inconvenience. Evans, shorter and stockier, with a mop of wavy black hair and overgrown sideburns, was brave – but beaten. By the ninth it was almost cruel, and Johnny sent Evans to the canvas. Legs splayed, mouth wide open and heart exposed, Evans rose at eight and bounced from rope to rope, throwing punches hopefully. 'He's wriggling around this ring like a fly on sticky paper,' Carpenter suggested.

At the end of the round Evans held his hand half aloft, as if in acknowledgement of his own courage. But the next round was a bridge too far. He came out to face a remorseless barrage and his efforts to hide and crouch were flawed. One more right hand on the chin felled him.

'Poor old Wayne Evans doesn't know where he is or what day it is,' the commentary cackled as he bent forward on all fours. His cornermen were quickly in and turned him on to his side, whereupon he collapsed onto his back in exhaustion. When he rose and fears about his condition evaporated, he was clapping his opponent, to the delight of the crowd and Carpenter.

'Isn't that marvellous?' he said. 'And Johnny Owen at last lets some emotion come across that poker face. At the age of twenty-two, Merthyr's Johnny Owen now has two notches on his belt. He needs one more to keep it. The best talent in Welsh professional boxing for a long time.'

The Owens celebrated with an eighteenth-birthday party for Susan at the Double Diamond Club. The Nolan Sisters were top of the bill and Susan wanted an autograph. As Johnny stood in the queue to the backstage dressing rooms, another queue formed as people sought the champion's signature. He happily obliged, as he would do throughout his career, albeit he got a specially made stamp to inscribe the publicity shots that were sent out. When he finally met the singing group, they exchanged autographs.

The family holiday that year was simple. They borrowed a local butcher's caravan for a two-week break near Barry. For Johnny it was no holiday. He ran ten miles before breakfast every day, each step taking him closer to his next aim of winning the Commonwealth or European title. The victories kept on coming too. He beat Dave Smith at the National Sporting Club on a card where his friend Billy Vivian was defeated by Jim Watt, the Scotsman on course to the world title. He also stopped Dave Lamour in seven rounds at the Double Diamond Club. During that fight, his father heard a punter say: 'Look John's got a leek.'

His friend replied: 'You mean he's taking the piss out of him?'

The first man laughed. 'No, he's got a Welsh leek taped to his sock.'

The leek had been a good-luck gift from the landlord of the Castle Inn in Aberaman, and fastening it to his sock would forever signal the end of Johnny's pre-bout routine.

As Johnny's stock rose, so did his marketability. Heddwyn Taylor, the mine owner, and Eddie Thomas, the former champion, locked horns in their own contest to stage the big fights. Thomas had more experience, but Taylor had the gift of the gab. He had the thick skin and wallet needed to succeed. He would often get Tommy Farr, a regular guest at his mansion, to be the guest of honour at his shows.

'Tommy would always say, "Just walking out into a ring makes my nose bleed now".'

One night Taylor and Farr watched a video of the latter's fight with Joe Louis. At the start of the fifteenth, Farr was up off his chair like lightning waiting for Louis.

'Jesus, Heddwyn,' he said with a shake of his head. 'I should have got a bloody Oscar for that. I just wanted to go to bed.'

Thomas had just as many contacts, but Taylor believed he had first say on Johnny Owen.

'Eddie was a good friend but he didn't want to know Johnny until I started him off,' Taylor said. 'Eddie did a lot of good for boxing in Wales, but he was fighting off the beaten track. He wasn't promoting the right fights and he lost a lot of money. I think he trod on Mickey Duff's feet too much.'

An offer came in to fight Paul Ferreri, a durable Australian who bore an uncanny resemblance to Carlos Zarate and had performed well in losing to him. Johnny would get £4,000 to take on Ferreri in Australia for the Commonwealth title. They might have signed but for the concerns raised by a letter from an altruistic stranger that dropped through the door.

'Don't go out there,' it read. 'You will never win out there. I lived in Australia nearly my whole life. Keep away. You will never get the verdict.'

Had Johnny been a big puncher, the camp might have ignored the letter, but they knew Ferreri was a quality man who had been in with the best, and the bout was likely to go the distance. It was a long way to go to be deceived, and they decided to bide their time. Perhaps it was this delay that led Johnny to lose focus. In training, Dick was alarmed to see his son forgo his usual defence and take numerous punches to the face. In the car on the way home, he asked: 'What's wrong?'

'I don't know,' Johnny said, 'but my nose is sore.'

Dick considered his son. They were on the way up, but he knew any weakening of spirit could ground the bandwagon.

'Tomorrow we'll go back and we'll practise on the bag,' he said. 'I want round after round with you using only your left arm. I want you to use that left not once or twice, but six or seven times to keep your opponent away. You've had all these contests and you've never had a black eye, but the way you're going you're going to have a black eye and a broken nose very quickly. I can get any boxer off the street to take punches in the face. Either buck up or we pack it in.'

Boxing is full of father-and-son teams, and there is a dichotomy at the heart of each one. Every father wants his son to have success and good health, yet the former inevitably risks the latter. Dick had recoiled when he saw his son take a hefty blow, but wanted him to fight a harder, more dangerous figure than anyone he had yet encountered. It is an impossible balancing act between risk and reward.

But with the Ferreri fight still not sealed, Dick and Johnny travelled to London to get their Lonsdale belt. They had given it to the British Boxing Board of Control to have it engraved. If Johnny defended his British title one more time, he would keep the belt that is the essence of British boxing's romantic ideals. In the office, Ray Clarke, the secretary, gave some surprising advice as he handed it back. 'Give up the title, don't bother with the Commonwealth and go straight for the European,' he said.

Dick could not believe his ears.

'What sort of advice is that?' he scowled. 'Every boy's ambition is to win that belt and make it his property. Thank you, Mr Clarke, but we won't be taking your advice.'

Clarke shrugged. He was the pragmatic side of the game, Dick Owens the heart of it.

Johnny stretched his unbeaten pro record to fifteen with a third-round stoppage of Wally Anglisson 25 September 1978, and finally heard the Ferreri fight was on. More importantly, it was to be held in Ebbw Vale on his home patch. It was a coup for Heddwyn Taylor and a blow to Eddie Thomas.

'I asked Eddie to go into a partnership and form the Sporting Club of Wales, but he declined,' Taylor said. 'Then he saw Johnny climbing the ladder and he wanted to promote him. At five in the morning my phone went and it was Eddie's wife playing merry hell, asking why I hadn't taken Eddie in on a joint promotion for the Ferreri fight. Well, I'd done all the donkey work and I wasn't going to take another guy in, because for the first few fights I'd lost a hell of a lot of money.'

Taylor met Ferreri's plane at Heathrow shortly after midnight and drove him and his manager, Jack Rennie, to the Maes Manor Hotel in Blackwood. Ferreri was tired and grumpy, but he was confident and talked of placing a bet on himself. With sixty-nine fights behind him, including the world title bout with Zarate – a fight stopped in the twelfth because of a cut eye – he had reason to doubt the ability of a rangy rookie to trouble him.

It was a fight that quickly captured the imagination. Paddy Maguire, the man Johnny had beaten to take the British title, offered to help.

'I so want Owen to win that I'm willing to come to Wales for nominal expenses to help with the final training,' he said.

Taylor said he would consider it. Those surveying the respective records noted how Ferreri had stopped Maguire in eight rounds at a time when the Irishman was at his peak. His career spanned ten years and had only six blemishes. Doubts dominated the headlines, although Colin Hart in the *Sun* predicted a 'shock points victory for Owen'. Some wondered whether, despite the CV, Ferreri was not the king of the mountain but rather a man in danger of disappearing over the hill. Most, however, thought he would win. Dennie Mancini, the agent who brought Ferreri over, explained that the Sicilian-born Australian saw the fight as a short cut back to another world title bout.

Johnny met Ferreri for the first time in a television studio. The chiselled features, dashing pencil moustache and armoured biceps jarred against the challenger's sallowness. Ferreri toyed with Johnny and handed him a fifty-pence boomerang.

'I'll get this back later,' he quipped.

Johnny was unmoved. 'You've got a little girl, haven't you?' he asked.

The comment jolted Ferreri out of his gloating. 'Er, yeah, I have.'

With that Johnny pulled out a knitted rag doll and handed it to the bemused Australian.

'Give this to her,' he said.

He nodded for Ferreri to take it and he accepted, edgily looking towards his manager. There was usually some sort of inference or joke to be gleaned from a gift. This, however, was just someone being kind and, as such, fell outside the boxing lexicon. Ferreri was an old pro, however, schooled in the mind games and statements that guaranteed headlines and ticket sales. He turned to Taylor and said: 'Tell me where you'll be sitting at ringside and I'll put him on your lap.' If his confidence was unbridled, his manager sounded a more cautionary note.

'He's like a big scarecrow,' Jack Rennie said, 'but we've seen clips of him in previous fights and it's enough to frighten us.'

There were concerns in the Owen camp, too. Dai Gardiner lived close to the hotel where Ferreri was staying and watched him pounding the streets in the morning.

'I knew he was in terrific shape and I was on to Johnny all the time,' he said. 'I told him this was going to be hardest fight, but he just said, "Dai, what are you so worried about, man?" That was the one where I did have concerns to be honest.'

Taylor told Gardiner that Ferreri was eating a T-bone steak with four eggs for breakfast. It sounded like a giant's feast. Taylor, though, was happy about his side of things. 'Harry Carpenter said, "They're hanging from the rafters in here," and that was music to my ears. That was a hell of a fight. Ferreri came here with the determination of a lion.'

Johnny was in better shape than ever. He had sparred with big-hitting Colin Jones, who, under Eddie Thomas's guidance, would go on to fight for the world welterweight title, and left nothing to chance. Dick warned him not to get carried away with the emotion and to give too much too soon.

The bell sounded and the chorus of 'Land of My Fathers' faded.

It was a contest for the connoisseur as Ferreri's counter-attacks and in-fighting rattled against Johnny's swarming blows. By the fourth round, the work-rate was taking the challenger into a healthy lead, but by the eighth the Australian was planting his feet firmly on the blue canvas and launching long, unerring blows. In the tenth they both stood in the centre of the ring, any advantage inherent in Ferreri's southpaw stance negated by the number of punches Johnny threw.

At the break, Jack Rennie pressed an ice-pack into his man's face, aided by Dennie Mancini.

'This will make him internationally,' Harry Carpenter intoned. 'The name of Johnny Owen will go right around the world if he wins this. They know it's coming to the crunch right here.'

The long left jab that he had worked on so much began to pick off Ferreri, but the Australian scored with uppercuts and hooks of his own. Johnny desperately sought to make the most of his reach and youth, but Ferreri had a filing cabinet of escape routes stored in his head and plundered it to ease the pressure. It was a thrilling, coruscating, primitive fight and Ebbw Vale lost its collective head.

At the end of the fifteenth round they touched gloves.

'Owen quite well out in front on my card,' Carpenter said.

Roland Dakin, the referee, called the men together, held their wrists and raised Johnny's gloved hand. He had made him the winner by six clear rounds. Ferreri claimed he had won, but the words were born out of his desire to secure a rematch rather than a genuine sense of injustice. Rennie offered a less jaundiced view.

'Owen is a world champion in the making,' he said. 'He has as much potential as any fighter I've seen all around the world. This Owen has everything – boxing ability, class and guts.'

The next mission was to secure the European title, but already some reports were tentatively mentioning Johnny in the same breath as Carlos Zarate, the world champion. What they did not know was that, by the time Owen was ready for the ultimate test, Zarate would have been sent mercilessly into retirement.

ROUND NINE

It was the wee small hours in Merthyr when the fight drifted off course. The ninth would give Lupe Pintor the conviction to overcome his injuries. At ringside, Allan Malamud, Tom Kelly and Little Red Lopez had Johnny Owen ahead by five rounds to three. Pintor needed something to pacify this hornet's nest that followed him around the ring, stinging his body at every turn. For the first time, with eight, hard rounds under their belts, Little Red talked of the prospect of a new world champion. The dedication of Johnny Owen was paying off. *I think that's the only way Pintor's going to win. He's going to have to land one of those big blows and put Owen out to win the fight. If Owen keeps rushing him and keeps the pressure on like he's doing, I think Pintor's going to lose it.*

Punches are thrown through a mixture of skill and instinct. Timing is everything and often involves a healthy dose of luck as a speculative blow lands plum on its desired target. Some boxers say they 'felt' it coming. Somewhere in their peripheral vision they saw a flash headed by a fist. Seeing is one thing. Getting out of the way quite another. In the ninth round of his world title fight with Lupe Pintor, Johnny Owen was knocked down for the first time in his life.

'It is not a bad feeling,' Floyd Patterson, the dethroned world heavyweight champion, once said. 'It doesn't hurt. You're just unbelievably groggy ... like floating on a pleasant cloud.' Then he said the feeling turned to anger and shame and an overwhelming desire to disappear through a magic trapdoor in the ring and be transported back to the dressing room. It is the ultimate humiliation. A man's hopes, dreams and boasts are lost in the most vivid exorcism. It is the knowledge that this is the apotheosis of boxing that makes it stand alone. It is the one sport where fans do not envy the combatants. Sport is a placebo, but boxing is the real thing – an addictive drug.

Johnny Owen's first knockdown came with twenty-two seconds left in round nine, and had been foretold by Malamud.

Somehow, I feel, somewhere down the line, Owen is going to walk onto a right hand. That's just a gut feeling. I think he's winning the fight and fighting beautifully but I have that suspicion that it's going to happen.

The round had started in familiar fashion. Although Pintor was visibly trying to up the pace and his punches were, if anything, carrying more weight, Owen stuck to his game plan. A left jab departed through Pintor's guard and Owen seized his opportunity to rush through the gate and back Pintor on to the ropes. Owen hit the body and the head, still lucid enough to vary his attack and keep Pintor guessing, to blue and bruise the chest, make the liver ache, test the guts.

It was, by the standards of any overseas challenger to have stood in the Olympic, a superb effort. A rare break in hostilities saw the pair step back and circle each other. They turned through 360 degrees and that alarm clock in the boxers' heads told both that they needed to attack. Owen threw out a cursory jab, an exploratory blow more than anything. And then Pintor was in. While Owen's punch was still travelling, the big one landed. A right hand slewed into Owen's left cheek and he stumbled. He had barely touched the canvas before he was up.

Marty Denkin was in front of him like a flash.

Denkin knew boxers. He had grown up in Spanish Harlem and Hell's Kitchen and had been the all-navy champion in another time. He remembered: 'I had twenty or thirty fights and then I went to a sparring session at the Main Street gym and someone said to an old pro, "Teach the kid some respect". I heard a crack and saw blood flying everywhere. I knew he'd broke my nose. The only lesson I learnt was to get out. I wanted to join the police force and they wouldn't let you in if you looked like a pug.' So Denkin, for the sake of his future and his features, quit boxing and joined the LA sheriff's department the same year that Johnny Owen was born.

Now he looked into Owen's eyes for a sign. He was focussed. Owen wiped his nose and mouth with his glove and looked almost irritated that he had been caught.

'When I first saw Johnny Owen, I thought it was a mismatch, but he was the strongest young man I've ever seen who didn't have the look of a boxer,' Denkin said. 'He looked like he should have been a librarian or something, but he was special. When the fight started Johnny Owen had a style that was smothering Pintor. It was not pretty but he was scoring and I can tell you he was ahead on two of the judge's scorecards. The trouble was he had a very bad laceration from an uppercut, the worst I've ever seen, and his lip was hanging off. Pintor had two cuts on his eyebrows that had opened from the last fight in Japan. The doctor, Bernhart Schwartz, went to look at them and, to avoid there being a riot, we looked at Owen's lip. His father kept pressing it back. I don't know if he was swallowing blood. He was putting up a hell of a fight, but it changed when he started to box outside. Pintor started fighting him the right way. When he went down in the ninth it was not a hard punch. I did the count and asked him if he was okay. He said, "Oh yes, sir." Imagine. He was the politest young man I ever came across. I asked if he was sure and he said, "Yes, sir".'

Denkin's recollections may have muddied with time, because there is no doubt the punch that felled Johnny Owen was a hard one. It travelled from a distance and was symptomatic of the greater intensity the champion was drawing on as he felt his title floating from his grasp.

Owen's down. A great right hand and Owen's down. The first time he's ever been down! He's back up. Marty Denkin is counting. Seven. Owen says he's all right. Five seconds to go in round number nine. Owen is in trouble. There's the bell. Owen is in trouble!

The bell came just when Owen needed it. Pintor landed a second heavy blow just before the chime stemmed his assault and Owen bounced on his feet before returning to the corner. Dai Gardiner, his white shirt hanging over his yellow tracksuit trousers, cut him off and led him back to his stool.

'It was the first knockdown in his life,' he recalled. 'He was up in a flash, he was so annoyed. We had trouble with his lip and it was bleeding, but it wasn't that bad. Johnny came back after the ninth and said, "Don't worry, everyone goes on the floor." Those were the very words he used to me. He was okay. "Get my gumshield in," he said.'

Ken Bryant remembers Gardiner being furious with the way Owen had got up.

'When John got back to the corner, Dai said, "If you go down, you stay down and get your faculties back. You bloody stay down and look across at me. You get up when I tell you to. If not, you go your own way. Those seconds can make all the difference. Get up too quick and you can catch a cold.'

The adrenaline coursed through Pintor in the other corner. He felt he could have won the fight had the bell been another minute away, but if seconds decide a fight, they can also determine a recovery. El Indio was discovering that Johnny Owen was as incredible as any he had fought, even Zarate. Some of the jaundiced partisans now knew this too. Prior to the first bell, an American at ringside had shouted, 'I don't believe this guy.' Now they were incredulous about his strength and courage rather than his physique.

Dr Schwartz had checked Owen's cut lip for the second time at the start of the eighth and deemed him fit to continue. Some would question his role in what ensued, but he would not have risked a boxer's health even for the sake of appeasing 10,000 Mexicans. Schwartz liked Owen and, as with all fighters, he prayed that, win or lose, he would not be seriously hurt. Prior to his pre-fight examin-ations, Schwartz had taken the trouble to do a spot of research into Merthyr Tydfil and Owen had been flattered and grateful for his interest. Much later, Schwartz would wonder why there had been no ambulance standing by and no neurosurgeon on call at the local hospital on Hope Street. It was only afterwards that such practices became the norm and boxers were given every chance. Then it was down to smelling salts and oxygen.

Pintor had sampled enough in their half-hour together to know Owen would not quit on his stool. It was impossible to put up this sort of display if the concept of quitting was anything but alien. So he went through his routine while Hernandez massaged the overwhelming feeling of power.

'You can tell things as a boxer,' Pintor said. 'From looking into the eyes of an opponent, but not only from that. You are so close together that you can sense when strength is draining from an opponent. Johnny was really hurting me early on but, as it continued, I felt he was starting to tire. I knocked him down in the ninth and they should have stopped the fight. He went down in a bad way, but every boxer has inside of themselves such heart that being knocked down just makes them want to come back for more. With boxers, even when you are spent, your spirit takes over and you fight as if you are not. It is a strange and beautiful thing. When I knocked Johnny down he went back to the corner and he told them he was okay. That was his spirit taking him on. From that point it was spirit. Just spirit. Only a boxer knows this.'

11

IN THE MATADORS' CHAPEL

On Christmas Day, 1978, Johnny Owen had his annual drink. He supped the tot of sherry with his family and listened to Slade toast the season on the stereo. It had been a good year, one that had brought him two titles and a modest income, though he kept his job as a machine-setter, and the inevitability of further private wars loomed. For Dick and Johnny it was thrilling, but for Edith Owen, pricking the turkey in the kitchen, it was horrible. Each mile post on the road to the endgame was struck through her heart.

'I could never ever go to one of Johnny's fights,' she told a reporter seeking a new angle on the man now being called the Matchstick Man. It was a nickname that stuck and was better than the Fighting Freak, one of Jimmy Wilde's old monikers, which was appropriated by more unimaginative writers. 'If I did I might pull him out of the ring. Boxing is his life and I've resigned myself to it, but that doesn't stop me worrying, especially if he is marked in any way.'

But on that Christmas Day they were just an ordinary family and Edith embraced the normality. It was the things that made her son extraordinary that tested her nerves and brought the journalists to their home. And she knew that it was a matter of three months before her son would be taken from her again and told to fight for the pleasure of another 10,000 voyeurs in a Spanish bullring. The on-off fight for the European title was now set in stone.

The European champion was Juan Francisco Rodriguez, a messenger with Almeria City Council, who had laboriously taken the title from Franco Zurlo, an ageing Italian who had twice turned down invitations to fight Johnny. Rodriguez's record of thirteen professional fights was modest but deceptive, given the Spanish hierarchy's preference to keep their better fighters in the amateur ranks and boost national pride with their medals. Rodriguez had done this by winning an Olympic bronze and, as well as a decent armoury, had the knowledge that Spain had one of the more blatantly whimsical approaches to scoring fights involving overseas challengers.

Johnny's innocence bucked such cynicism and fuelled his appeal. The Welsh rugby team won the Grand Slam in 1978, but it was Johnny who was the Welsh Sports Personality of the Year. *Boxing News* had named his bout with Ferreri as their fight of the year. He was also voted best young fighter by the Boxing Writers Club and even gave a speech at the dinner at Quaglino's restaurant in London.

'Boxing is said to be a one-man sport, but don't you believe it,' he told the audience. 'You need a team behind you and I'm very lucky to have Dai Gardiner as my manager and my father, Dick, as my trainer. I sometimes think they are slave drivers, but it's all for the good.'

Dick was shocked to hear his son so vocal in public. 'That was quite a speech from the quiet man,' he recalled. It also glossed over the growing friction in the triumvirate. Almeria would be an entirely new experience for the team, and they had reservations even before boarding the plane out of Heathrow.

Gardiner was well aware that Colin Power, another British fighter, had been forced to wait in a cold hut on a building site until gone midnight before he defended his European light-welterweight crown the previous September. Meanwhile, Dave Needham and his manager, Mickey Duff, had been threatened with jail if they did not agree to a fifteen-round fight, despite an edict from the European Boxing Union stating that bouts should be twelve rounds following the death of Angelo Jacopucci after his fight with Alan Minter. Both boxers had lost. Spain was a short flight but a world away. And there had been a litany of stories, some true, some urban myths, of poisoned food, polluted water and prostitutes. The stories inspired a caution that drove the camp to travel to the airport in three cars in case of a breakdown.

They made it to Madrid before encountering problems. The party, including Byron Board, Owen's principal cheerleader, and Heddwyn Taylor, the promoter, made their way through a hangar. Board's thirteen-year-old daughter, Helen, had knitted Welsh leeks for the group. Her mother had given her daughter a letter asking the school if the class could make them in needlework class, but Helen was too shy to hand it in and so she had done them all on her own at home. The largest belonged to Board, but a policeman brandishing a machine gun was unimpressed.

'I couldn't understand a word he was saying but he kept prodding the leek,' Board said. 'He wanted to see if there was anything in it. Eventually, he could see that it wasn't going to bite so he let us go. The rest of them were killing themselves laughing.'

On the bus taking the group and the British press to a different terminal for the flight to Almeria, Johnny tried to ease the tension by pulling out a bag of sweets. He handed them out to each of the group. 'It summed him up,' Gareth Jones said. 'Your average champion would not have done that and, even if he had, he would have got some lackey to do it for him.'

However, the troublesome beginning proved portentous. A row about accommodation followed. Gardiner had expected the group to be staying in the four-star La Parra Hotel, a quaint place overlooking the Mediterranean in the small village of Aguadulce, but they were instead directed to the Grand Hotel in the centre of Almeria. Gardiner accepted the switch when he and Dick scouted the hotel and decided it was suitable, despite its busy, central location.

One thing Dick was adamant about that was his son should only eat the food they had brought with them. This included a selection of enormous steaks cut by Bryan Walbeoff, the New Tredegar butcher who had lent the Owens his caravan for their last holiday.

'They laughed at us for taking our own food, but we weren't taking any chances,' Dick explained. 'The only problem was where were we going to cook them. Byron went to a café called the Robin Hood and we were in luck. It was run by an American girl and her Austrian husband, and they allowed us to use their kitchen. The steaks were so big I could hardly get them in the pan. After I cooked it, she said, "Who's going to eat all that?" I said, "See the little boy in the middle?" She couldn't get over it.'

That night they dined out. The promoter griped about the size of a party that included Les Roberts and Pepe Forbes, two agents, as well as the regulars.

'He says he will only pay for John and Dai,' Forbes, a Spaniard, said.

Dick had an answer for that.

'He doesn't need to pay for John,' he said, whereupon he

pulled out a freezer box with his own food stocks, complete with bottled Welsh spring water.

Their suspicions were soon shown to be more than paranoia. The following morning a car with a loudspeaker attached advertised the fight outside their window at 6 a.m. Then Johnny, having been told he could train at the same fire-station gym that Rodriguez was using, was made to stand in the baking midday sun for an hour while they waited for the champion to finish. It got worse. At the weigh-in Rodriguez stepped on the scales and, given the precise parameters of boxing, was considerably overweight. Extra ballast in the bantamweight class can prove decisive, so the Owen camp naturally objected. As tempers frayed and fingers were pointed, Rodriguez made his way to the bar and ordered a pint of orange juice. Dick's jaw dropped. He had never seen such a cool disinterest in a weight problem, and he reasoned that the fight would be postponed.

'Come on, John,' he said. 'We're leaving. Let them sort it out.'

Back in the hotel bedroom, Johnny tucked into his tuna sandwich, yoghurt and honey, washed down with a flask of tea and his vitamin tablets, just in case. He had barely finished when Gardiner entered with a sweaty shirt and deep-set frown.

'The fight's on,' he said.

'But Dai, he's overweight,' Dick responded.

'Yeah, but now they say he's okay. The contest is on and there's nothing I can do.'

'It's a mess,' Dick added. 'They're pulling one.'

'I know, Dick, but what can we do?'

What they did was what any boxer does when the rug is being pulled from beneath his feet – they battled back. The fight was scheduled for 11.15 p.m., but by now they were well tuned to the intrigues of Spanish boxing and they all expected the start time to be well past midnight. As they made their way to the dressing room, the crowd, fuelled by cheap wine and beer, jeered them. Johnny noted with interest that the Boxeo posters on the flaking walls of the ancient bullring billed him as Jhony Owen. They were led to the matadors' chapel, a tiny, whitewashed room with a small altar and a cross on the wall.

'They were trying to wind him up, but Johnny was unflappable,' Gareth Jones said.

Graham Walters, a fan who liked talking boxing with Johnny when his runs took him over to the Rhondda, pushed his back against the door. 'There were no locks on it and the Spanish were trying to get in,' he said. 'It was chaos.'

Gardiner, whose emotions always bubbled closer to the surface than his phlegmatic charge's, was nervous.

'There was just a partition that separated us from the bulls,' he said. 'They kept banging away. The Spanish tried everything. Looking back now, there was an awful lot of stuff done. They'd mess with the food, put women on to you. There weren't the drugs around like today, but even then we did hear they'd try things to sap your strength.'

In this hostile atmosphere, with Rodriguez's fans trying to force their way into the matadors' chapel, a raging bull next door and a brass band bedecked in red and white reaching a discordant climax outside, Johnny Owen prepared for the biggest fight of his life.

'Owen was like an apparition out of the darkness,' a Spanish journalist wrote. 'He had the shoulders of a vulture and the face of a dead man. He was like a skeleton. Only when the fight began did we see that this skeleton was alive ... and very dangerous.'

The fight encapsulated all that had gone before, veering between the comic and scandalous, and winding its way to the inevitability of a wrong verdict. The footage of the fight shows Johnny as the constant aggressor, his pale body against the coal-black sky flickering like a candle in the breeze. Rodriguez's only response was to hold and butt and throw elbows. It was ugly and it was cheating and it went unpunished. He knew that surviving would be enough, that he was in on a carve-up. The drunken fans, including Rodriguez's brothers, crowded the judges.

'They were all drinking and every one of them had a knife,' Walters said. 'All the women and the children had to be taken out before the fight started, because if Johnny had got the decision, it would have been bloody murder. They were all looking at me and making gestures, all screaming at Johnny behind his corner. They were out of their minds.'

Midway through the first round the Owen corner had caught a whiff of wintergreen oil. Now they realized why Rodriguez had held out a glove and waved it in Johnny's face. He was smearing the illegal substance into Johnny's eyes, temporarily blinding him and causing him a lot of pain. Heddwyn Taylor still believes a member of the Spanish Boxing Federation was the guilty party.

'He was assisting in the corner and I had a feeling he was the one who put the oil on the gloves. He had really got my back up at the weigh-in and now this. Tactics like that were for thugs.'

Harry Vines, the experienced chief inspector from the British Boxing Board of Control, jumped up as soon as he smelt the stench. He raced over to Rodriguez's corner, but was shoved away. Policemen then carried him from the ring and left him to the mercy of a crowd demanding blood and injustice.

'Rodriguez went back to his corner and blatantly wiped the oil off,' Taylor said.

Dick was apoplectic. 'I'm furious and shout at the referee about the oil, but he just ignores me. I'm shouting at the top of my voice and there are 10,000 people in there wanting my head, but I couldn't care less. It's my son in there and they are stacking the odds against him.

'Harry Vines went over but he was pushed and shoved and abused. I couldn't believe it. They were manhandling an old man. John Lloyd, the journalist, went over to tell them who he was, but he was told to shut up and sit down. It was a total farce. The rounds were only about two minutes long and the intervals were about two and a half. They wanted Rodriguez to catch his breath. He was holding, butting and putting his thumb in John's eye, but he never had a warning. John would have had to shoot him to win.'

To make matters worse, one of Rodriguez's brothers had taken it upon himself to stand in the Owen corner and hurl abuse at the challenger every time he returned to it. Johnny sensed what was happening and warmed to his task, even taking on the crowd as well as the overweight champion. He walked back to the corner after another ugly round and fixed Rodriguez's brother with a stare. 'Quiet, boy,' he said. 'You're making too much noise.' Then, as Rodriguez again made him wait through an interminable interval, he rose, walked to the centre of the ring and blew kisses to the crowd. It was the boxer's way of acknowledging the risible antics and accepting that he was handing out a hiding for nothing.

Dai Gardiner was as frustrated as the rest of the corner, but was surprised by Rodriguez's durability. 'I didn't think he'd come out for the thirteenth or fourteenth, but he did. His father was his trainer and he just kept pushing him out.'

It was a nonsense decision. One judge scored it a draw, but the other two, including Marcello Bertini, the referee, gave it to Rodriguez by a single point. 'I was in the corner with Johnny that night and a Spanish guy kept hitting me on the leg,' Taylor said. 'It was crammed at ringside, you were tight in and this fella kept kicking me. At the end of the fifteenth I turned round and smacked him on the chin. Then I got beaten by a policeman with a truncheon. It was a crazy night.'

The pressmen referred to it as 'moonlit robbery', but the theft turned to grand larceny when the Spanish Boxing Federation then withheld £1,200 of Johnny's purse as revenge for a similar measure taken by their British counterparts when another Spaniard, Antonio Guinaldo, had been denied his full pay for giving up in a bout against Jim Watt. A trio of British journalists – Jones, Karl Woodward and Ray Parker – argued with the Spanish officials, but it was to no avail, and Johnny Owen returned home having been robbed twice. Harry Vines nursed his injured groin and bruised arm, while Walters's anger was at least tempered by the visit he had from a group of Spanish fans apologizing for the behaviour of others.

Meanwhile, Edith battled the snap of the night, walked up the hill and waited by the phone box until the allotted hour. She rang the *Western Mail* number in Cardiff and asked if the result had come in. Her disappointment at the verdict was countered by the relief of knowing her son had emerged unscathed from another fight night. Vivian had parked up and waited for the news to come in on the radio. He was anxious and kept turning the dial, endlessly hoping for some comforting words. When the BBC told him what had happened he was so angry he pulled the speakers out of his car. He went to Tiffany's nightclub and got drunk.

The fallout from Almeria lasted for weeks. To the chagrin

of Taylor, Gardiner applied for his own promoter's licence because he felt the fight should never have been allowed to go to Spain. Harry Vines said his official report was as thick as a novel, and Dick smarted. Johnny Owen, meanwhile, tucked into a slice of his beloved Black Forest gateau at a party held in his honour by the Board at his pub, the Ruperra Arms. The British Boxing Board of Control eventually made up the lost £1,200, although the exchange rate denied Johnny what would have been another £400, and Gardiner's foray into promoting ended when his first fight, a testing points win over Guy Caudron, left him £200 out of pocket.

Almeria was a lasting gripe, but Johnny had other things to concern himself with as he started to get complaints from his manager at the factory where he had worked since leaving school. Nobody doubted that Johnny was a hard grafter – he had been promoted from machine operator to setter – but the time he needed to take off to prepare for increasingly taxing fights, coupled with the popularity among his colleagues, left Tom Baker unimpressed.

'The trouble is, every time Johnny fights, his friends go along to support him, even if it means missing a shift,' he groused. 'And some of them have turned up for work the next day still the worse for drink after celebrating a victory. I've had to suspend a couple of them.'

Johnny resigned and started boxing full time. His father was pleased, as he felt work was becoming an unnecessary burden. There was also the prospect of winning the Lonsdale belt outright, with a second successful defence to build towards. The omens were not great: Johnny had to work hard to chalk up wins over Caudron and Lee Graham.

'I got caught so many times,' he said after his mediocre points win over Graham, a journeyman who was written off when announced as a late replacement. 'I'm disgusted with myself.'

Dick had no doubts that it would be different when his British title went on the line.

'In my heart I knew that belt was John's. I mean, hadn't the quiet man told me it was his? I only hoped that God would look after him because I knew he would fight until he dropped for that belt.'

It was a comment that sounded like an eerie echo of the remarks Lupe Pintor had made as he tried to explain the boxer's psyche.

'At the top level in America, you get knocked down and you come back for more,' he said. 'You are ready for that, you are prepared for that. You are ready to die if that is what it takes.'

This time it was easy. Heddwyn Taylor had secured the fight for Ebbw Vale by delivering his purse offer in person to the British Boxing Board of Control in London, five minutes before the deadline. In his favoured arena, Johnny pounded out a one-sided beating to Dave Smith, whose corner retired him at the end of the twelfth with his left eye closed and his forehead horribly mangled. Johnny shook hands with Dennie Mancini, Smith's manager and a person he liked despite his habit of turning up in opposing corners.

'Hey, Dennie,' he quipped. 'You'll have to come over to my side if you want a win.'

Mancini smiled.

On the way home, Johnny turned to his father.

'This is my belt, Dad,' he said 'but the next one will be yours.'

It was 13 June 1978, one week since Lupe Pintor had dethroned Carlos Zarate in Las Vegas. That result, however contentious, had sent shockwaves around America and Mexico, but the tremors barely reached Caerphilly as Johnny Owen sat in the back of the car and rubbed his Lonsdale belt.

Johnny's commitments were now piling up. He attended a function at the Aberfan Community Centre and did a charity run for deaf children over the mountain from Brecon to Merthyr and, despite getting lost, still came second. He also bought a grocer's shop in Merthyr against his father's wishes.

'I wanted him to finish with boxing before he turned his attention to anything else,' Dick explained. 'But he was a good buyer and the shop did well.'

He kept totting up the wins, too. He beat Neil McLaughlin, his old adversary, on points in Glasgow, but it was not one of his better performances, and he stopped Jose Luis Garcia, a late Mexican replacement rated no. 8 in his homeland, in five rounds at Ebbw Vale. His last fight of 1979 came against Davey Vasquez, a New Yorker, at Ebbw Vale. It was a more normal affair, with John's signature salvos eventually thwarting a game opponent.

'Owen's world-class material,' Art Curley, the American's manager, said.

As they celebrated the win, nobody in the Owen camp gave a thought to the fact Vasquez had been knocked out in two rounds by Lupe Pintor the previous year, or that their disparate paths were arcing towards each other.

On Christmas Eve, 1979, Johnny Owen finished training in the afternoon and went to the Ruperra Arms, his New Tredegar HQ, to discuss the future. Dick was surprised to overhear someone saying that Gardiner had landed Johnny a shot at the world title in America, but the purse was a mere £5,000, plus expenses. Dick told his son what he had heard as they went home to get changed for a Christmas party back at the pub.

'He must be joking,' Johnny said. 'I could get double that for defending my British title at home. I'm not fighting for that sort of money.'

His father agreed, but added the caveat; 'Let's see what Dai has to say.'

When they returned to the pub that night, Gardiner pulled Johnny to one side and began talking about the fight. In another corner, Dick bristled.

'What's Dai talking to John about?' Edith asked.

'It's all right,' he replied without conviction.

Board had also noticed that the conversation had a secretive air about it.

'Dai's trying to persuade John to fight for the world title,' Dick told the landlord as he supped his pint. 'But John's told me he won't fight for that money.'

The subject was dropped, but Dick remembered how he had been excluded from the talks. While they still talked of being a family in front of the media, the truth was the tight-knit bond was fraying. The snub would fester for some time, even as Johnny Owen sipped his annual tot of sherry around the groaning family table the following afternoon.

The conflict between the promoters, Heddwyn Taylor and Eddie Thomas, was also escalating. Friends once, their relationship was worsening amid their dual desire to stage Johnny's major bouts.

'When I wanted money to stage the European title fight, I went straight to the top and met Cliff Morgan, the top man at the BBC, in the Café Royal,' Taylor said. 'I said, "I'm about to promote this fight and I need television coverage." Cliff was

Welsh and I emphasized how I thought it was a disgrace that the TV coverage was always in London. We had a three-course meal and he never put his cigarette out once. Then we got slated out of our brains and took a taxi back to Knightsbridge because we couldn't find the car. As I got out he said, "How much money do you want?" '

The purses were opened at 5 p.m. on a winter's day at the European Boxing Council office. The phone rang in the corner of the Station Hotel where Taylor was fretting. He picked it up and was told he had the fight. It would cost him £26,000, and he admitted the public would have to pay dearly for his victory.

Three weeks before the fight there was a drama in the Owen camp. Johnny's right hand was sore and it emerged that he was having to train with only his left.

'Johnny often skins his hands during fights and he has got an infection on his right knuckle,' Gardiner admitted. 'It may prove a blessing in disguise because in recent fights he has used his right hand too often.'

It was not much of a silver lining.

On a crisp day in New Tredegar, the sky a patch of blue bullied by dreary greys, Srikumar Sen, the boxing writer for *The Times*, strolled along the high street. He spotted two little girls in cotton dresses sitting on a wall.

'Is this where Johnny Owen trains?' he asked politely.

One of them laughed. 'He doesn't train on Sundays,' she said.

Sen told them that Dick Owens himself had said that he would be there. He later wrote: 'They jumped up like startled owls and fled downhill screaming "John-nee is coming", their screams carrying across the narrow valley to the terraces of the Old Powell Duffryn house like coal seams along the face of Capel Mountain.'

The gym was a 'weather-blanched stone building with an iron gate and an old step, doused in last year's Autumn leaves'. Sen met Dick and was invited inside the building where he watched Johnny spar with Mike Pickett. He was impressed by the power in both hands and the effectiveness of the body punches. His timing, he noted, was immaculate.

'Owen could emerge as Britain's most exciting prospect,' he noted in his pad. 'The Matchstick Man has fire in his fists.'

One warm-up fight against Glyn Davies at the National Sporting Club had been enough to polish Johnny's ring-readiness. 'I've lost to the next world champion,' Davies said afterwards, but platitudes never inflated Johnny's self-regard and he pencilled an entry in the new green pocket diary that would detail his ascent to the ring in Los Angeles.

Monday, January 21. Fighting Glyn Davies. Won the fight in the fifth. Didn't fight well. Café Royal.

Ten days later he made another note.

Thursday, January 31. Got to train hard for the most important fight of my career.

He was true to his word. His only break came when he helped police investigating the stabbing of Ann Cuesta, an infant-school teacher. It was a shocking crime that stunned Merthyr. For a craggy town, Merthyr had a large heart, and Cuesta's funeral was a mammoth affair, with a thousand people lining the streets as a 130-car cortège crept between them. Her husband of ten months was inconsolable. Johnny was asked to aid a reconstruction of the murderer's escape through Cyfarthfa Park to the village of Cefn Coed and gladly agreed. There had been twenty sightings of a man wearing a bobble hat fleeing on the night of the attack, so he donned his grey sweats and his red and white cap to run the six miles. Detective Chief Superintendent Viv Brook said: 'Johnny is fantastically fit and his run has proved vital in establishing the timings of the assailant's escape.' Johnny put the ghoulish thoughts of the murderer's escape from his mind. Ann Cuesta's death was just another life-shattering tragedy that was terribly sad but, ultimately, beyond the boundaries of his existence. Other people's nightmares.

Juan Francisco Rodriguez had never heard of Ann Cuesta, but he knew of Merthyr and had now accepted that he would have to travel from the loving embrace of Almeria to defend his title. And yet, when his comfort blanket was discarded, Rodriguez was a better boxer.

'I don't think much of Owen,' he said on his arrival in Wales. 'He is just a sticky fighter who comes at you like an octopus, but why do you rate him so highly? I will surprise him by my fitness and battle plan. I am still the greatest bantamweight in all Europe and I will prove it.'

Johnny, though, was ready. In the dressing room before the fight, he even indulged in a few rounds of sparring, the theory being that the new rule curtailing bouts to twelve rounds worked against him. 'We can't take any chance of Owen having a slow start,' Gardiner said.

Thursday, February 28. Ebbw Vale. European title fight. You have got to put everything into your training and life so that you can achieve what you only dream of. You must pull out all the stops on the night from round one to twelve. Put every drop of sweat and blood and energy into winning. All your dreams must be fulfilled tonight. All the very best boyo. Cymru am byth [Wales for ever].

Back in the greying council house by the sodden green, Kelvin wrestled with himself. He had not watched his brother's last twenty fights. Susan, Vivian and Dilwyn were regulars, Dick was in the corner and Edith stayed away until the time was right to trek to the phone box. Even Shereen was going to the Rodriguez fight. But Kelvin, closer to Johnny than any of the other siblings, had not seen his brother box since the lacklustre win against Neil McLaughlin in Merthyr almost three years before.

'I think it hurt John a bit, but I thought I was a jinx and so I stayed away,' he said. 'He'd lost when we fought on the same bill for Wales as amateurs and he'd been poor against Mc-Laughlin. But when he fought Rodriguez I wanted to go and see him. I thought I was bad luck, but I thought if I went on my own then nobody would know. So I bought a ticket, without anyone else knowing, and went over to Ebbw Vale very late and crept in the back of the hall. It was just before John was due on. I watched the fight from the shadows and scored each round in my head. I thought, "If it starts to go bad then I'm out of here."'

The Owen camp had demanded a strict referee this time, and Rodriguez was warned for holding in the opening round, but he surprised many by fronting up to the challenger and, midway through the fight, even began to plant a seed of doubt. Perhaps Johnny's weight was also a factor. Heddwyn Taylor remembered him being a pound overweight at the weigh-in at the Royal Oak on the afternoon of the fight.

'He had an hour to get it off,' he said. 'So they rolled him over in boiling hot towels and, when he went back on the scales, they even took off his underpants. He stripped right to the buffers to come in on the limit.' In fact, Johnny was well inside the weight, but so was Rodriguez.

By the seventh the two inspectors from the British Boxing Board of Control cried foul after they saw the Spaniard's corner use illegal smelling salts to revive their man. In the tenth a Rodriguez uppercut knocked Johnny's head back forty-five degrees, but by the end few doubted that the title had changed hands. It was an easy decision, but Rodriguez had relinquished his title in a fashion few believed him capable of. It was the only way to go, fighting hard, reputation intact, down but not out.

At the back of the hall, Kelvin had not moved.

'John was winning, but Rodriguez came back for a couple of rounds,' he said. 'I had him fairly comfortably ahead, by four or five rounds, though. If I hadn't then I'd have been out of there like a shot.'

The Danish referee did not give a single round to Rodriguez. The Belgian and Italian judges deemed it closer, but the victory was assured and Kelvin now made his way to the ring. His brothers were already in there, wearing their Johnny 'Bionic' Owen T-shirts, hugging the champion and holding his head in their hands.

'John! John!' Kelvin shouted.

Through the pandemonium, Johnny heard the voice and looked down to see the beaming face by the ring.

'Kel! What the bloody hell are you doing here?'

It was all Kelvin needed. He clambered quickly into the ring and ran over to his brother. 'Brilliant, John!' They hugged.

'Glad you made it,' the new champion said.

Johnny succumbed to tears at the end. His supporters revelled in the moment. The party lasted all night, a meal followed by a session in a beer cellar in Blackwood. Board presented Johnny with a plate bearing the Welsh emblem of three feathers and the words 'Johnny Owen – British, Commonwealth and European Boxing Champion'. Dick welled up. 'What would you have done with that if he'd lost?' he asked his friend. 'I'd have gone out the back and quietly smashed it,' the landlord replied. Jeff Pritchard, his faithful sparring partner, had also won that night on the undercard against Frank McCord. It made for a happy group.

Johnny sought out Pritchard at the party and handed him a box.

'What's this?' he asked.

'Open it and see,' Johnny said.

Pritchard did, and pulled out a silver St Christopher's medallion on a chain. He read the inscription. 'Thanks Jeff'.

'For good luck,' Johnny added. Neither could imagine that this would be their last year as boxers.

Johnny lived up to Board's faith, and was also true to the words he had scrawled in another diary entry three weeks prior to the fight.

> When you win the European title, give mam and dad some money and treat the whole family to a night out. And you can order that ring and dream.

In the aftermath, the press attention increased tenfold. A girl fan sent him a cardboard skeleton. There were more analogies and more talk of his Adam's apple vying for magnificence with his biceps. Gardiner admitted he was worried in case Johnny burnt himself out with the rigorous training and fight schedule. David Hunn, writing in the *Observer*, spoke of Taylor paying Pintor £55,000 to come to Wales, but suggested a British title defence and a couple of European ones would be more prudent. And, of course, much was made of his never having kissed a girl.

'Wouldn't be fair!' he protested. 'Up at half-six every morning, on the road, training every night. Can't marry like that, can you?'

It had been a long road and he was now the British, Commonwealth and European champion. There was only one place left to go.

ROUND TEN

It was a new day in Sydney and the staff at the Lidcombe Dancers' Club were getting ready for another shift. The previous night Paul Ferreri, the man whom Johnny Owen had beaten to the Commonwealth title two years earlier, had won his bout there. He was rebuilding his career, fighting in half-empty basketball halls and working men's clubs, and was the new Australian super featherweight champion. His hands hurt and his head throbbed but he had beaten Big Jim West for the second time in seven months. He was on his way to the Commonwealth title. He would fight until he was almost forty and would reflect in later years that losing to Owen did not do him much harm.

All over the globe it was fight night. Professional boxers at varying stages of their careers stood in rings in Kamloops in Canada and San Dona di Piave in Italy. It was the night that the Philippine featherweight title was being decided in Quezon City. In Belgium and Argentina and Mexico they bought tickets, squinted into the spotlights and drank their beer.

Few boxers would have stopped to ponder the big picture that night or wonder how fate might pool their histories and mark them with tragedy or triumph. In a tiny house in Culiacan in the Mexican countryside, the son of a railroad worker was sitting quietly and contemplating his upcoming bout against Jesus Lara in two days' time. He was nineteen and had just given up his engineering studies. This was

Julio Cesar Chavez at the start of his career. As Johnny Owen and Lupe Pintor traded dreams at their peak in the Olympic, the most renowned Mexican boxer of all was an unknown teenager from nowhere.

Among those Chavez would defeat was Adriano Arreola, a decent journeyman from Los Angeles. Arreola was feeling pleased with himself as Owen and Pintor fought. Having dispatched Paz Mena easily, Arreola had showered, changed and was heading for his favourite bar by the time the bell sounded for the tenth. Another three years would pass and Arreola would beat a waning Lupe Pintor in this same ring in the Olympic on a night when Marty Denkin was again the referee. And within twelve months from the moment he sipped his first drink tonight, the riotous noise from the Olympic encased by those harsh, concrete minders, he would take on an up-and-coming fighter named Francisco Graciano Bejines, whom everyone simply called 'Kiko'.

As Owen climbed from his stool for the start of the tenth, Alberto Davila, at ringside, wondered if the Welshman could come back. Davila was still recuperating from his own fight with Terry Pizzarro at the Freeman Coliseum in San Antonio the previous Saturday. It had been his forty-sixth pro fight, even though he was only twenty-six. Twice he had fought for the title. Twice he had had lost. But there is always another fight, and it was coming towards Davila now. He was ready. In knocking out Pizzarro, he had put himself in pole position. He was ready to fight the winner of the bout that was taking place in the open cage before his eyes at the Olympic.

For Johnny Owen and Lupe Pintor tonight's bout was everything, but for others theirs was a stepping stone towards or away from their goal. Everyone on the undercard that night had a story and a motive. The main support bout had been the swansong of Alfonso Zamora. He was only twenty-six but he was past it. The sudden descent had started. But this was Zamora and the crowd loved him. He had delivered the WBA bantamweight title back on that intoxicating night at the Great Western Forum in Inglewood, but the wounds of that loss to Zarate went beyond the holes breached by Vaseline. He lost his belt seven months later and tonight, when he met Rigoberto Estrada, another Mexican, his time was up. Estrada was not in the same league as the peak-time Zamora, but he dismantled the former champion in less than three rounds. Zamora's father held him tightly at the end. He knew. By the time Johnny Owen heard the bell for the tenth, Zamora had retired and the cold, dark chill of reality was biting into his excavated wounds.

Pintor, now, has got to be thinking 'I'll nail him for sure', and Owen has got to be wary of that right hand. He looks to be the stronger of the two now, Danny. The knockdown has had to do a lot for Pintor's self-confidence. Nails Owen again. And again. Owen is in trouble. Owen is in trouble. Johnny Owen, of Wales, blood streaming from his nose, was down in round number nine, and he's in trouble in round ten. Owen has fought a magnificent fight, but the superior punch of Pintor appears ready to take its toll. One thirty-eight remaining in round ten.

After being down for so long, Pintor had managed to turn the fight around. The commentators spoke in twisted terms shorn of perspective of Lupe Pintor moving in for the kill and of 'putting him away' and of 'taking him out'.

Right back when the bell had sounded, Pintor had sensed he could finish the fight in this round. The perfect ten. He wasted no time. The first punch was a big one. It swept through the air with a silent fury and missed, but the intent and power were ominous. Boxing history is littered with the laurels of those who contrive incredible revivals. Seconds can see a fight lost and seconds can make a head clear. The task for Johnny Owen in round ten was to hold out, survive, carry on.

Part of the appeal of the sport is in its ability to take men out of themselves. Johnny Owen fought so heroically in the tenth round of his world bantamweight title showdown with Lupe Pintor. And Pintor ignored the blood in his eyes and went for broke.

These were hard yards for Owen the marathon man. Pintor was now exuding the authority that had given him such a lengthy record of knockout triumphs. Two lefts preceded a weighty right. Pintor was now refusing to be shoved backwards at Owen's will and was holding his own in the centre of the ring, sharing the initiative with his assailant. Owen was still thinking and was sticking to his plan of trying to tie Pintor up and score with his pressure, but it was becoming more difficult and his blows seemed less meaningful. Meanwhile, Pintor now appeared utterly convinced, where once he had been ravaged with questions. Three uppercuts were brandished with haste and anger. As Owen's head nodded under their weight, a right hand struck. This was now ugly stuff. 'There was unmistakable evidence that the strength had drained out of every part of Owen's body except his heart,' McIlvanney would write of the tenth.

Yet the tenth round summed up the simple bravery that made Owen so special. He tried to get in close and cut down the space. He tried to stifle Pintor and engulf him as he had done so effectively. He tried to force a break in the assault.

Allan Malamud suggested to Tom Kelly that Pintor was looking for another big right hand. *That's Allan Malamud the prophet. He called it and you saw him throw it and narrowly miss.* Kelly had seen enough bouts to know this one was now lurching towards Pintor, but Owen had made him stagger and had a tough core that might yet stem the tide. Owen might yet call on unseen undercurrent that would sink Pintor. *You have to admire the courage and stamina of Johnny Owen. Backing up Pintor on to the ropes.*

Graham Walters had never felt pride like it when he had carried the Welsh flag into the ring less than an hour ago, and the sensation had not left him yet. Owen was fighting heroically. This was a trying time, but, hell, Johnny's career had been a procession of tests. Walters knew him too well to write him off. This was a man who had lived by confounding people's expectations.

'It was like going into a cauldron that night,' Walters would remember. 'But you are that proud that you don't care. People underestimated Johnny. They went on about his physique, but his whole body was sinew. It was tough, like leather. When you shook hands, it was like shaking the calloused hand of someone who had been on the plough. When you shook hands you could feel the power in that man.'

Owen was not beaten yet. He needed to regain his composure and start the gradual process of dissolving Pintor. Walters still believed Owen could win and so did Dick Owens and Dai Gardiner.

Nails him again. Owen had his knees buckled. Comes back, driving Pintor back. But Pintor is the stronger of the two now for sure. Half a minute to go. Owen still on top of his man, but Pintor with the heavier firepower.

The round had been a three-act drama. Pintor had started well and sought a knockout blow in that first minute. He had hit his man fiercely, even hurting his knuckles, but Owen had hung in there. In the second act, Owen had pushed Pintor against the ropes and thudded away. It was a brief respite, though, and in third act Pintor had landed a right on the corner of Owen's jaw when he found a break. Thereafter, he again threw hard and fast. When the bell sounded, Pintor jogged to his corner.

Far away in Sydney on this September night, Paul Ferreri did not give the Olympic a second thought. In boxing you just look after yourself, and things were on the up for him. Who could tell where he would go after the Lidcombe Dancers' Club? Who could tell whether Chavez would fulfil his potential or fade away to the periphery? Who could guess that Davila and Kiko would come together in the Olympic for a night nobody would ever forget – or, indeed, what would happen to Johnny Owen and Lupe Pintor after the next bell?

12

THE LITTLE GREEN DIARY

The list was simple enough. Seven items written in the back of his green pocket diary that revealed the purpose behind all the sweat-soaked pain. Seven motivations. Johnny Owen chewed the pencil and wrote them down in capital letters at the start of 1980.

A) SUCCESSFUL BUSINESS

B) HOUSE OR HOUSES

C) PLOTS OF LAND

D) FREE HOUSE

E) HOLIDAY

F) ENOUGH MONEY TO RETIRE, 27–29

G) GOOD LUCK

It was a world champion's shopping list. The seven things that would bring him happiness. The boxing ring can be a way out. You fight and dig and make magic. Black magic. Conjure worlds from the flesh of others. Sweat and bleed and cry until your ribs ache and your heart is banging against them. Johnny Owen knew what he was fighting for: friends, family and Wales. For better houses for the family, for the pub his parents wanted, for land to develop. For a holiday and an early retirement from the sport he loved but which he knew was draining him, putting him through an emotional mangle. He would ignore the hurt, the punctured eardrum, the lacerated lip if there was some hope that he might be blessed with the good luck that would make his list reality.

One day after Johnny Owen had fought Jose Luis Garcia, a Mexican bricklayer, at Ebbw Vale on 4 October 1979, Lupe Pintor stepped into a boxing ring for the first time since he had sent Zarate bleating into retirement. It was a brief workout in Reynosa, a clubbing right knocking out Aucencio Melendez in the first round. He took another fight that month but was lacklustre in defeating Jose Soto in ten rounds. Both were non-title bouts and Cuyo Hernandez quietly wondered whether Pintor was resting on his laurels after his catharsis against Zarate. He had heard of the problems at home with Coti and knew how domestic disharmony could blight a boxer's prowess. It was a fear that was realized when he lost inexplicably to Manuel Vasquez, the man against whom he had started his career four years earlier.

'That was crazy,' Pintor said. 'Before the fight this guy was saying I was a lucky champion and that I hadn't deserved to win. He was going to do this and that to me. But when we actually came face to face, he was literally shaking with fear and he didn't even want to look at me. I actually felt sorry for him because I knew I was going to hit him so hard. During the fight he was actually running away from me, but the doctor stopped the fight because I had a tiny cut on my face. I don't know what he was drinking, but it must have been good.'

Pintor's relationship with Coti became more joyless with each passing week, but despite her grievances, Pintor is adamant that, like Johnny Owen, he was fighting for his family.

'When you box at world championship level, there has to be a lot of give and take,' he said. 'You fight for money, but you also fight for respect from the public and from your friends, and for national pride. You represent your country and your race; that's why I called myself El Indio. But above everything else, you're fighting from a responsibility to your family. You do everything for their well-being, because they will always be at your side; at every given moment, now and in the future, when you're no longer a champion and not on TV and nobody remembers you.'

Christmas 1979 was not a happy one in the Pintor household. Despite it being his seminal year, the one in which he climbed to the very summit of his ambition, he could not pretend the marriage was recoverable. 'You fight for everyone else, why won't you fight for me?' Coti asked. For Pintor, her grievance hurt because he was doing precisely that. Coti was now living with her mother, and he busied himself getting ready for the first defence of his world title against Alberto 'Superfly' Sandoval, a flashy contender from Pomona.

It irked Cuyo Hernandez that Pintor could look so ordinary in training and be transformed into a great champion when the spotlights shone. It made it difficult to gauge his progress. But Pintor was no fool. At the age of twenty-five, he knew that it was reckless not to train religiously for fights, so he mirrored the regime of Johnny Owen, pounding the streets before breakfast and then punishing himself in the gym until his lungs burnt and his head spun.

'I often remembered the fight with Gabi Cantera,' he said. 'It was the fight where I learnt that you can even be unconscious and come out victorious. I still can't stop that thought giving me the shivers. How can it be that you just switch off your consciousness and your body stays alert and defends you?

'It's clear you don't get that without good preparation. That's when you most appreciate the value of tiring training days. The body, if it is well conditioned, begins to work by itself, and that will save you in the moment when you need it most. It's closely related to spirit and there hasn't been a single champion who has lacked this capacity.'

Three weeks before Johnny won the European title, Pintor stepped into the Olympic Auditorium. Sandoval was ranked the no. 10 contender and had a huge following in LA, where his flamboyant skills were symptomatic of a city that thrived on ostentation. However, inside the arena, it was the Mexicans and Hispanics who filled the seats and Pintor was ready to feed the ten thousand. Outside in the parking lot another thousand waited for news and begged for tickets.

Their eagerness was understandable as the fight was a classic confrontation between artistry and brute spirit. Sandoval's pin-point jabs and fluid rights bounced off Pintor's head as the champion tried to study the methods of the challenger. This was Pintor's way. Like Johnny, his was a slow-burning style that afforded him the chance to test his rival's power and tricks. His gloves were held high in defence and he looked ponderous early on. That encouraged Sandoval, who was thrilled to see Pintor's knees shake in the third round, but Pintor survived and retaliated in spectacular fashion. A vile uppercut drove into Sandoval's chin twice like a pneumatic drill. 'Superfly' wriggled and found himself snared by the ropes and deadly clubs. Only the bell saved him.

It was a close fight, but Pintor always improved in the later rounds of long fights, and now the *gaucho* slewed into Sandoval's kidneys. The bludgeon blunted the rapier with a power that almost lifted the skin off the bone. Slowly, Sandoval found himself fleeced of his style. All he had left was his spirit, and that merely delayed the inevitable.

In the twelfth, Sandoval turned his back on the champion to signify he had suffered too much. The referee called a halt and Pintor was chaired around the ring. In the corner, Tony Torres punched the air while Hernandez smiled. They had $100,000 in their pockets from the fight, and the chance of another payday. Pintor already had plans to buy a small stable and fill it with racehorses. For Sandoval the end of the road had reared up in front of him. He would fight once more, two years later, and retire, broken by his fight night in the Olympic.

Four months later Marty Denkin packed his bags and checked in for the flight to Japan. This was a big moment for him. He was officiating in a WBC world bantamweight fight and that meant something. The fight in question was Pintor's second defence, against Eijiro Murata at the Budokan, a cavernous arena in Tokyo more famed for sumo wrestling and pop concerts. Denkin considered it an honour. He was on the way to becoming a legend among referees, and he'd earned it. Back in Hell's Kitchen, the kids from 108th would fight the kids from 106th. Denkin had taken up boxing so he could avoid being called names by his friends when he went home before 10 p.m. to avoid a hiding from his father. He boxed, joined the police force, transferred to the district attorney's office and investigated organized crime. He spent two years in Vietnam and worked with the toughest street kids. He saw drugs and death and, by

1980, was investigating job discrimination. His solace was boxing.

Pintor did not perform at his best in Japan and only just retained his title, courtesy of a draw. It had been a risk to take a fight in Japan, where the unfamiliarity of the culture and the time difference conspired against him.

'I went for the money,' he said candidly. 'It was a good offer.'

For Denkin it felt good to be refereeing a world title fight again, and he felt it had been a good fifteen-round effort.

'Going the distance has two definitions,' he said. 'For a fighter it means you have gone the distance and can fight another day; for me it means I fulfilled my obligations and did the best I could. I've looked into the eyes of fighters and seen that they have gone. You have to do what you think is right for those men. You have two lives in your hands and you can't let anything come in the way of what you think is right. When there's fifty thousand people there, believe me the pressure is huge, and you have fifty thousand thoughts in your head, but you stay true. If I had a nickel for every life I've saved I'd be a wealthy man.'

Denkin scored the fight a 144–144 draw. It was scarcely a dominant performance by Pintor, but he was still the champion, and he had another big purse to feed his horses.

The draw meant the talk of a meeting with Johnny Owen intensified. However, the boxing scene in Wales went about its normal routine, the mundanity of real life winning out against the hazy prospect of a world championship bout. Jeff Pritchard was negotiating his purse for his fight against Ricky Beaumont.

'Dai came on the phone and said I was getting £450,' he recalled. 'I said I'd fight him for £600. Dai came back to me and said I'd got it. You had to try it on. In those days you got £600 for being top of the bill. It was crap money.'

Billy Vivian was training in the converted garage at the Butcher's Arms. He had been working there ever since an acrimonious split with Gardiner.

'I got fed up with Dai,' he said. 'Bev Walker came down to the pub from Reading and he took over as my manager, but I had to wait for my contract with Dai to run out. I twice went to meet Dai and the Welsh Boxing Board and he never turned up. I had to wait months to fight and, when I did, I got £200 more for my first eight-rounder.'

Martyn Galleozzie had lost a final eliminator for the British featherweight title on points in January and knew, deep down, that he was spent. Boxing is a hurting business and to succeed you have to believe in the sacrifice. Galleozzie wanted to start a family. He would spar with Johnny before his trip to America, but, like Pritchard, he would be an ex-boxer by the end of the year.

In a small house in Pomona, Alberto Davila had no such doubts. Since losing in his second attempt to win a world title, he had chalked up an impressive sequence of wins. The injustice of his world title defeats was still there, but he was happy in his work. His silk ensnared the press, his home life with Roberta and his son, Gabriel, was settled and he had a zealous belief that providence would bring him a world title. Had he known that it would do so in the way that it did, then he would have joined Pritchard and Galleozzie by quitting in 1980.

Johnny was being typically hard on himself as talks progressed. He was scheduled to fight John Feeney, one of the scrap metal brothers from Hartlepool, for his British title on 28 June. It would, he hoped, be his last bout before a world title showdown, but the brief entries he made in his diary hinted that everything was not going as smoothly as he might have liked.

At the top of the page he wrote:

Fighting John Feeney. Got to win it to earn money and keep the British title. Good luck.

Saturday, May 31. Four weeks to fight.

Saturday, June 7. Three weeks to fight.

Sunday, June 8. Bad week.

Monday, June 9. Long run. Pull yourself together.

Saturday, June 14. Two weeks to fight.

Sunday, June 15. Father's day.

Saturday, June 21. One week to fight.

In the back of the diary he wrote a few more words.

Fighting John Feeney. Defending the British title at Wembley. Must put everything into training and go to bed early so I can win and start earning money for a pub or hotel. A good win on national TV will do you a power of good and, if you can stay unbeaten through 1980, you will have achieved all that you wanted.

The Feeneys were a tough family and John was a genuine talent. Originally, Johnny was going to have to put all his three belts on the line, but in the end the boxing chiefs deemed it should be only a British title bout. Only twenty-two, Feeney had won seventeen straight fights, including victories over opponents Johnny knew to be tough – Neil McLaughlin, George Sutton and Ahmed Younis. Indeed, both Feeney and his brother George would go on to become British champions.

They were also full of self-belief, as Graham Walters discovered when he bumped into the Feeney party on his way into the arena.

'We've come to take your title, Taff,' one said.

Walters was taken aback by the next comment.

'We're going to take his body away. Look at him. He's only a skeleton. We'll take his fucking body away.'

Feeney exuded confidence, boasting beforehand of what he intended to do.

'He was doing all the Ali stuff,' Dick recalled. 'John said, "He'll cop it tonight for trying to make a fool out of me."'

Like Wayne Evans, Paul Ferreri and, most recently, Rodriguez, Feeney was about to pay.

The fight was the main support for Alan Minter's defence of his WBC and WBA middleweight crowns against Vito Antuofermo, the rugged brawler from Italy, at Wembley's Empire Pool on 28 June 1980. Minter was at the peak of his popularity and it was an exhilarating atmosphere. Johnny boxed well to take advantage of a tiring Feeney and get the points verdict.

However, others were less happy. Heddwyn Taylor claims he was well down the road to bringing Pintor to Wales to fight Johnny, and says that that night in London confirmed something was amiss.

'My matchmaker, Les Roberts, said there's a smell in the air. I noticed Mickey Duff hanging around them all night. We all went to the Aberdeen Angus Steak House and Duff wouldn't leave them alone.'

According to Taylor, he was due to fly out to Mexico the following week to arrange the fight. He had arranged for an interpreter to be present and had been in touch with Cuyo Hernandez. Before he departed, he said, he opened the *Western Mail* and saw a banner headline saying Johnny was to fight Pintor in Los Angeles.

'I was amazed and disappointed,' he recalled. 'They'd have got more money from me. I'd already arranged for a friend of mine to do a seating plan for Ebbw Vale. It was going to be 27 September. We never signed a contract because we always shook hands and that was it. But I felt robbed. I don't know how Mickey Duff persuaded them to go over. I was friendly with Dick and Dai, but I couldn't understand why they allowed Johnny to box on that canvas. It was an inch and a half thick, like sponge, and Pintor trained on that every day. I was devastated because it was my ambition to promote a world title fight and I felt I'd been promised it.'

This version differs markedly from the one offered by both Dick and Pintor.

'No one else but Mickey Duff approached us about a world title fight,' Dick said. 'There were rumours going around that a promoter in Wales had offered us £10,000 to fight in this country, but we'd have jumped at that if it was true. John and I were never told about any other offers.'

Pintor, who had just travelled to Japan to defend his title, said that he would have gladly fought abroad.

'The Johnny Owen fight almost took place in Wales, but for the sake of $50,000 it went to LA. Whoever was organizing it could not come up with enough money. They couldn't raise $100,000, and you go where the money is.'

It was the last time that the three members of the team – Johnny, Dick and Dai – would take a vote on a major issue. That had been their policy for the course of their partnership and, despite the friction, they were unanimous.

'We had a big offer to defend the Commonwealth title in Denmark,' Gardiner said. 'But we got offered the world title at the same time and Johnny's attitude was, "I might as well go to America." I would have gone to Denmark, but don't get me wrong, I didn't say, "Don't go to America", and we all agreed we should. It was Johnny who more or less decided it. He wanted the world title – that had always been his aim. Win it, secure it, have a few defences and get out at twenty-seven.'

Some doubted that Johnny was ready. Michael Katz, a writer with the *New York Times*, had been present at the Feeney fight and was both impressed by Johnny's skills and left cold by the lack of a big punch. He predicted an easy win for Pintor.

'Why? Because the guy can't punch. If he could he would be illegal because he's got so much else.'

The deal was done. It was the culmination of a decade's dreams, yet the words Johnny wrote in the back of his little green diary, fuelled by the souring of his father's relationship with Gardiner, showed his mixed emotions.

> Problems all this year so far. Nothing is going right. Hope to put it all together. Beaten John Feeney in a good fight. Talking about a world title fight in August against Lupe Pintor in the USA.

When the deal was struck he added another entry on a blank page.

> Fighting for the world title on Sept 19 in the USA. Must go out and fight like never before. It only comes once in a lifetime. You must take a chance and try your best to achieve the impossible dream and turn it into reality.

The excitement flowed like lava around the streets of Merthyr. Byron Board immediately started arranging a trip for some of his regulars at the Ruperra Arms. Idris Sutton beamed as he worked a shift at the Ukrainian Club, feeling proud that he might have helped the boxer in some small way. A gruelling daily schedule was set in place, comprising a nine-mile run in the morning, an hour and a half chopping trees in the afternoon, half an hour skipping, an exercise routine in the gym and then between four and twelve rounds of sparring.

Gardiner knew they were facing their biggest test.

'They had a show on Saturday afternoons and I'd watched Lupe Pintor box,' he said. 'He had big hair, that stood out, but he was very, very strong. I said to John, "This one may try to push you back," but, as it turned out, even he couldn't do that.'

Johnny sparred 263 rounds in the month leading up to his flight to America, but some raised doubts about the lateness of his departure – just one week before the fight – and why the camp took no sparring partners. In the *Sun*, Colin Hart wrote: 'Johnny Owen has put his chances of winning the world bantamweight title in serious jeopardy because he stubbornly refuses to travel to Los Angeles early enough.' Gardiner explained that Johnny, ever the home boy, had put his foot down and insisted he complete his sparring in Wales. The vastly experienced Hart remained incredulous.

'Johnny may never get another chance to win the world title and somebody . . . should make him listen to reason. Otherwise he will face Pintor feeling listless and lethargic.'

He suggested Ray Clarke, of the British Boxing Board of Control, but it is doubtful Dick and Johnny would have listened to him, given the advice offered when they had gone to retrieve the Lonsdale Belt.

Billy Vivian could not afford to take up a place on the special charter plane to go and watch his friend fight, but he visited the gym one last time. 'There were three of us there – me, Mikey Pickett and Jeff Pritchard – and we'd known each other since we were babies,' he recalled. 'After splitting with Dai

Gardiner, I hadn't sparred with John for eighteen months, but I went over to see him.'

Shortly before the day they were due to fly to America, the differences between Dick and Gardiner again surfaced. It stemmed from something as simple as the choice of hotels, with Dick dismissing the ones Gardiner came up with.

'It was like he was going on bloody holiday,' Dick said.

In a rage, he walked out of the gym and caught a bus from New Tredegar to Dowlais, where he sought refuge in the Antelope pub. A search party was dispatched to find him and, eventually, at 10.15 p.m., Johnny and Kelvin wandered through the door of the snug.

'I'm sorry, John,' his father said as they stumbled out into the pitch of a depressed night. 'I'm not going to LA.'

There was a stony silence. They could hear the bleep of the fruit machine inside and the chink of glasses. Johnny rubbed his face.

'Well, I'm not going without you,' he said.

That jolted his father out of his introspection.

'Don't be daft, John. This is the world title. You have to go.'

He knew how stubborn his son was. It was another crossroads. Now he was considering giving up on the very reason he had climbed every obstacle.

'Not without you,' his son repeated.

Eventually, after the gentle pressure exerted by Board's phone calls and the glum-faced demeanour of his son, Dick relented. The fight was back on, but the partnership with Gardiner, dying by a thousand self-inflicted cuts, was all but over.

'I gave in to John and went back training,' Dick reflected. 'Oh, I wish to God that I hadn't.'

When Gardiner took a holiday with his family on the south

coast, it added to the tension. The press found out and questioned his decision to have a break so close to a world title fight. With that and the discontent about sparring partners and departure dates, the tension increased to breaking point.

Johnny did his best to remain focussed and seemed happy and content in those last weeks at home.

'He never changed,' Jesse Harris, his old friend and pupil, said. 'The last time I saw him was in town. He had a sheepskin coat on, but he was the same old John. My old man and Dick were talking away and John just said, "You going to come back down the gym?" '

Sometimes his brothers played on that humility. Vivian and Kelvin loved to walk with him through Merthyr and casually drop back a pace or two. Then they would point at him and shout, 'Look, there's Johnny Owen, that's Johnny Owen, the famous boxer.' He hated it. 'You bastards,' was his reply.

Yet there were doubts he kept hidden. In the appointments section of his diary he had summarized five months in the space of one page.

May. Disappointing year so far.

June. Nothing going right so far. If only?

There were ditto marks beneath July and August

September. Fight for the world title. If only I could win it. What a dream. Must go out with determination and pull out all the skill, courage and heart like never before. Bring it back, then three more fights and retire with your dream. Got to do it boyo.

As the final days drifted away, Dick came up with a special fitness drink that had been given him by a professional cyclist.

'It was a jar of white powder which they used on long tours, full of vitamins and minerals,' he recalled. 'When you added water it turned blue.'

They began training and eating to correspond with American time. Dick reasoned that, for all the contrary arguments, his son would be happier at home, where he was familiar with the runs and could continue chopping down trees.

On the day of their departure, the Owens woke early to a commotion outside their council house. Five cars were parked and one was playing a tape of 'We'll Keep a Welcome in the Hillside' at full blast. Dick remembers that, curiously, no neighbours came out.

'We all got into the cars and went to New Tredegar where they gave him a marvellous send-off, with all the streets decorated with flags and bunting.'

Some cars followed them all the way to Heathrow. And then they were gone.

The previous day Jeff Pritchard had met Johnny for the last time. They had sparred. Pritchard was disappointed that he would not be going with his friend into the maw of the unknown.

'I'd been asked if I'd go as a sparring partner and I said I would, but nothing came of it. I'd have done anything to help Johnny. Maybe it was down to money.'

Dick says only Gardiner knows the reason why no sparring partners travelled, but he would have taken them.

On that windswept night, Pritchard did not voice his opinion that Johnny should not be going to America.

'Johnny was good enough to fight Pintor, but I just thought he should have had a couple more fights first,' he said. 'Why rush him? But if you'd said to Johnny, "Don't go to America, you're not coming back," he'd have gone anyway. It was his life. When I'd lost to Ricky Beaumont at the Albert Hall, I was knocked out in the third. Bang, bang, whack. They could be still be counting now. As I walked down the stairs to the dressing room, I said to Dai, "I won, didn't I, Dai?" He said, "Won, you bloody idiot? How many times have I told you not to go off your left on to your right, but off your right on to your fucking left?" The point is you don't feel pain as a boxer. You don't worry about what might happen. You couldn't stop Johnny. I told him he was coming home as the world champion and that he could give him one from me. Then I shook his hand.'

That night, with a new alarm due to be fitted the following morning, Johnny's grocery store was broken into and six hundred pounds' worth of stock was taken. Dick heard that police were questioning a youth, but ensured nobody told his son about the incident. Pritchard, meanwhile, kept another secret. He had lost Johnny Owen's St Christopher.

ROUND ELEVEN

In April 1958, Harry Carpenter travelled to Los Angeles to cover a fight between the world featherweight champion, Hogan 'Kid' Bassey, and the local hero, Ricardo Moreno. The venue was the Olympic Auditorium and Carpenter experienced first hand the messianic appeal of a Mexican legend. Just as was the case twenty-two years later, the Hispanic crowd had unleashed a fanaticism that was almost frightening. Moreno's huge popularity had involved being christened 'Little Bird' and, on that balmy April night, the Mexicans left the sweat-shops, the kitchens and the car washes armed with cages.

'Moreno had this extraordinary fan worship,' Carpenter recalled. 'All the Mexicans came to this fight with real birds. It was quite a sight. But Bassey did Moreno in the second round and, from this huge babble of noise, you had utter silence. There was not a word. Then they dumped the cages on the floor and left.'

Carpenter was not there this time. He planned to go into the BBC studios in London the following morning, watch a recording of the fight and add a commentary. The bout would then be screened during *Grandstand*. In the end, it would never be shown on television. A quarter of a century on, Carpenter proffered a possible explanation for why the fight had turned against Johnny Owen.

'The strange thing about the Pintor fight was Johnny Owen did very well in early rounds, but then he changed tactics and started keeping Pintor at long range,' he said. 'I think it was about the seventh. Where he had been smothering, now he began to get caught. I read one report of the fight in my cuttings and the writer commented that it looked as if Johnny didn't see the right hand coming. I thought that was very interesting. There might have been a problem. Maybe something had happened on the left side of his head and he wasn't seeing properly. It could be. Whether he had suffered something early on and it had changed his perception, I just don't know. But it's worth thinking about.'

The two big punches in the eleventh round were right hands from Pintor. The first was a hook, the second an uppercut. The way Pintor threw his hook meant it travelled a long way from his body before curving back into the target area of his opponent's head. Who knows whether there was something wrong with Owen's peripheral vision, blighting his prospects and handing the initiative to Pintor?

At the start of the eleventh round there were fifteen minutes to go. It is an insignificant period in most sports, but boxing is condensed drama and fifteen minutes is an age. Johnny Owen had to do more than merely clasp and run and count if he was to win, so he dredged up the core of his spirit and attacked again. He forced Pintor on to the cushioned wire and shrugged off the right hook. He thrust out his jab, shoved Pintor with the crook of his arm and tried to regain the backbeat of attrition that had been so successful. It was a good round in the circumstances, although Pintor won it with the weight of his punches.

'Every time Owen was hit solidly in the eleventh his thin body shuddered,' Hugh McIlvanney wrote later that night, but he was still holding up his guard and still throwing jabs.

Lupe Pintor, the third title defence of the WBC bantamweight title, he has grown in confidence. The knockdown seems to have taken the snap out of Owen's punches.

Pintor got the right hand in then, right through the gloves, the defence of Owen. One minute to go in the eleventh. Pintor has done most damage to Owen at long range, not inside, where you would expect.

Owen had been winning the fight, and he still was on some cards. Hindsight always has 20–20 vision, but he was still game in the eleventh. He had suffered from the knockdown and Pintor was looking stronger as the bout progressed, but the outcome was still uncertain. A couple more rounds like this, taking the initiative and avoiding the worst of Pintor, and he might discover a second wind. He was unbelievably fit, and it was hard for his followers to believe that he would run out of steam. They glowed in his honesty and burned with indignation as they were doused by more urine from the balconies above. There would be no dumping of metaphorical bird cages tonight. Whatever happened, Johnny Owen was going home a hero. It had been a performance that could stand resolutely alongside the best of Wilde and Winstone.

Pintor, the stronger of the two now in the eleventh. Despite a great effort from Johnny Owen, who continues to throw punches and take them, he's not the sharp puncher he was four rounds ago. Those gloves now feel like eight pounds of lead.

There were chimerical signs in the eleventh round that Owen was still thinking with a degree of clarity. He recognized that Pintor had been more clinical when there had been clear blue space between their feet and now sought to close it. At one point Pintor took a step backwards, felt the divots in his face and cast a cursory look at Marty Denkin. It was a beacon of hope for Owen and showed that Pintor was still concerned about those clotted brows. It had not been a butt and Denkin ignored Pintor's grousing. Dr Schwartz looked carefully at Pintor's bloodied face and at Owen. The punches might not have been as hard as they were, but this did not seem like a spent boxer. He was punching, thinking and attacking. The pendulum had swung, but it was a good fight.

Denkin, too, was working overtime. It was a simple fight with little call for him to intervene, but he was a passive student of hurt. Owen's lip was a sorry sight and Pintor's forehead was a messy red. Yet he had no concern about the fight continuing. 'Your sixth sense comes into play,' he said. This was a huge night for Denkin. When the trauma of the fight unfolded, Denkin would be on his way to the airport for a flight to Puerto Rico and a date that would change the course of his own career.

The Olympic was a tough place, as Carpenter knew. 'It was rough and ready, but it was the sort of place you'd regard as a proper boxing arena,' he said. 'You don't want to go somewhere glitzy and plush. The old Liverpool Stadium was a sparse, bare arena, but that's as it should be for boxing. Lots of reports on the Pintor fight talked about the crowd and how very pro-Mexican they were. But you get that over there. It is a passionate place.'

In Owen's corner there was the normal concern, but nobody knew him like his father, and Dick Owens felt he could still win the title. Ken Bryant, the cornerman, believed it too, though he could see that Pintor was coming back and he could hear the crowd's excitement.

'Johnny got up a bit quick from the knockdown in the ninth, but he seemed to have all his faculties,' he said. Later, Carpenter recalled what had happened when he had travelled to Los Angeles in December 1969 to watch Alan Rudkin, a rugged Liverpudlian, take on Ruben 'El Puas' Olivares, the undisputed star of the Inglewood Forum.

'Olivares was a hard, seasoned fighter and Rudkin got knocked out in the second,' Carpenter said. 'That, in a way, was a blessing. You don't really want to get involved in a fight that goes on and on and you get knocked about. I later thought that maybe if Johnny Owen had been knocked out in the second none of it might have happened.'

Pintor echoed the same thought, suggesting that it was the resilience of Johnny Owen that proved so dangerous to both men.

'I don't blame the referee,' he said. 'When you are fighting in America, especially in world championship fights, bad things can happen, because you have two guys of such high quality and such strength. It's almost more dangerous. In Mexico, you will get a guy who is world class against a guy who really shouldn't be in there. That guy will get knocked out and that will be the end of it. He won't come back for more and does not take so much punishment. But in America, at the level Johnny Owen and I were fighting at, if you got knocked down then you made yourself come back for more. That's probably what happened that night.'

By the end of the eleventh round, nobody could say for sure whether the caged bird would find its wings and soar again. But Johnny Owen was still in there fighting. It would be another three minutes before the door slammed shut and the deafness and darkness descended on him.

13

TEN DAYS

The Gala Inn Motor Hotel had seen better days. It was a scruffy, weather-baked block flaking at the seams. It was also located in the heart of Los Angeles' Mexican quarter and was the favoured stopover of Lupe Pintor. The world champion had a floor to himself and would lie on a sunbed by the pool with an entourage of handlers ensuring he had as much peace as he wanted.

And now here was Johnny Owen, besieged by a new crop of cameramen and writers, and struggling to come to terms with the brouhaha of a world title build-up. The flashbulbs and shouted questions were new to him, and the anarchy outside his barred window did little to make him feel at ease. It was ten days to fight night and Dick wondered about the wisdom of allowing the promoter to pick a hotel.

'Mickey Duff said he'd stayed there before, but I doubt it,' he said.

Colin Hart, the *Sun* journalist covering the fight, agreed.

'We were in another part of town,' he said. 'It wasn't a palace by any means, but at least there were no sirens going off all the time. The promoters did it on the cheap. There were bloody drug dealers everywhere and they were on the ground floor. It was terrible.'

Pintor was used to it. He had been for his morning run and was feasting on his usual pancakes and syrup in the hotel restaurant when the Owen party arrived.

'Someone said come and meet Johnny Owen,' he recalled.

Pintor got up, daubed the syrup from his chin and wandered over. It was the first time he had seen Johnny in the flesh. The challenger offered his hand.

'It's nice to meet you,' he said. 'You are a great world champion and I hope to have a good fight against you.'

The words were interpreted and Pintor nodded in appreciation.

'I hope so too,' he replied in Spanish. 'I've heard a lot about you.'

The pair hugged and Dick smiled. Even then, his son's height advantage resonated. He also studied Pintor's brow for the telltale scar tissue that they could exploit. This was it. They were here. At that moment in the foyer of the Gala Inn Motor Hotel, reality sunk its teeth into Dick Owens.

In the ensuing days, everybody was canvassed for an opinion. Ken Buchanan, the man who had been cut by Eddie Thomas's razor at Madison Square Garden, said Johnny would need to climb Mount Everest to win, while Howard Winstone, the Merthyr man who had taken on Mexico's finest in a bygone age, said that Johnny was 'a bit special' but still gave him only an even chance. The bookmakers made him a 4–1 outsider, and Don Chargin, the West Coast's most famed promoter, voiced some doubts privately. 'I couldn't believe it when I set eyes on him,' he told friends. 'The kid looks so thin and undernourished it looks impossible for him to be a fighter. I'm terrified that, if he doesn't put up a good show, the Mexicans are likely to tear my arena apart. They've done it before.'

One man who didn't underestimate him was Pintor. He was

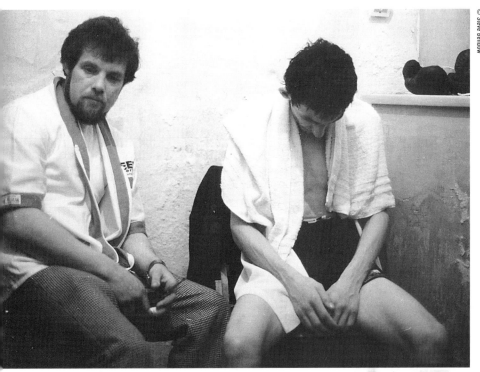

Devastated after losing in Almeria.

The rematch against Juan Francisco Rodriguez at Ebbw Vale.

Jubilation after beating Rodriguez
Heddwyn Taylor is extreme left

The spoils of success.

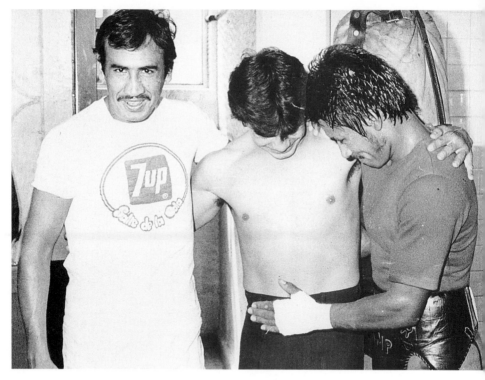

'The Z Man', Carlos Zarate (left), with Pintor (right) and friend.

Cuyo Hernandez studies a cut.

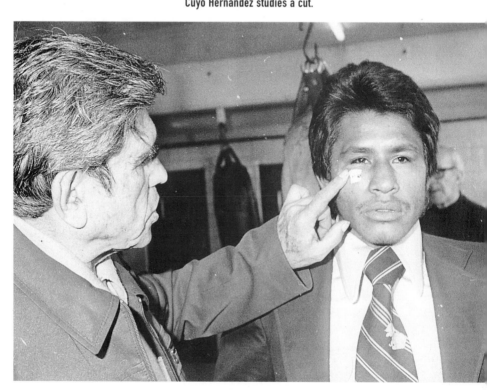

Above. Rope burns against Alberto Davila in Las Vegas.

Right. Pintor behind bars in 1979.

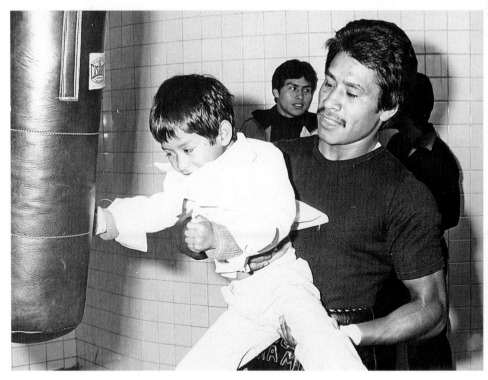

Pintor with his son, Lupe Junior.

Pintor and Tony Torres.

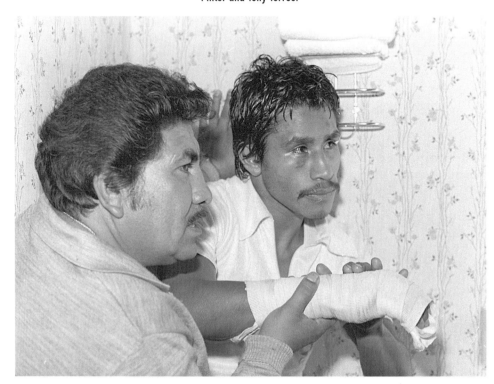

Right. Johnny training in Los Angeles.

Below. Action from Owen v Pintor.

Lupe and Virginia Pintor.

Pintor the trainer.

Dick Owens and Pintor
at the unveiling of
Johnny's statue.

sunning himself by the pool one afternoon when Johnny walked through the glass patio doors. The Pintor party turned as one and, when Johnny removed his top, a couple sniggered. Pintor emptied his mind.

'People in the build-up to the fight were telling me how easy it was going to be,' he said. 'They said there would only be one winner. I never believed that. I just knew that he was the European champion and that he was a really, really tough guy. A warrior. It is easy for other people to make judgements when they do not have the heart to get inside a ring.'

There were those who agreed with him. Jackie McCoy, the man who guided Carlos Palomino to the world welterweight title, was more upbeat.

'Owen's work-rate is fantastic and, if he can reproduce the form he showed against Feeney, he is going to prove a real handful,' he said. 'Pintor has looked sluggish in recent fights and, although he punches harder than Owen, he may find that the challenger, who is superbly fit, is capable of withstanding his best blows and handing out plenty of his own punishment.'

Trouble, though, was brewing in the Owen camp. There had been a string of issues – sparring partners, hotels, departure dates – but it was the Californian boxing authorities who decided the latter bone of contention, pointing out that their rules stated that boxers had to be in the country for eight days. In the end it was ten hot, stifling days.

There was also a row about the contract. After consulting with Mickey Duff, Gardiner returned to the camp and told them low blows would not result in disqualification. Given Pintor's lack of inches, it sounded to Dick like they were agreeing to give the champion carte blanche to fight dirty. He argued with Gardiner, who said there was nothing he could do, but Dick felt the manager was not standing up for his boy. It was a fracture that was only held together by the boy who looked almost translucent in the LA sun.

At 5 p.m. on day one, Johnny was forced to give an impromptu press conference at the hotel. It was a side of being a boxer that he did not relish, and the intrusiveness of the American media, who followed him into the hotel restaurant and even into his bedroom, irritated him. Johnny and his father shared a room, and Gardiner had another. Dick felt the most important thing that first day was to sleep, but the phone kept ringing. He went to see Gardiner to tell him to take the calls, but the manager was dressing to go out.

'I told him it would be better for all of us to get a good night's sleep, but he didn't listen,' Dick said. 'Dai went out and wasn't right for days.'

Although the arrest of a man outside his hotel window left Johnny shocked – 'We don't have things like that in Merthyr,' he told Colin Hart – boredom also set in.

'We got there Wednesday and I wished we'd been fighting that Friday,' Dick said. 'John was ready.'

Days were spent training in the morning, escaping the media glare and clock-watching by the pool. The Mexican press could not believe that Johnny was not sparring and suggested he must be resting an injured hand. Dick, though, was happy with his son's condition.

'We were training in the gym until 12.30 p.m. and then we'd have the rest of the day to ourselves,' he said. 'We were bored stiff, but John was in good shape. We weren't allowed any sparring partners, but we'd done the hard training back in Merthyr. I believe in easing up a bit and resting the body anyway. At home he'd been sparring fifteen rounds a night, against middleweights and heavyweights. He'd take on seven or eight fellas a night. Out there it was just a case of ticking over.'

Johnny found a running track in a local park. It was sandy and so had more give, which he felt would be useful preparation for the spongy canvas at the Olympic.

'There were two gyms, one for us and one for Pintor,' Ken Bryant, the cornerman, said. 'There were loads of boxers and I remember loads of women ones too. Johnny got introduced to the lady bantamweight champion of the world. She was very attractive, petite and dark-haired. Johnny was embarrassed. I remember thinking, "How the hell can someone like that box?"' It was the same thing many Americans were thinking about Johnny Owen.

The second night he was there, Johnny made another entry at the back of his diary.

Must train like never before. Early to bed. Stop eating chocolate. Bring back the world title for my family and friends and supporters, and show others that, with luck and dedication, you can achieve almost anything.

On another floor of the hotel, Pintor was relaxing after venting the full fury of his strength in the gym, boxing two rounds with three different sparring partners. Each was left gasping for breath with ugly red marks on their midriffs.

'That's what I'm going to do to Owen,' he said for the benefit of the writers. 'Only twice as hard.'

The Owens had been given a six foot, five inches tall gentle giant named Van Barbieu as their public relations officer. He had a booming laugh and warm face and would be an anchor during the ten days in America. He also helped in negotiating the problems that quickly arose. The first came on the fourth day, when Johnny found his father and said: 'Dai says I've got to spar for the public down the Olympic.'

Dick bristled when he heard that.

'Don't worry, John,' he said. 'Forget about it.'

Later that afternoon, he sought out Gardiner.

'What's wrong with you?' he said. 'John is physically and mentally fit and you and no other bugger is going to ruin it.'

Gardiner said the Americans were insistent, so a meeting was hastily arranged.

'I don't like it,' Dick told Van Barbieu. 'He might get knocked off. They might put anybody in there with him to try to soften him up. I'm not having it.'

Van Barbieu managed to douse Dick's fears, and his son did spar in America after all, though, in an age before wall-to-wall television, internet access and ubiquitous news feeds, Dick had wanted to retain an element of surprise. They had seen very little of Pintor and the champion had only read of Johnny.

'In the end I let John do it, but I told him to stand up straight and retreat,' Dick said. 'That wasn't his way, but I told him that's all they think British fighters can do. So he did it.'

On day eight it was arranged that Johnny would give a speech on television. Again the fighter was unhappy. His lack of confidence meant the prospect made him anxious, but on Wednesday, two days before fight night, he walked into the Brown Darby Hotel, a lush and lavish place that exposed the Gala Inn's impoverishment.

'The chandeliers were bigger than our front room and the carpet was so soft you sank up to your knees,' Dick said. 'We had a wonderful four-course meal.'

The speeches trundled on, and then it was Johnny's turn. For him, this was worse than facing any opponent.

'I'm Johnny Owen and I come from Merthyr Tydfil,' he began in his thick Welsh brogue. 'It's an iron and coal town in Wales, which is part of the United Kingdom.'

He warmed to his task and it was soon time for the agreed question-and-answer session.

'You haven't got any marks on your face and don't look much like a boxer,' the inquisitor started.

'They don't pay me enough to get marked,' came the quick reply and the diners chuckled.

'I know your ambition is to win the world title on Friday, but do you have any other ambitions?'

Johnny paused and looked around the cavernous room, stuffed with wealth and the overfed middle classes.

'Well,' he began, 'I'd like a hotel like this in Merthyr for my mother and father and brothers and sisters.'

The place guffawed as one.

It was a brief foray into the world of celebrity. Tom Jones, the Welsh singer and boxing fan, wanted to meet the remarkable young fighter. He left messages at the hotel inviting them to the Bel Air mansion he had recently bought from Dean Martin, but by the time they picked them up, Jones had flown to Lake Tahoe. He was performing there on Friday 19 September. It would be a run-of-the-mill, forgettable night in the career of a singing legend and Welsh hero. For Johnny Owen, it would be anything but.

A trickle of Welsh supporters flew into the City of Angels during those last days. Byron Board was using a stick when he arrived.

'What's the matter, Hopalong?' Gardiner shouted. 'You got gout or have you fallen off your wallet?'

Everybody was pleased to see 'Lord' Byron and his friends. It transported the warmth and comfort of home into this alien land. Yet all the time the reminder of the task was there, and at every turn at the Gala Inn, Pintor seemed to appear.

'We started calling him John's shadow,' Dick recalled.

No words were exchanged. It was the respectful silence of two men biding their time, waiting to be judged.

On the ninth day, the eve of the fight, Dick gave his son a massage with the usual mix of oils. His mind drifted back to the time Edith had gone to the shops to get the mix of oils Dick had asked for. By mistake she had been given turpentine for paint, rather than the oil of turpentine Dick wanted. It had burnt Johnny, who had torn up the stairs, knelt in the bath and started splashing water over himself. This time Dick made sure the recipe was correct. He smiled.

'After I'd finished, John stood in front of the mirror,' he said. 'I couldn't believe it. His stomach muscles looked like they were chiselled out of concrete.'

Johnny caught his father's eyes. 'Tomorrow night I'll be world champion,' he said calmly.

'Yes,' Dick replied. 'I know you will be.'

And then they had one of only a handful of disagreements in their limpet-tight relationship.

'Now you listen to me,' Dick said. 'You win tomorrow and you retire undefeated.'

Johnny Owen's laugh subsided to a half-smile. 'No, Dad,' he mouthed. 'I must make two or three defences and then call it a day.'

Johnny got into bed while his father decided to go and enjoy a drink with Board and the boxer's other supporters at the Figaro bar next door. He had a good time. They spoke about how Johnny could beat Pintor and what a great son Dick had. He glowed with pride and wished Edith could have been there to hear all the praise.

At 12.45 a.m. he made his excuses and went back to the Gala Inn. He didn't put the light on for fear of disturbing his son, undressed and got into his bed. Dick's thoughts were rampant. After a few minutes he sensed Johnny was not asleep either.

'John,' he whispered. 'Are you awake?'

'Yes,' came the soft reply.

'How long you been lying here?'

'Just now. Thinking.'

And then Dick felt compelled to do something he had never previously done on the eve of a fight. He got out of his bed, walked over to his son and put his arms around him. 'Come on, Dad,' the boxer said. 'Don't get emotional.'

In the years that followed, Dick wrestled with why he did that.

'Was it my subconscious mind telling me something?' he said. 'I fell asleep and, when I woke up, I was in the single bed and John was in the double. I've never said a word about that until this day. I try to fathom out why I did it because it wasn't like me. Before a contest I always prayed that John would be all right during it and after. That's all I ever asked for. I don't know why I felt the need to hug him that night.'

The sun rose on day ten and cast its shadow through the barred window. It was Dilwyn Owens's nineteenth birthday. It was also the day Johnny Owen had lived most of his life for.

They had breakfast and then went to the weigh-in at the Olympic. Despite his habit of gorging on pancakes, Pintor had sweated and pounded himself into perfect shape. Johnny, too, was at his peak. Dick did not want to hang on to his son's coat-tails and shuffled to a corner of the room. A couple of Americans began talking to him.

'If your son wins,' one said 'you want to piss off out of here. Get the first plane out of town. Don't stop here whatever you do.' The advice was issued out of concern and they wished Dick all the best.

The boxers shook hands. Pintor had not brought any gift as a token for his opponent, so the Welshman kept hold of the miner's lamp he had with him and gave it to his driver, a man named Johnny Carbrerra.

They were thinking of Johnny Owen in all sorts of places that night. His family at home hoped for the best. So did his friends. Jeff Pritchard and Mike Pickett kept their fingers crossed. They wished they could have gone and sparred, but that was history. Idris Sutton was in the Ukrainian and Heddwyn Taylor in his mansion. Everyone wondered.

In the Olympic, people took their seats. Rick Farris leafed through a programme and Alberto Davila let his mind wander to his own world title bouts. In the press row, Gareth Jones was excited but had work to do. Danny Lopez chatted with Tom Kelly.

In Merthyr, Vivian Owens hoped his sense of foreboding would be rendered needless anxiety. 'I didn't know much about Pintor, but thought John could win,' he said. 'But I had this premonition beforehand. A couple of nights before. We were all there in a room. We're dressed in black with black ties, and the only one you can't see is John. We all have our dreams, but it's only afterwards you start to think about it. I remember speaking to him on the phone and him telling me about the police having this guy on the floor. He was very excited about that.'

Vivian stayed up all night trying to find out some news on the radio. The streets in Merthyr were deserted by the time Johnny Owen had his hands bound with ten feet of bandages. Marty Denkin met both boxers and gave his instructions.

Inside the Olympic, the place was shaking. The Welsh sang. Keith Davies, a bartender from Santa Monica who had been raised in Merthyr, was in their midst. Byron Board, Johnny's number one fan, held the skeleton banner high and marched down into the Olympic. Graham Walters waved the Welsh flag high. This was it. Ten days had brought them to fight night.

'John was fine,' Dick said, although others were angered and shocked by the way they were scratched and taunted as they walked through the mob. 'We had to go up a flight of steps and there were lots of spectators who were pushing and pinching John. When we reached the top he held his arms up high into the air and bounced down into the arena.

'The adrenaline was pumping. I felt nice. I was proud. All the fights I went to, if he won, I just walked away. I didn't jump in the ring or anything. This was his domain. It was no business of mine. All he did, he achieved on his own. The atmosphere was terrible, and now I think we were lucky, because there were only four policemen there, but John didn't have a trouble in the world.'

'Attack,' Dick told his son. 'And keep your hands up high.' They knew that Pintor, with his lack of height, would be sucked in by the thinness of Johnny's waist and direct his punches to his body. But they were ready. The count of ten was over. It was time.

Yet back in his hotel room the lingering doubts lay unseen in his pocket diary. The last entry expressed Owen's frustrations:

Dai seems to be lost. He is causing problems when he should be helping me to win the title. Without Dad I'd be lost too. If only I could win it and defend it twice I think I'd retire. It all seems to cause more heartache than enjoyment, through Dai's lack of understanding and the foolish words which hurt me and Dad.

He added an afterthought, 'P.S.,' he wrote. 'Hope everything comes right on the night. If only. It's a big if.'

14

LOST

Dick Owens was lost. For the first time in his life he rushed into the ring. He crouched by his son and repeated his name, oblivious to everything else but that ghostly visage. He was cocooned in his own personal nightmare. Dr Bernhart Schwartz was there and was worried by the boxer's eyes and the spasms. Dick Young, one of the judges, untied Johnny's boots. They got him on the stretcher and carried him from the tumult of the ring. More cups of urine were hurled at them. They were pushed, shoved and scratched. Ken Bryant was one of the bearers.

'They'd told us not to leave any valuables in the changing room,' he said. 'I had $600 in my wallet so I put it in my whites and took it in with me. As I was helping Johnny out of the ring on the stretcher I could feel this bastard with his hand in my pocket. I turned around and there was a copper with a .45. I said, "He's nicking my bloody wallet." He just shrugged. I was so annoyed but I was not going to let go of that stretcher, not even if my life-savings had been in it.'

Marty Denkin, the referee, and Mickey Duff, the promoter, also had their pockets picked in the chaos. The Mexicans celebrated and mocked the losers. The British writers were stunned by the misanthropy. It was a hell of a place.

At the California Hospital on Hope Street, Dick cried fresh tears as his son was taken away from him into an operating theatre. Colin Hart, the *Sun*'s boxing writer, paced the floor, trying to offer solace, but the words failed to penetrate the dislocated world Dick now inhabited. He heard nothing, traumatized by what had happened and paralysed by doubts. Should he have pulled him out? Why had he not stopped it when he could, when the lip was bad and future still bright? But it had been going well. For two minutes of the twelfth round he had looked okay. He had only had sixty seconds to get through before he could grab another breather. That was all.

Those willing Johnny to victory had had reason to cheer as the twelfth wound its circuitous course to tragedy. The boxers were again like duelling stags of old, heads locked side by side, suffused in the smells and tastes of combat. Johnny fired off a couple of punches to the chest of the bowed champion. This was the way to win. It was a bigger if now, but the question was still there, lingering like fading light.

And then time froze and the enormous golden digits on the cubed scoreboard stopped. Pintor edged to his left and, from point blank distance, heaved his body into an uppercut. The blow had scarcely been shrugged off when the right connected squarely on the left side of Johnny's jaw. As he went down, Pintor almost half-heartedly threw another right, as if perfecting the punch.

Flashbulbs exploded. The cacophony was squeezed to a fuzzed growl. People leapt from their seats in slow motion. Everything was paused.

But there were only seconds remaining. If Johnny could hang on, they could get him back to his corner. Again, Dai Gardiner was furious with his man for getting up so quickly. Barely had he felt the canvas on his legs than Johnny was putting a gloved hand on a thigh and dragging himself back for more. He wiped his cut nose as Denkin held his fingers in front of him and gave him the mandatory count of eight. He might have salvaged another five seconds had he stayed down. Who could tell whether that would have made a difference?

Marty Denkin says, 'Are you all right?' Only the second time he's been down in his life. Pintor the heavier hitter now.

Nobody knew what Johnny Owen was feeling in those last seconds. Nobody knew whether it was the unbelievable grogginess or the confused pain, as Floyd Patterson had variously described being knocked down. But almost everybody accepts the damage was done before the last blow. Summing up his incredible will, Johnny still threw two more punches, but they were shrugged off and Pintor managed to spin him around and back him into his own corner. That was when he threw the last punch and Johnny crumpled like a rag doll. 'Like a tap had been turned on and the strength drained away,' Colin Hart said.

He's in trouble now. A right hand and down he goes. And that I think will do it. He won't get up from that one.

Lupe Pintor arrived on Hope Street too. He was badly marked over both eyes and they were glazed with sadness. The corridors were flecked with people and voices. It was just another day in Bedlam. Pintor made his way through the miasma until he saw Dick sitting on a bench, head bowed.

'Normally at the end of a fight you feel total happiness and excitement,' Pintor said. 'It is an adrenaline rush. The defences I made before Johnny, I always got that feeling. But at the end of the fight with Johnny, there was a really bad atmosphere; we knew something really bad had happened. I went to the hospital as soon as I could and I wanted to see him, but he was already in intensive care and they were operating on him. They wouldn't let me in. I saw Richard. Obviously, he was very worried, but when he saw me he hugged me. "No problem, no problem," he said. "It was a great fight." And it was.'

Dick was pragmatic enough not to blame Pintor for anything. 'He told me he could see the title slipping away, that he couldn't hurt John,' he recalled of that meeting.

A phone call to Merthyr in the early hours of Saturday morning changed everything. For Edith Owens, it was the realization of sixteen years of anxiety. 'Are you hurt?' she always asked Johnny the moment he rang after a fight. It was her only concern. Winning was a distant second. And now the boy she had scolded for having the semblance of a black eye all those years ago was helpless with hurt. Edith felt sick.

Kelvin initially failed to appreciate the message's import. 'Somebody phoned, a journalist, and said John's in hospital. My first reaction was surprise that he'd been knocked out, but I wasn't too worried about him being in hospital because that's standard if you're knocked out. I didn't think it would be anything serious. It was only the next morning when we began to realize. They were trying to keep the seriousness of it away from us, but when we saw it on TV and heard them talking about a brain haemorrhage, we started to get scared.'

The journalists had a job to do. They visited the hospital and then went back to the hotel.

'I remember Hugh McIlvanney at the hotel bar,' Gareth Jones said. 'McIlvanney hardly spoke to anyone and was having a whisky. He must have had two or three, a quite nice type I think, and then he went and wrote one of the most brilliant bloody pieces I'd ever seen.'

McIlvanney began: 'It can be no consolation to those in South Wales and in Los Angeles who are red-eyed with anxiety about Johnny Owen to know that the extreme depth of his own courage did as much as anything else to take him to the edge of death.'

It had also been the edge of glory, the very brink of answering the big if with a resounding affirmative. It had been a gruelling, soul-sapping fight, but both men had acquitted themselves well, and some clung to the meaningless belief that Johnny would have won had he lasted the course.

'Unless it was a bent decision, Johnny was going to win,' Graham Walters said. 'Pintor couldn't understand how this man could stand in the middle of the ring and fight him. Neither could the Mexicans. Looking back I don't think he had time to train. It would have been better to go earlier and get used to the air, but as far as I'm concerned, he was big enough, strong enough, good enough.'

Dai Gardiner was trying to come to terms with events, but it was hard. Johnny was undergoing a three-and-a-half-hour operation to remove a blood clot from his brain. Everything was blurred. There were photographers and journalists and doctors and nurses. How had it come to this when a few hours earlier they had been climbing the mountain?

'The fight was going great,' he said. 'Even after the first knockdown. The tenth was very good for us. Up to the twelfth it was going fine. I said, "He's looking for the big uppercut, he's trying to draw you in." He said, "Okay, I'm all right, I'm watching for everything. I've got him worked out." And he did. He had him worked out. Then that punch. Unbelievable. I was in shock. In the ring in a flash. Oh, I'll always remember it. I didn't know instantly. I just thought it was a knockout. When he hadn't come around in the ambulance I started to think, "What's wrong?" It was my worst nightmare and still is.'

In the hospital foyer, Dick and Bryant sat side by side. They did not talk about the fight, they were only interested in Johnny. It was later when Bryant would start to go over what had happened, the way the challenge had crumbled, the decisions they had made, the treatment in those minutes when the boiling cauldron spat and hissed.

'John got cut early on the lip,' he recalled. 'I don't think Dick, Dai or myself realized how serious it was, but I have thought about it a lot since. Johnny must have been swallowing a lot of blood and I wonder if that had anything to do with it. The hotter the body gets, the faster the adrenaline flows and the thinner the blood gets.

'I wasn't worried with the first knockdown. He did get up a bit quick but he seemed to have all his faculties. But he was more cautious and Pintor was getting more aggressive. Johnny went backwards for the first time, the Mexicans saw it and they responded. They screeched and roared like hell. They had been quiet before, but now they saw some hope, they saw Pintor making a comeback. That heightened the adrenaline in Pintor, because I am quite sure he realized he was going to lose.

'When Johnny went down the last time we knew he was not going to make the count. We were in the ring before the referee had even finished. "What a bit of bloody bad luck," I thought. I never thought for a minute that it would be anything bad. I thought we'd just tap Johnny on the side of his face and he'd come round. But the doctor was all over him, checking his pulse, using smelling salts. He couldn't bring him round and said, "We'd better get him to hospital." I thought, "Oh no, bloody hell!" They didn't have a stretcher at ringside so there was a delay. I helped carry him out. I can't remember who else was there because your mind is a muddle. There was no oxygen. People all around were jeering at us. We went to hospital and were devastated, but we expected him to come round.'

They sat in the foyer and waited. There was little anyone could say. They had plotted and planned and now they were at a dead end.

'Dick and I just looked blankly at each other,' Bryant said. 'I have never seen a man look so despondent in my life. We were trying to console each other, but I don't think we were doing a very good job.'

Dick tried to convince himself of the best. 'He's a fighter, man. He's a fighter. I've all the confidence in the world that he'll make it.'

'Let's hope so, mate,' Bryant said. 'Let's hope so, because, Christ, he does not deserve this.'

By that time, Marty Denkin was in the air. He was on his way to San Juan in Puerto Rico to officiate at a WBA world lightweight fight between Hilmer Kenty and Ernesto Espana. He had been to the hospital on Hope Street and was unaware of the storm brewing in his wake.

'I'll tell you the truth,' he said, 'the tension was there but I got on the plane and fell asleep. I didn't know how desperately ill he was. I know this sounds cold, but that's the way it was.'

When he touched down in Central America, it hit home. A newspaper offered him a small fortune to say he had jet lag and was putting the lives of Kenty and Espana at risk. He declined but realized he was at the centre of a controversy.

'CBS had the tape of the Johnny Owen fight and said I shouldn't referee,' he said. 'Someone else told me it would look awful if I got into the ring the day after what happened at the Olympic. I was told I'd be crucified. Now, I'm a warm and caring man, but I'm a professional. So I did the fight and stopped it after four. They penalized me and I never refereed a world title bout for two years. They thought I had no feelings, but I did. That wasn't the real me.'

When Denkin got back to the States he visited the hospital again because he needed to look Dick in the eye. Although his pocket had been picked at the Olympic, he gave his wage to Dick to help foot the bills. Now he says he has no regrets about his role in the fight and puts it down as one of the tragic accidents that scuff the surface of the sport.

'He was in control of all his faculties,' he said. 'When he went down a second time it was not a hard punch, but he said he was okay. Then twenty seconds later ... the kid went down, he collapsed totally. I knew he was in trouble from the way he fell. I showed the tape to some young referees. We don't prepare for those things, but a referee has a second responsibility. I came in to help. I remember the concern on the doctor's face. I'd never change anything I did about that fight. I visited the hospital and a newspaper man said it looks like you think you're guilty. I didn't feel that way. I prayed. I'm not a religious man but I am spiritual. I prayed hard.'

Inevitably, the roles of Denkin and boxing were subjected to rigorous scrutiny in the days that followed. His decision to fly to Puerto Rico lost him much public sympathy, but opinion is divided about whether the fight should have been halted earlier.

Rick Farris, a former boxer in the crowd that night and a friend of Denkin, believes it should have been.

'Although I hate to place the blame on a referee for a boxer's death, Marty let the match go on far too long,' he said.

Dr Schwartz, though, told the media that there had been no legitimate reason for pulling Johnny out.

'As far as I was concerned there was no question of stopping the fight,' he said. 'Owen was doing very well and seemed to be ahead on points. In the thirty-eight years I have been a fight doctor, I have never seen a braver fighter.'

In fact, by the end, all the judges had Pintor ahead. Chuck

Hassett had scored 105–103, Dick Young 106–102 and Denkin 107–102. The sad truth, going into the twelfth round, was that Johnny needed a knockout.

Walters remembers the medical provisions being inadequate. 'When Johnny was laid out, all they were doing was turning him over and sticking smelling salts under his nose,' he said. 'It was a good ten minutes before we got him out. It was the Welsh and the English boys all together, getting soaked in urine, all completely distraught.'

Pintor believes the fight should have been stopped earlier. It is not a judgement made with the benefit of hindsight, but from the boxer's ability to gauge the strength of a rival.

'I was really surprised by the way Johnny came at me to start with,' he said. 'He had a longer reach and he cut me early. There was a distinct feeling at the start of the fight that I was going to lose from cuts because he was really hurting me. But from about the eighth round, Johnny started to drop a little bit and, in the ninth, I knocked him down for the first time. They should have stopped it then because he went down in a bad way. He was still hitting as much, but not as hard. When he went down in the twelfth, again I felt they should have stopped it.'

Linda Roberts, with a brown bob, high cheekbones and a maternal manner, liked her job as the public relations officer for the California Hospital but was affected by the tragedies that tempered the good-news stories. It had been a busy night. At the same time that the boxer had been admitted to the building on Hope Street, an 83-year-old college professor was receiving treatment after being stabbed in a park with a sandy running track.

Roberts issued the first of many statements on Saturday. 'Johnny Owen was admitted to the emergency department at

California Medical Center last night, Friday, September 19, in a critical condition. He was operated on to remove a blood clot from the brain and was in surgery between approximately 11.30 p.m. and 3 a.m. He was subsequently transferred to the ICU, still in a critical condition. He remains in the ICU in a critical condition and will be in the ICU for another seventy-two hours. No surgery or tests are scheduled and there is still no prognosis.'

It was the second day of a vigil that would attract the sympathy of people around the globe. Keith Davies, the bartender from Santa Monica, had taken a call early that morning from John Hiscock, a friend who worked as a stringer for newspapers on both sides of the Atlantic. He was told Johnny was in a coma and hooked up to a life-support machine. Davies travelled downtown to the Gala Inn to find Dick. There he found a dazed, dumbstruck figure, and offered to help. Dick, almost passively, agreed, and Davies began helping as a chauffeur, running people to and from the hospital.

'He does it because he's a Taff, and I'm grateful,' Dick told a journalist.

Walters could not believe the young man he had supped tea with back in the Rhondda was now fighting for his life in LA. It seemed incomprehensible. He went to the hospital with some friends.

'There were about thirty of us,' he said. 'We weren't allowed to see him, but at least we were in the same place. There were lots of reporters there and I was so upset. We were in the depths of despair and they just wanted news. I threatened to shove a camera down someone's throat.'

Back in Wales the wait for news was agonizing. The first call had come through at 6 a.m., but by 5 p.m. on Saturday they had heard nothing new from America. All they had to go on were the bulletins on the television and the radio. It was an awful vacuum, the silence fanning their fears and fraying their nerves. That evening Kelvin rang Melanie Doel, a reporter with the *Merthyr Express*, to ask if there was anything the newspaper could do to help get Edith to America. It set in motion a chain of events that would see Ted Rowlands, the local MP, arranging a passport and ringing the American embassy in London to fast-track a visa. Duncan Hill, the manager of the Midland bank, footed the bill for tickets for Edith and Susan. All the flights were booked up for Sunday, but Freddie Laker himself stepped in and got them seats on the 15.15 from Gatwick. Eddie Thomas drove them to the airport.

Harry Carpenter had received a phone call early on Saturday from Jonathan Martin, the head of sport at the BBC. 'Harry, we're not putting the fight out.'

'What?'

'Come in and have a look. It's too disturbing for the relations.'

Carpenter liked Johnny and drove to the studio in reflective mood. He watched the tape and knew Martin was right. Instead of screening the fight, Frank Bough introduced Carpenter on that afternoon's show and he gave a report of what he had witnessed.

'I must express the concern of everyone in British boxing at this awful news,' he began. 'It comes as a particular shock because Johnny Owen is one of the fittest and most dedicated men in boxing. His whole ring strategy is based on the fact he has the most enormous stamina which is built up by running over the Brecon Beacons. I have just watched a recording of the complete fight and I must say at once that Johnny Owen, for eight rounds, put up what was for me as good a challenge by a British boxer as I have seen from anybody in an American ring. After eight rounds I had Owen five, Pintor one and two draws.'

After giving a narrative of the fight, Carpenter picked up a phone and spoke to Mickey Duff, who was at Don Chargin's home.

'Probably the best performance by a British boxer abroad for years,' Duff said before disagreeing with Carpenter's assertion that the celebrations had been distasteful. 'The crowd were rowdy in a playful manner rather than hostile,' he said, forgetting the urine, the pick-pockets and the man who had threatened Bryant with a knife. 'It became a contest between too many Mexicans and too few Welshmen. The worst they did was throw paper cups over the balconies.'

It was an insensitive appraisal.

'It's always sad when something like this happens but these are the hazards of boxing,' Duff concluded. 'You can't whitewash it, but when it happens in a minor bout the public do not seem to notice. All we can do is keep our fingers crossed and hope for the best.'

The passage of time has not altered Carpenter's views on the morality of boxing.

'People forget about how well Johnny Owen did in that fight,' he said. 'But it was the first time he'd been knocked down, as an amateur or professional, and not being a boxer, I don't know what effect that has on a young man. It must be terrifying when it happens for the first time because it's not something you can practise. He got up very quickly, but who knows whether it would have made a difference if he'd stayed down? You don't know what's going on up in the head. He might well have suffered a fatal blow earlier and it only takes one more to put you over the top.

'But, even with what happened to Johnny Owen, I tell people I have seen boxing give people so much more than it has taken away. I remember Roger Bannister telling me he didn't like boxing. He was a neurological surgeon. I told him I hadn't seen too many fights where people had taken a lot of punishment, but he said I had it wrong. You don't need to take a lot of punishment. You could get a brain haemorrhage from stepping off the kerb. It only takes one punch in the wrong place at the wrong time to do damage.'

Over in America, another seasoned boxing watcher had become the spokesman for the family. Tom Lyons of the *Daily Mirror* explained: 'I didn't seek the bloody job, but the Mexican press has been knocking on my door and I am closest to the family. When I finished my story I went down to Our Lady Chapel and said five decades of the Rosary.'

Another supporter asked not to be named in the media. 'People go to fights to see a man half kill another man,' he said, 'but then, when a boxer is half killed, they feel guilt and sorrow and try to help out as an apology.' It was a cynical assessment but not entirely groundless.

Davies had arranged to drive to the airport to pick up Edith and Susan the following day. Dick was still in a morbid stupor. Board and Gardiner were concerned enough to take him to the hospital to have his blood pressure tested. The doctor confirmed he was in a state of shock, but Dick refused to be sedated. He landed a bill for $65 for his trouble.

That night he went to back to Hope Street. He asked the policeman on duty if he could visit his son. The policeman nodded and accompanied him to the room. As soon as Dick saw his son wired up to a life-support machine beneath a maze of tubes, he broke down in tears again. In turmoil he walked out of the room and the hospital and wandered aimlessly into downtown LA, floating among the crack dealers and the whores. He walked and walked, getting deeper and deeper into the labyrinthine den of thieves.

'I don't know what I did or where I went,' he said. 'That night my heart broke. I cried and cried and thought it would never end. When or how I got back to my hotel I don't know. I don't remember anything.'

Eventually, with the blind night dwarfing this middle-aged man from the valleys, a blue light flashed and a police car drew up. As chance would have it, one of the police officers recognized Dick as he had spoken to him a few days earlier. He put him in the back and drove him back to his hotel. As Dick got out of the back and shook their hands, Tom Lyons was passing on his way to church. 'What's wrong?' he said, wondering what else could have happened.

'Nothing,' the trooper replied. 'But no white man usually gets out of downtown LA alive. If you know this man then make sure he doesn't go down there again. He was very lucky.'

Lyons looked at Dick and knew he was anything but lucky. It was like staring at an empty shell. Dick went back to the room where, two nights earlier, he had held his son and told him to retire. He was home, but lost.

15

HOPE STREET

At around 7 p.m. on the first Sunday, Byron Board found Dick and asked what he thought about Edith coming out. The sunken father had no idea about how his personal tragedy had engulfed the wider world and thought he could hide the trauma from his wife.

'No, Byron,' he said. 'She would break her heart if she saw John like that.'

Board shrugged. 'Too late, Dick,' he said. 'She's already here.'

The duo packed a few clothes and made the trip to the nearby town of Torrance where it had been arranged for Edith and Susan to stay with a couple of friends named Ron and Frances Evans. The reunion was painful.

'We cried all night long,' Dick said. 'It was unreal. We couldn't believe it was happening.'

The following morning, Keith Davies drove them to the hospital. Dr John Holly, the neurosurgeon, invited Dick into an anteroom and fixed him with a meaningful but sympathetic expression.

'How many fights has your son had, Mr Owens?' he said from behind his desk.

Somehow, remembering John's prodigious skill, his infallibility and his raw strength buoyed Dick.

'He's had 124 amateur contests and this was his twenty-eighth as a professional.'

Holly's eyes dropped momentarily and he paused, as if sifting through his words for the right ones.

'Mr Owen,' he said in a dulled monotone. 'This could have happened at any time to John because he has a thicker jawbone than an ordinary man, but a very thin skull. This happened because, instead of the jawbone breaking, it went up into his skull.'

It took Dick a few moments to take in the irony of the doctor's words. It was John's abnormal strength that had felled him; yet this scene could have been played out at any time during his career.

The family got into a routine. Dick, Edith and Susan would make daily trips to the boxer's bedside and did all they could to pull him out of the coma. They spoke about his grocery store, of friends, of Manchester United. They played the tape that the football team had made for him. It was desperate stuff, daily leaps of faith over black holes of depression. In Merthyr the remaining family could only hope. Every pub and shop had a picture of the jug-eared, big-nosed gentleman boxer and an ice-bucket or a whisky bottle to collect money. Davies had set up a support fund to help at an American bank. Another was created at home. The money poured in, as did the cards, telegrams, presents and phone calls. One Mexican girl sent a crucifix to prove not all of Pintor's compatriots were unthinking hooligans, and Dick hung it at his son's bedside.

Another Mexican also visited the hospital, often unseen by the family, knowing they might hold him guilty. Ken Bryant noticed the small, muscular figure.

'There was an alcove at the hospital in the foyer,' he said. 'There was a crucifix on the wall and I saw Pintor there a lot. He was just in the corner on his own, praying. I thought that was marvellous.'

In Merthyr they kept hearing conflicting stories. One day Johnny would be getting better, the next he would be worse. Kelvin and Marilyn were photographed reading some of the hundreds of letters that poured into the family home. Everyone wanted to believe that there would be a miracle on Hope Street, but the truth was he remained in a deep coma and, a week after the fight, underwent a second operation to relieve cranial pressure.

'The doctor is pleased with Johnny's improvement, but it must be made clear that he is still critically, critically ill,' Dick told the *Merthyr Express*. 'I think people have got the wrong impression. The muscles are moving, but I don't think we are getting through to him at all. People have been running to the phone saying things they shouldn't.'

Such were the contradictory reports that Dick also rang his flock at home and told them no decision had been taken to turn off the life-support machine. Not yet.

That question hovered over Dick and Edith. For a while it was unspoken, but with each passing day and no sign of improvement, they knew it was coming. Doubts about how long the insurance money would cover the spiralling medical bills persisted, and they knew that one day they might be asked to make the impossible decision.

The intensity of the spotlight gradually faded. Some friends, like Bryant, simply could not stay indefinitely, and so, after ten days, he shook hands with Dick, embraced him and left. Walters was also forced to return. A giant card arrived on Hope Street signed by eight thousand people, but the family felt increasingly on their own. For all the sympathy and affection being offered them, this was their own personal nightmare. Others could go home and find diversions. For Dick and Edith Owens, their life became an obsessive game of patience.

Then the day came.

'One morning, just like the rest, we had breakfast and went down to the hospital,' Dick began. 'When we arrived we were told Dr Holly wanted to see us in his office. There was me, Edith, Susan and Dai there. He told us John was clinically dead and he wanted permission to turn the machine off. He said, "I won't be back for your decision for a while." We were all crying and Edith said she could not make any decision and that it was up to me, but she would stand by whatever I said. I replied it wasn't fair that I had to make all the decisions and that now it was up to me to make the last one. I thought God was very cruel. I thought it over and over.

'All our hopes and prayers were there on Hope Street, but after a lot of thought and tears, I decided to turn off the machine and take him home to his beloved Wales. Susan was on the floor in the corridor crying her eyes out, screaming, "He's not dead! John's not dead!" She was breaking her heart and so was everybody else.

'When Dr Holly came back I told him my decision, and he said, "You've got a lot to do and I'll phone you later." That was so awful. He went and that was it. There was this sense of emptiness. We went to see John again and cried a lot. Then we left. We had barely got back to the hotel when the phone went.'

The caller was Dr Holly. 'Is that you, Mr Owens?'

Dick's voice was strained. 'Yes.'

'I can't quite believe this, Mr Owens, but everything seems to be working. I haven't turned the machine off and everything's working.'

It took a few seconds for Dick to realize what he meant. It seemed that, having spent an hour mourning his son and trying to fathom some meaning from the tragedy, an hour comforting his traumatized wife and daughter, that Johnny Owen was now back from the dead. It was like Lazarus or Lew the Milk's son in the Aberfan disaster.

'We were crying again, but this time with joy and laughter,' Dick said. 'It was like someone had listened to our prayers. Dai said he was so happy that he was going for a swim with the boys up in Santa Monica. We were all delirious with joy.'

At 4 p.m. that afternoon the first call came from a journalist asking if it was true that Johnny Owen had died. Dick denied it, but the phone kept ringing. Then Kelvin rang and asked what was going on. 'Don't believe it, Kel,' Dick said. 'It's not true. John's alive. He's getting better.'

However, when newspapers actually carried the story saying Johnny's life-support machine had been switched off, the confusion turned to anger. It was clear somebody had told the media that the boxer was clinically dead. Dick rang Linda Roberts, but the hospital PRO said it had not come from them. Later, Dr Holly called Dick. 'I can assure you it was nothing to do with us, Mr Owens,' he said. 'We can't do things like that. You could sue us for millions.'

It was when Eddie Thomas called from Merthyr in the early hours that Dick's confusion turned to rage.

He recalled: 'Eddie said, "What's up, Dick? Dai's been on and ordered the hearse to come up to Heathrow to pick up John's body. He phoned me yesterday." I was furious. Les Roberts then rang and said the same thing. The following morning Ron Francis took me down to see Dai. I confronted him as he came out of the lift. I said, "Did you tell them, Dai?" He denied it, but I said, "Come on, Dai, no more lies. Did you say John was dead?" Then he started crying and admitted it. He said he'd lost his head. I told him I'd have knocked the bloody thing off if it wasn't for seeing the headlines about the father and manager of the boxer in a coma being in a brawl.'

With both men high on emotion, Dick said: 'I could smash your face in for what you have put us through. In future you shut your bloody mouth and I do the talking.'

Why Gardiner would alert the media is debatable. Perhaps he had wanted to help by making the arrangements for the family when he was told Johnny was dead. However, he later denied he had done so. 'How could I do that?' he said. 'It's impossible. It's news to me and I'm shocked. If Dick blames me then say it, but he knew I couldn't pull Johnny out of the fight. There was no reason at all.

'That first week I didn't think he was going to make it. Then we got another call saying he was coming round. Then we got another. It was terrible. You'd press his hand and there would be a bit of a reaction. At least you thought there was.'

Dick believes Gardiner could not help himself because he was in thrall to the media. Whatever the truth, it was a divisive intrusion, but there was still the belief that Johnny was nearing the surface of his coma to divert the pair. After eighteen days, Susan felt confident enough to go home and tell the family that there was hope. Board accompanied her on the flight, and the choking claustrophobia tightened on Dick and Edith.

'It was one of the days I was absolutely dreading,' Dick said. 'To have Susan go and Byron too, John's number one fan and our great friend, was terrible. I didn't want him to leave, but he had to. We missed him very much. Everything seemed to be black then. Edith would come down from Torrance on the Sunday night and we stayed in the same hotel room at the Gala Inn. There were thick bars on the window and we couldn't go out because it was too dangerous in downtown LA. It was very depressing.'

When they read the paper they realized they were not alone in suffering. Muhammad Ali, the greatest, had been admitted to the nearby UCLA Medical Center after being beaten by Larry Holmes and his age. 'Like watching an autopsy on a man who's still alive,' was how Sylvester Stallone described the derobing of the Ali legend. A friend, Howard Bingham, remembered that Ali, who had had to deflect stories that he had been suffering from brain damage even before the fight, had not wanted to go into hospital for tests. 'He didn't want people reading that Larry Holmes put him in hospital,' Bingham said. 'We told him it was better than it would be reading that Holmes had killed him.' This was boxing. It had given the world Ali and then dismantled him.

As Ali tried to ignore his sudden helplessness, the Owens felt an upsurge of hope. At last, their son did seem to be improving. The next day a British newspaper carried the headline 'BOXER JOHNNY WINS LIFE FIGHT'. Dick was reported as being elated after being told his son would recover, even if it took months. 'His eyes are flittering, he is swallowing positively and his cheeks have more colour,' he was quoted as saying. If it was never quite as good as the tabloid writers suggested, never that black and white, there was a burgeoning of belief. Indeed, Ron Evans suggested a break from their routine and invited Dick and Edith to join him in Torrance for the weekend. With Dr Holly confirming the coma was lighter than it had been, they accepted. There the relationship between Dick and Gardiner plumbed new depths.

'Ron, Frances and Edith were sitting around a table,' Dick recalled. 'Dai and I were on stools by the bar. The television was showing the news and it flashed to a piece about John. Dai turned to me and said, "Do you know what, Dick? I'm a celebrity now." I couldn't believe my ears. I said, "What did you say?" He said, "You know – me, you and John, we're celebrities."'

Dick was incredulous. 'Celebrity, you bastard! My boy is fighting for his life down the road and you're a bloody celebrity!' Gardiner got up and walked out of the bar, but Dick was not finished and followed him.

'Dai, do me a favour and go home,' he shouted. 'You're doing nothing for me by staying out here and your wife needs you. Go home.'

That Sunday the family were driven from Torrance to church to hospital. Gardiner said he had taken what Dick had said on board and would be leaving, but there was still time for more clefts to appear in the once solid bond.

The next morning, Dick was greeted by Aileen Eaton at the hospital. Eaton was a pioneering promoter and a living legend of West Coast boxing. Now seventy-one, she was in the last of her thirty-eight years promoting fights at the Olympic. Nick-named the Redhead and the Dragon Lady, she was a domineer-ing, street-smart negotiator who could intimidate many a rival with her presence. Now she spoke to Dick and said she would like to see John.

'No, I'm sorry,' Dick replied. 'That's not possible.'

Eaton was used to getting her own way and replied: 'Wouldn't it be better if you flew home?'

Dick sighed. 'My dear lady, I would be only too glad to get on the plane and get out of this godforsaken hole and this bloody nightmare, but John has gone down to the next floor for more tests. How can I leave?'

Van Barbieu, the public relations officer, then interrupted with some news that cut like a knife.

'Dick, I'm sorry, but it seems we've been misled about your son's condition.'

The one sentence twisted everything.

A few moments later they were seated by his bedside once again. Dick, as was the ritual, began talking to his son, messages of hope and family and trivia delivered in a stream of consciousness. He held Johnny's hand and did not see Gardiner pick up a form and sign his name. Edith did, though.

'What's that?' she asked. 'Dick signs everything.'

Gardiner passed it reluctantly to Edith, who read it and handed it to her husband. According to Dick, it was a brief note giving permission for Eaton to visit Johnny in his room. It was, to Dick, another example of Gardiner forgetting his priorities, and he ripped up the form.

'I would not have let anybody see John like that or take photos because he was a very proud man,' Dick explained. 'I wanted him to keep what dignity he could. Things like that, with Aileen Eaton, all added up. I wanted Dai to leave.'

For the purposes of the media, Dick realized a united front would be easier. So he told the journalists: 'He has done a great deal while he has been here, but there is little more we can do other than wait.' Gardiner jetted out of LA to return to life as a gas fitter in Blackwood. There is no doubt he cared deeply for Johnny but the partnership was now over, as foretold in the little green pocket diary.

If only I could win it and defend it twice, I think I'd retire,
as it seems to cause more heartache than enjoyment through
Dai's lack of understanding and the foolish words which hurt
me and dad.

Dick also claims Gardiner told him that the promoters were cancelling the hotel room at the Gala Inn. Dick rang Don Chargin. His recollection is that Chargin said: 'You got it wrong, Dick.

The rooms are yours as long as you need them, but I told Dai that I would only pay for the phone bill up to a week after the fight.'

'That seems fair,' Dick said and hung up.

He checked the phone bill and paid $1,200.

'Those things were so annoying,' he said. 'We were at our wits' end and Dai would say these things. I don't know why. He just didn't think sometimes. We got into a routine of staying the morning at the hospital, going for a walk, staying in the hotel room until morning and starting over. Dr Holly kept telling us to keep talking to him because he was getting lighter in his coma and he would be all right.

'It was Sunday, November 3rd, and we were with Ron Evans and wondering what tomorrow would bring, praying that he would come out of his coma and everything would be all right again.

'We woke and it was a beautiful morning. It was forty-six days since the fight. The sun was shining and the sky was blue. We went to the hospital as usual and Edith pointed out that John must be getting better because the window was open for the first time. We met Dr Holly, and he said John was getting lighter and lighter in the coma and should come out of it next week. Things were looking a little brighter so we walked out and had some food before going back to the hotel. There was a lot of press about how the insurance money was running out and I was worried. Out there, if you can't pay, nothing gets done. I talked to Dr Holly, who told me not to worry and that he'd do it all for free if he had to. It was a relief.

'We thought John was getting better. I wanted to buy him some winter clothes, because I was convinced he was going to be okay and was going to get through it, but they stopped me. I was so sure he was coming out of the coma. And then, at

7.40 p.m., the phone went and they said John was dying. He had pneumonia and they couldn't clear it up. We rushed down to the hospital, our minds in bits, and he died in my arms. It had been almost seven weeks since I'd held him in the hotel room on the eve of the fight.

'I don't know how long Edith and I sat with him, but the next thing I remember is ringing Ron, who came down to pick us up and take us back to his house. We cried all night.'

It was much later when Dick began to go over the vigil and let doubts deepen his depression.

'Why was that window open? My wife is still convinced that gave him pneumonia. We've no proof, but the window had never been open before. He'd had pneumonia not long after the accident and they'd cleared it up, so why not this time? They said we can't. He was brain dead. The other organs had packed up. His lungs were filling up and he couldn't cope with it. It was a father's worst nightmare come true.'

Linda Roberts issued a statement. It could be an awful job, but they were doing good. After all, the 83-year-old college professor who had been stabbed in the park had recovered.

In Merthyr, the press were quick to set up camp outside the little council house that encased the grief of seven siblings. A neighbour had been sent to tell them the news at 6 a.m. and the early hour meant they had suspected the worst even before he had stepped in from the outer world.

'We'll have to do something or they'll never leave,' Kelvin said as he looked at the press through a crack in the curtains. It tended to be Kelvin and Marilyn who took charge of the brood. 'What if we spoke to them? That might get them off our backs.'

Kelvin opened the door and the flashbulbs peppered the grey sky like little explosions.

'I spoke to one guy I recognized and said we'd let him in

and he could share the information with the others. I told him there were things I didn't want to discuss. I didn't want to talk about the fine detail of John's passing or the last round. I told him I'd throw him out if he crossed the line. I know from watching television that silence is a great weapon for a journalist. When you give them an answer, they don't respond, and so the interviewee feels obliged to say more.'

The journalist did as he was told, little good that it did. The throng rose to around forty and showed little sign of diminishing. In the end the brothers and sisters lined up behind the door. Kelvin was at the front. He flung it open and, as they had agreed, the Owens ran, down the path, away from the media scrum and dived into the car. Kelvin revved it up and it tore away.

'If I had one fault as a kid it was my driving,' he said. 'I was never in trouble with the police for anything apart from my driving, so I tore away like a lunatic and we went to Marilyn's house. We never saw them again and we stayed there for a week.'

The next day was just as traumatic for Dick. Ron Evans took him to Forest Lawn Glendale, the sprawling cemetery of the stars, to pick a coffin. In keeping with LA's crassly idiosyncratic ways, Glendale had long become a tourist attraction, with replicas of Michelangelo's greatest sculptures nestling alongside the last resting places of Clark Gable, James Stewart, Nat King Cole and Sammy Davis Junior. With his mind a myriad regrets and memories, Dick endured a torturous day.

'That was one hell of a job for me,' he said. 'It was a massive cemetery, bigger than Merthyr borough itself, and the office was in a mock Tudor mansion. It was like a bad dream as I sat there, sipping tea from bone china and eating biscuits, while a man with a deep voice gave me his sales talk. "What suit do you want him to wear? What colour complexion do you want him to have? Which way do you want his hair parted?" If I thought this was bad, there was worse to come and he took me into a big hall filled with literally hundreds of caskets. It was like a supermarket for the dead. There were metal ones that would last a thousand years. He pulled up the mattress on one to show how well sprung it was. I thought, who the hell would want padding with springs? In the end, I decided that John was made of Welsh oak and so I chose Californian oak.'

They flew home courtesy of Freddie Laker. A man from the British consulate, Mr Backhouse, carried their bags on to the plane. They were given a secluded part of the jumbo, out of sight of the rubberneckers, and they finally left America six weeks and an eternity late. They had hoped to bring home the world title, but now that was a trivial matter of forgotten value. All they were doing now was bringing home their son. Laker Airlines booked a suite in an airport hotel at Heathrow and ferried the couple there. They laid on tea and sandwiches. 'We were all in there waiting for our parents,' Kelvin recalled. 'When they arrived there was a lot of crying.'

Dick agreed to speak to the media for ten minutes in an effort to appease them. It was a hard time, but he actually found a morsel of solace in being able to talk about his son's achievements. Next to him, Byron Board stood and drifted.

It was raining on the way home. It was a long journey and they decided to go through New Tredegar, the home of the gym where the dream had been born and where his support was strongest, rather than stick to the dual carriageway. They followed the hearse, and Dick let his own mind wander through his memories, glimpsing ephemeral pictures that intensified in colour before vanishing. In one they were travelling back from Evan Taylor's funeral in Bedlinog a few years before.

'When I die I want a funeral with plenty of singing and I want the Welsh flag on my coffin,' John said.

Dick sniffed. 'Don't tell me, John,' he said. 'I'll be long gone before you so you'd better tell your wife.'

Now he realized he would have to do as Johnny had wished, and he wondered about the fickleness of fate, that it could let a 24-year-old die before his 54-year-old father.

'My mind was in turmoil. I was thinking, "How am I going to get the casket through our front door, because the American coffins are so big?" We arrived at Merthyr Parish Church and I wanted to take him home, but they kept telling me that people would be coming to the church to see him. It is the Welsh tradition for the coffin to lie in your front room, but they said he belonged to the people and so they put the casket in the parish church.

'Now my heart ached because the children wanted to see him. I asked them to leave the casket closed, but the children said they needed to see him for one last time. So they removed the lid and they said their goodbyes before the lid was put back in place. We all broke down and cried in the church that night. John stayed there for a few days, and thousands walked past his flag-draped coffin. One little girl from Aberdare put a rose on it.'

As she went through her son's things, Edith came across the little green diary. She read it and wept again, but kept the diary from Dick, fearing it would deepen his despair.

The practicalities of grief did little to lessen the burden and, that night, they discussed who would be the pall-bearers.

'I'm carrying my brother,' Dilwyn said.

'No,' his father replied. 'You'll get too emotional.'

Dilwyn was adamant. 'Dad,' he said with an air of finality, 'I am carrying my brother. I won't let anybody down.'

Jeff Pritchard, Martyn Galleozie, Billy Vivian, Mike Pickett and Ceri Collins, another boxer from Court House, also carried their friend. They had all sparred with him, all knew his power and his resilience, all struggled to accept what had happened.

More than five thousand met beneath another pewter sky. The High Street Baptist Chapel only held seven hundred and fifty, but another three hundred sat in the church hall while a loud speaker relayed the service to the mourners outside. The wreath from his brothers and sisters was shaped like a boxing ring, while his parents' bore the message, 'To our champ, with all our love, Mam and Dad'.

Tom Jones never did get to meet the boxer, but he sent flowers. So did Henry Cooper. Muhammad Ali and Prince Charles sent messages of condolence. Colin Hart and Ken Jones were among the national journalists to travel to Merthyr. The streets were packed as the funeral cortège made its way through Dowlais to the Pant cemetery.

Kelvin looked out of a car window. 'Nothing can comfort you in that situation, but it was wonderful to see how many people held John in such high esteem,' he said. 'Don't get me wrong. Nothing could make you feel better, but it was better that they were there. They lined the route all the way to the cemetery, and the graveyard was black with people.'

The Reverend Herbert Price told the mourners that Owen was a man of courage. 'The measure of a man's life is not the number of years he has lived. It is in the way he has lived them,' he said.

'John had his singing by his grave,' Dick said. 'There were thousands in that cemetery. Then we all got in the cars and went home for a good cry. I told my family that people had come from a long way and we must compose ourselves and thank them all.'

After the funeral Gardiner approached Dick. 'Will you come and be my trainer?' he asked.

'It's not the time or the place,' Dick said, 'but if you can find somebody like Johnny . . .'

Gardiner shook his head. 'You'll never find another Johnny.'

'Then I'll never train again,' Dick said. And he never did.

16

HUMAN DEBRIS

The press coverage was blanket. Even Jim Murray, the renowned columnist who had rejoiced in Johnny's physique, questioned the validity of the sport. In the *LA Times*, he wrote: 'The human debris boxing puts in the mainstream of society is far out of proportion to the numbers who practise it. Proportionately, only a few world wars or plane crashes exceed it.'

At home the debate was reopened. How to justify a sport that is so inherently dangerous? How to validate the violence? How to paper over the graves without demeaning the dead? There had been eleven deaths in British rings in the previous thirty-four years, 421 globally since the Second World War. 'The fault only lies with the game,' stated an editorial in *The Times*. The Mayor of Merthyr said: 'It is rather incongruous that this gentle person should die in such a violent way.' Brad Pye, the chief of the Californian Athletic Commission, added: 'Boxing is a vicious sport, the idea is to knock out your opponent. Every time you enter the ring you have to realize there is a possibility someone may suffer a permanent injury.' Even Patrick McGrath, the physician superintendent at Broadmoor Hospital, had a view. Writing as one 'not unaccustomed to violent or dangerous personalities', he sent a letter to *The*

Times bemoaning these public blood-lettings. 'How many more fit, young men have to join the litany of the dead and grievously injured before this obscene sport is outlawed?'

In Merthyr, Jeff Pritchard searched for his St Christopher medallion. 'I couldn't believe I'd lost it,' he said. 'I always put it on my chair at the gym and I think someone took it. When Johnny died I asked if anyone had seen it, but nobody had. It broke my bloody heart.

'I remember phoning Ivy, Dai's wife, the morning after the fight and asking how he was. She told me he was in a coma. It was so sad. He was such a nice boy. They say there's a God, but who's up there? You couldn't have stopped him going to America. If you get killed you get killed. That's how I felt too. I never thought it would happen to me and I never thought it would happen to Johnny. As a boxer, you think, "As soon as I go in there I'm going to splatter your face to a pulp." It's the same with most contact sports, but there's nowhere where you're more alone than in boxing. It's a hard sport but one I loved. I don't know why.

'When they said he had a thin skull, I thought, Jesus, I could have done it to him. I sparred thousands of rounds with him and this could have happened at any time. Thank God I didn't.

'Ivy phoned me one day and told me Johnny had died. The gym just collapsed. When Johnny died the heart and soul got ripped out. I finished in 1980. I had two or three years left but just couldn't do it after Johnny. Later my son, Sean, started to box so I went back as an amateur trainer. He had six pro fights. They call me Punchy now, but I take that with a pinch of salt.'

Martyn Galleozzie retired on the same night, on a run-of-the-mill professional bill at Wolverhampton Civic Hall. It was 1 December 1980 and both Pritchard and Galleozzie lost their last bouts. It was hardly surprising that their heads were not right, given it was less than a month since the death of their friend. Having been stopped in six rounds by Paul Chance, Galleozzie left the ring for the last time at the age of twenty-six.

'I don't speak about boxing at home,' he said. 'I change the subject if it comes up and I wouldn't let my kids go that way. I had all my plaques, Welsh vests, gloves and trophies at my father's house and, when he died, I said, "Chuck them out." I've got a couple of photos in a scrapbook left. That's all.

'I realized you have to be very, very lucky in boxing to be successful and come out the other side. I fought Tommy Glencross in a professional bout in Solihull and the only thing I remember about that fight is the bell going for the start of the first round. I threw a jab and then the darkness came to light. I was stopped in the first round. The following day I had a terrible headache. I sat talking with my father and my brother. They said I'd got up and gone down three times. I didn't remember anything about it. A total blackout. When I think about it and what happened to Johnny, I know I was lucky.

'When I fought Paul Chance, my eye was torn open. I had six stitches. The referee put his arm around me in the sixth. I was twenty-six and strong as a horse, but my wife was pregnant and my son was due in March. I'd always said if I had children I wouldn't box. I never thought it right to be sitting there with your kids with a normal face one day and to be cut and bruised and scarred the next. It's frightening for them. My kids will never box and neither will my grandchildren if I have any say in it. It was terrible what happened to Johnny and my father was deeply hurt by it. He was a quiet man who didn't show his emotions, but when John died he shut the gym. It took the heart out of him.'

Another of the pall-bearers, Billy Vivian, boxed three days after Johnny took on Pintor. He lost to the unbeaten Micky

Baker, but while his thoughts inevitably stretched out to America, he had no imminent thoughts of retirement.

'I never felt like giving up,' he said. 'It wasn't hard to go on because I wasn't working at the time and I needed the money to pay for Christmas. Calling it off never entered my mind. My wife didn't say anything. We were upset, because Johnny and I had been much more than sparring partners, we'd been great friends, but you need to make a living.

'The funeral was the biggest thing I ever saw in my life. We couldn't carry the coffin because it was a big American one, so they wheeled it out of church. Jeff and I had to run to the graveyard to make sure we were there in time. Merthyr shut down that day.

'It was the following year, December, when I took on Vernon Vanriel up in London. That did it. I was fit, but ended up thinking, what the fucking hell are you doing? That was the end. He beat me up in two rounds. Everyone wants to be a champion, but there's kudos in just being a boxer. I don't put my hand in my pocket when I go back home. It's respect.

'You need to be more than hard. You need to have brains, not in an academic way, but you have to be sharp. I'd have ended up in more trouble without it. It's a cliché, but a lot of boxers have done a bit of bird. Bernard Hopkins is the best fighter in the world in my opinion, but he's been in jail. Every boy should have a try. Schools should give you the opportunity. I believe that, even though I've never been able to watch Johnny's fight with Pintor and even though I well up when I read about him.'

For Dai Gardiner, the impact would be just as telling. 'Dick rang at three in the morning and he was very down. I asked him what was wrong and he told me Johnny had died. I had six months off. I was completely shattered. I couldn't do anything.

I couldn't go shopping or even get out of the house. I was badly depressed.

'One minute he had been getting better and the next he was gone. Work said take as long as you want, but I couldn't have cared less about that. I was devastated. I wondered about whether we should have pulled him out. We couldn't have, but it will prey on my mind for the rest of my life.

'LA was a nightmare. Dick and Edith went to stay with a family, so I was on my own. I had to drive in seven lanes of traffic and I wasn't used to that. My daughter was ringing me saying, "Daddy, when are you coming home?"

'I was a wreck for a while, but some of the other boxers, like Jeff Pritchard, kept ringing me. Going back to work for the gas board helped, but I never ever went back to that gym. I never even went up the same street. There was another gym seventeen miles away. It had burnt down and when it reopened I thought, I owe it to Johnny. He's always in my heart. He was like a brother to my girls and was always in my house. The gas board helped me get all the material to do the gym down the valleys. I dithered for a bit, but thought I needed to prove something to all those who doubted me. I wanted to show I was good enough to get a world champion.

'It changed me for a time. I always feared how I'd react if someone went down. It happened with Jeff Pritchard. He was coming to the end of his career. I had a good word with Jeff and retired him. I saw boys get put on the floor and eventually got used to it. And then they started bringing in brain scans. We had none of that before. Johnny wouldn't have boxed at all if we had. Boxing helped me, but it took me a while to get some good boys.'

One of those was Steve Robinson. Thirteen years after Johnny's death, Gardiner took a man considered a journeyman in boxing circles to the top. The Cardiff fighter had only forty-eight hours' notice that he would be taking on John Davison for the vacant WBO featherweight title on 17 April 1993, when it was found that the champion, Ruben Palacios, had failed an AIDS test. Robinson, who had won just thirteen of his twenty-three pro fights, took the opportunity. He won a decision that proved a cathartic triumph for his trainer, and went on to defend his title seven times before Prince Naseem Hamed humiliated him two years later.

'Steve is working with all my boys now,' Gardiner said. 'I direct him but Steve's a good trainer. It took me two years to get back into boxing. If it's in your blood, that's it, but I'm starting to lose that now. I tried to shake Dick's hand at functions afterwards, but he refused. It's a shame. We were a good team. Life goes on, but I think of Johnny Owen every single day.'

The death of Johnny Owen touched all who knew him, from the family struggling to deal with it, to those who were just interested observers in his recent history.

'I went back to my flat and waited for news,' Idris Sutton, his old amateur trainer, said. 'The punters at the Ukrainian knew about me and Johnny and they commiserated. I watched the TV and was thinking about him. That's what you do. You leave the boxing world but you still feel the thrill. I was with him in the corner. I felt for Pintor too. In that era you knocked someone down but were always concerned about them afterwards. He must have gone through hell and he's going to be haunted for ever.

'I remember being excited the night of the Pintor fight. To think I may have helped in any small way, even if it was just letting him develop his power by hitting me. I was always rooting for John, it was always "That's my boy." When he was ahead on points you felt he was there, but then that bloody punch. Whether it dislodged a clot or whether it was an act of God, who knows? Those looking for excuses blame boxing.

'He'd taken punches on the jaw before. I think his time had come and he was in the ring – there's no other way of putting it. I couldn't get to the funeral because I was working away, so I watched it on television and my sister-in-law kept the cuttings from the paper.

'When we started in boxing, you were the champion of the world, and that was it. Now it's a business. People like Johnny and Howard Winstone fought for peanuts, and I think they did the dirty on Dick. The art of boxing is gone now. They drop their hands, taunt each other and showboat.

'Eventually, I saw Dick again and we chatted. I got a pub around 1990 and sometimes he'd be in there until 3 a.m. and I'd get a call from Edith. We still talk about Johnny now.'

Sutton's partner at the old Hoover gym, Don James, also remembered Johnny with undiluted affection. 'I wasn't very, very close, but I followed his career, like we all did,' he said. 'We moved in the same circles and he'd be at the other side of the room and give that wink and wry smile, just to say everything was okay. That was nice.

'You have to take your chance. Some people said he shouldn't have had a world title shot. If you read the reports I'm not sure Johnny was ahead at the finish, but he'd given a marvellous account of himself. That punch came out of the blue. We all thought Pintor was tired.

'When I heard John was knocked out I thought, "That's bad luck, innit." Then I heard he was in a coma and, as that continued, Merthyr was a very sad place. It hit the town. This is a boxing stronghold – there's a special boxing section in the local library. People loved Johnny Owen. It was a tragedy for his family, a tragedy for the way he lived and a tragedy for mankind. A guy tried so hard to get to the top and, when he got there, the lights got blown out.'

Heddwyn Taylor's bitterness over his perception that he had been wronged over the title fight vanished alongside the tragedy.

'I'm convinced that if Johnny had beaten Pintor, and I'm sure he would have if the fight had been in Wales, then he'd have beaten anybody. I told Johnny that if he won I could foresee a few payments of £75,000. That was a lot of money for a bantamweight. The bigger you are the more money you get and the longer you last. It's the same as a baritone and a tenor.

'I took a fighter from Swansea called Robert Dickie after Johnny. As a promoter you have to concentrate on one man. I did four or five fights and decided I'd done all I wanted. It's a tough old game. I went to Madison Square Garden once and they introduced the great Sugar Ray Robinson. He could barely get in the ring.

'I loved boxing, and Johnny Owen and Howard Winstone were true gentlemen. When Howard was going through bad times I'd slip £50 through his door every Christmas. I did the same with Joey Erskine, a great fighter. Henry Cooper said if Joey had had a knockout punch he'd have been world champion. It's sad that a lot of boxers end up with so little money when they give so much pleasure to so many people. Howard went into property, but he had a lot of hangers-on. The same with Joey. My mam died the same year as Johnny. Snow was belting down on our little terrace house and my mother's body was lying in our home and the front door was open for the bearers. Then I saw a man standing on the other side of the street with just a handkerchief on the top of his head. It was Joey. I asked one of the family to go and tell him to come over and he stayed the night with us.

'I used to be well known in Wales. I'd say I was making £200,000 a year in the 1970s. A lot of money then. I knew Oliver Reed and Sean Connery. I've had an interesting life, but if I could choose which bit I'd like to live over it would be my boxing years.'

The death of Johnny Owen revealed boxing's naked core. It is life stripped to the bone, not just sport. Colin Hart admitted he was deeply affected by what he saw in the Olympic Auditorium that night. He wrote his article for the *Sun*, was told by his editor that it was up to him whether he stayed in LA, and recorded a report for BBC Radio Four. It went out without a musical intro as a mark of respect. 'I nearly gave up afterwards,' he said. 'I thought, if this sport can do this to a kid like Johnny Owen, then is it worth covering? He lived for boxing. Eventually, I thought if I didn't do it then somebody else would. But he was such a nice kid.'

Harry Carpenter was well aware of the impact a ring fatality could have on the steeliest of minds. 'If you have a man die against you then there's no telling what effect it might have,' he said. 'Joe Bugner was always accused of not being fiery enough, but I had the feeling afterwards that Joe held back a little because an opponent had died from injuries sustained in one of his early fights.

'You always knew you were going to have a hard fight if you had a Mexican in front of you, especially if he was world champion, but nobody at the time thought Johnny Owen shouldn't fight Pintor. I mean, he'd done it all apart from the world title in only four years.

'I can understand the arguments for banning boxing. It can

be barbarous, but I've known hundreds of boxers who would have been nothing without it. Boxing took them out of their environment and turned them into respected citizens. It's a very disciplined sport, and that's good for people.

'It's a much more humane sport now than it was fifty years ago. Fifteen-round fights were really too long and took too much out of people, but in Joe Louis's day they fought twenty. I don't go to boxing any more. I'm a has-been. There are too many governing bodies and too many championships. Nobody understands the weights, and that's all down to TV. Governing bodies have sprung up to get money and TV has leeched itself on to boxing. There are too many phoney titles. The public knows that, but you can't stop it.'

Marty Denkin had thirty-eight more world title bouts after he flew to Puerto Rico on the night of Johnny Owen's last fight. Snubbed for two years afterwards, he went on to make the Hall of Fame and become a renowned referee, but he has never forgotten the polite young fighter from Merthyr.

'I've had 168 title fights. The biggest I ever did were in the *Rocky* movies. I did the first fight of the new millennium, and when I got home my mother had died four hours earlier. Boxing was my life for thirty years. I remember there was a fight in Wales once and I begged to go because I wanted to go and visit Johnny's grave. One day me and Johnny Owen will meet up again and I hope he says I did okay.'

Ken Bryant is another who will never be able to erase 19 September 1980 from his memory.

'They came from all over the valleys and beyond for the funeral,' he said. 'We had a job to get through to the church. It was like they were burying royalty and, in a way, they were.

'I stopped boxing after. I'd been looking after the kids for twenty years, but I didn't go down for over a year. They kept asking, when are you coming back, and I'd say maybe next week, in a while, one day.'

On a hilltop outside Merthyr, Jesse Harris is still thankful that Johnny made him go to the hospital when his vision started to go.

'He told me to go because we were sparring and I started to lose the vision in one eye. It frightened the life out of me because boxing is about getting punched in the head under fluorescent tubes. I suffer with headaches now and have got a balance problem in my ear. The doctor said, "I see you used to box." I told him it was nothing to do with boxing and my mother, her twin sister and my brother all had the same problem. But I can't go on the computer now. My daughter's got one, but the screen flickers. I can't play games with kids any more.

'I followed John's career, God, yeah, and I couldn't watch that fight for a long time afterwards. When I did see it I thought John was battering him because his way had always been long distance. It shouldn't have happened, and today it wouldn't have. There were all these people saying he should not have been in with Pintor, but he should. Telling him he couldn't have fought would have been worse. His whole life was geared to that one thing. Knowing him the way I did, what else would he do? His head was totally focussed on that one thing.'

Harris still lives high above Merthyr, the computer screen flickering in the back room, the noise of his family breaking the silence of the dark. He has returned to his roots. He only ever boxed to get off the mountain. By contrast, Johnny Owen boxed to scale it.

The guts were removed from Byron Board that night in the Olympic and his interest in boxing evaporated.

'It's all money now,' he said. 'If I had a heavyweight now

with the same skill and dedication as Johnny, then I'd be a multimillionaire. He was so polite, so humble.'

Board still lives with his wife, Esther, a stone's throw away from where the gym once was.

'What a tragedy, losing your son,' she said. 'When you are in the corner, you are going to wonder if you could have pulled him out. He just wanted to do it for his family, to get them on and give them a better life.'

The Owens family themselves struggled on. Vivian set up a successful taxi firm, while Kelvin ensures his brother's memory survives via a superb website – www.johnnyowen.com. Johnny Owen's legacy was in the £123,250 raised in the wake of his heroism. When the fund closed, it was decided to give the bulk to the Prince Charles Hospital. Two of the region's biggest health concerns – poor eyesight and bronchial complaints – stemmed from its industrial past, and some of the money went to buy new equipment to counter them. There were also two foetal heart monitors, a mammography scanner and a blood gas analyser. The remainder of the fund was ploughed into community projects, from buying a new church organ to helping a diabetic association that Owen had been the president of. It ensured that he would always be remembered in the place that made him.

Johnny's parents had no life cover for their son. After his death, the WBC said his life was insured for $50,000, but Dick and Edith received nothing. One official from American Home Insurance, the San Francisco-based insurers, admitted the policy was, in fact, limited to $25,000 and all medical expenses would be deducted from any possible pay-out. The bill came to $94,000.

As a high-profile tragedy, Johnny posthumously helped

improve the safety of a sport that had flouted safety consider-
ations for so long. CAT scans became the norm, but deaths
continued. In 1980 there were five ring fatalities. In the next
twenty years there were 104. One study claimed there were 1.3
cases of life-threatening injuries for every 10,000 boxers. It was
possible to twist the statistics to fit any argument, but the issue
of intent – that only boxers try to maim an opponent in the
name of sport – lingered like a cancer.

Yet boxing survived, and slowly life returned to normal for
those involved in this story. Dick battled his pain and the rank
and file went back to work and play, hoping there might one
day be another transmitter for their hopes and dreams. And in
Mexico, Lupe Pinto continued to box.

The message went from California to the WBC office in
Mexico and then to the yellow house with the marble floors and
the doorstep cat eyeing the cockerel. The clank and roar of a
truck and the sound of shuffling wings were the mourning song.
Lupe Pintor closed his eyes and his body crumpled beneath a
sigh that sucked the strength from his body. Coti watched her
husband and knew.

'It was extremely difficult,' Pintor remembered. 'Extremely
difficult. A fighter has a very special respect for a fellow fighter,
especially one who proves to be his match in the ring. When he
died it was like I lost a close friend. I was distraught, and
thought hard about my future and life.'

Many writers have since said that Pintor almost quit the
sport in the aftermath and that he was never the same fighter.
It was as if the graphic realization of a killer instinct had left
him bereft of the things that forged it. Lupe Pintor was now the
naked boxer. However, those reports were disingenuous. Pintor
was deeply affected by the death of Johnny Owen, but he never

seriously thought about retiring. Instead, he thought about what had happened and how he must be at his peak for the next fight, another title defence against Alberto Davila. Just five weeks after Johnny died and three months to the day since he had watched the Welshman fall in the bowels of the Olympic, Pintor was back in action.

'Life goes on, and I went straight back to training,' he said. 'I knew I had to get over it. I never really considered stopping and just threw myself back into the gym. I thought about Johnny the whole time. I felt he was with me, pushing me on in every fight. I felt his spirit lifting me and I was carrying him in my heart. It was the right decision.'

It sounds crass and cold, but while the Owens scooped up the pieces of their lives, and as the pictures on the television channels and in the newspapers faded, Pintor went over the fateful fight with a ruthless pragmatism. Johnny had exposed weaknesses in the champion and, for all his success, he knew he needed to improve if he was to win against Davila. Hernandez and Torres knew it too, so they worked their man harder than ever, driving him through sweat and exhaustion.

'It was Johnny's physical condition and mental state that made him carry on,' Pintor said as he reflected on that last round. 'After the first knockdown it was his spirit that took over. It was a hard fight. I couldn't get close to him to wear him down, because as soon as I did my face was getting damaged. So I had to find the space to hit him with one-off knockout punches.

'Johnny probably shouldn't have fought me because his style was more like an Olympic boxer – scoring points, not hard shots, but fast and lots of them. For him to have someone in front of him who was capable of hitting him with hard shots over fifteen rounds in a world championship bout, that was going to tell. Keeping up that rhythm – that endless rhythm – was going to wear him down in the later rounds.'

One day, soon after Johnny had been laid to rest in the Merthyr earth, a telegram arrived at Pintor's house. He read it and his eyes glazed over. LUPE PINTOR STOP YOU ARE A GREAT CHAMPION STOP YOU MUST CARRY ON BOXING IN MEMORY OF JOHNNY STOP FROM RICHARD & EDITH OWENS & FAMILY.

Those simple words expressed the spirit of boxing at its purest. Those who wonder how the bereaved could find such forgiveness when the wounds were so painful ignore the pact made by boxers – an unwritten, unspoken contract.

'It is an agreement,' Pintor said as he tried to explain this exclusive world. 'I believe in God, and I believe you get what's coming to you. It could have been me, and if it had been, there would have been no reason for Johnny or anyone in his corner to feel guilty. Lots of children of all ages die for no good reason, and you ask yourself why. But Johnny died for something marvellous. He died in a fight for life.'

In the months and years after his son's death, Dick would torture himself. It was the natural recourse of the condemned father. He had travelled down the road with Johnny Owen and never once taken the route out when they had come to a crossroads. Perhaps only Dick had the power to stifle his son's talent, to smother it with kindness. But he liked boxing too. And his son was good. But the lip. The lip. And the two knockdowns, the two unheeded warnings.

Pintor can empathize with Dick, and is adamant he should be spared an iota of guilt.

'I never felt that I was at fault,' Pintor said. 'And the beautiful thing is Johnny was fighting for prestige for his family, prestige for his country and prestige for himself. Despite what happened, he got those things. He is now remembered. Even though he died, he got everything he wanted.

'There are many world champions that just come and go. There are many world champions that everyone forgets. Johnny will always be remembered. That is the most important thing. At the end of the day we were both out there fighting for a beautiful life. Fighting for the right to be remembered. Even though he lost the fight and his life, he won that right. We both went into the fight knowing death was a possibility, but we didn't care because we were dying for something we really believed in.'

It was the same when Pintor fought Davila. Johnny Owen hovered over that fight, as the build-up was dominated by dissections of Pintor's mental state. In those few weeks, Pintor ignored the debate about boxing's morality and worked the smoky streets like never before. Twin motivations urged him on – the need to prove something to Johnny Owen, and the desire to avenge his earlier defeat by Davila.

The fourth defence of his world title took place in Caesar's Palace in Las Vegas. It was a big deal: an eagerly awaited rematch between the big-punching champion and the boxing aesthete from the American south-west. In the dressing room, Torres clad Pintor's hands and called him champ, but Pintor's mind was elsewhere. He thought of the telegram and of Dick Owens and the nights spent praying in the hospital chapel.

'That message gave me great support,' he said. 'They told me I had to carry on and they wanted me to fight in memory of Johnny. They told me I was a great champion. It meant a lot to me.

'I'd been beaten by Davila before and was desperate to win. I had so much desire. And I was extremely determined to beat him for Johnny. Everybody thought that I would lose because of my mental state and because of what happened in our first fight, so they all wrote me off. They didn't know I had a special motivation. I felt really confident going into the fight because I'd made a commitment. I had a responsibility to Johnny.'

ONE MORE ROUND

Alberto Davila was not one of those who doubted Pintor. He had been in the Olympic that night too and had prayed for Johnny Owen.

'I liked to go and watch the big fights and he put up a gallant show,' he said. 'I felt terrible, real sick over it. He put up a great effort, real brave, but he didn't have the power and took a lot of punishment. People made much of Pintor's mindset before our fight, but I knew he'd be ready and, if anything, even stronger after what had happened.'

It was Davila's big chance. Twice he felt he had been cheated out of world titles, and those slights rankled, drove Davila on. He kissed Roberta and left for Vegas. He had triumphed against Pintor before and felt sure he could do it again. In his changing room he crossed himself. In her living room, Coti Pintor again watched the television and said: 'Lord protect him with your blessed cloak.'

Well, here we go. Pintor in white trunks, Davila in yellow. The WBC bantamweight title on the line. Pintor, fighting for the first time since the tragic defence against Johnny Owen, knows Davila has already beaten him once. Could be an interesting night.

It was a manic night of hammer and fist. For three rounds Davila used his fast hands and feet to slip Pintor's blows and counter with his own. He spun a web and ensnared Pintor time and again, manoeuvring him around the ring and using his deft right hand to damaging effect. In the fourth Pintor found his range and drove the *gauncho* into Davila's teak-coated liver, but he was cut in the fifth, reopening the split in his brow Johnny Owen had created, and was in serious trouble by the end of the round.

He had not been worried when his first huge right hand had struck Davila firmly on the jaw. This was boxing. Fate could not be that cruel.

'I never ever thought that it could happen again,' he explained. 'The only thing I thought was it could happen to me if I didn't prepare myself properly. It gave me the heart to always be in the best possible condition.'

Davila breathed in. The water swished around his mouth. He spat it out and bit on his gumshield. He stared straight ahead and narrowed his eyes at the sweating brown hulk across the ring. The sixth, seventh and eighth were tight affairs, Davila's quicker punch and higher work-rate impressing the judges, while Pintor's busy mid-sections, all upper-cuts and devilish combinations, counted too. John Beyrooty was impressed. He had written much about Pintor and Johnny Owen in recent weeks, forced into defending the sport as it came under repeated attack, and was happy to see his favourite fighter back. And this was a classic. 'Pintor-Davila was one of the greatest bouts I ever covered,' he said. It was the ultimate boxer-slugger match-up.'

You would not want to predict a winner at this stage. It's a gruelling fight, both men landing good shots and both men having to take punishment. Pintor's blows are heavier, Davila's more stylish.

Pintor nailed Davila in the ninth, but he ran and recovered and the fight oozed desire, will and brutality. Nobody doubted that Davila had more grace, but Pintor was strong and his innate reservoir was deep. The late rounds were his time.

'Things changed when they made fights twelve rounders instead of fifteen,' Beyrooty said. 'Rounds thirteen to fifteen really separated the fighters.'

Like Owen, Pintor loved the long haul, the pain and the drudgery.

It was enough to get him the tightest decision. Duane Ford scored the bout a draw, but Anselmo Escobedo and Angel Tovar gave it to the champion by one and four rounds respectively.

Davila, in intense pain now that his body had stopped fighting, felt physically sick. Not again.

'I feel in my heart I won the fight,' he said. 'Maybe nine or ten of the fifteen rounds. But in the thirteenth I realized I couldn't catch a second wind. He came on and I slowed down. You know what I mean, I was looking for the bell in those last rounds. I was devastated.

'You know, the funny thing was, from the time I beat him to our second fight, he hardly ever talked to me. He seemed to be mad at me and I guess he was. After that, though, he was friendly. He's a great guy.'

Coti switched off the television set, and Pintor smiled. Some in Vegas might have seen him cast a fleeting glance heavenward.

'If I had lost that night it would have been the most destructive moment in my whole career,' he said. 'It was a pivotal moment in my life because once I beat him it gave me the strength to carry on. I wanted to do it for me and Johnny, and suddenly I knew I could.'

17

BROTHERS (2)

When the novelty of his physique is removed, Johnny Owen could be seen as just another boxer who died for his sport. He was not an Ali or a Chavez or a Wilde. He was just another naked boxer, another statistic on the files. Yet he was much more too. Though he never became rich through his popularity or was fêted globally for his skills, he was a reminder that the sport could wear a dignified, respectable face. When the Mexicans threw cups of urine and when the British showered Marvin Hagler with bottles after he beat Alan Minter at Wembley ten days later, they threw into relief the untainted principles of Johnny Owen. He did it the right way and he touched all he met, not only with his genius but with his genuineness.

Twenty years passed. And then, in 2001, Graham Walters, the flag bearer and loyal supporter, was talking with some friends after a Joe Calzaghe fight. The name of Johnny Owen came up. It was decided, there and then, to build a statue.

Not long before, Walters had bumped into Dick in Merthyr. The intervening years had been hard on the bereaved father. About a year after Johnny's death, Kelvin had told his father that he would start boxing again, thinking it might work as some sort of therapy, but Dick had seen through the good-

natured gesture. He tried to concentrate on the rest of his
life, but it was not always possible. His mind would fly back
to Los Angeles, and his marriage strained beneath the burden
of unshakeable memories. He drank in Idris Sutton's pub and
watched the rest of his children grow, always wondering what
would have happened to John, always missing his quiet
presence.

'They've forgotten my boy,' he said to Walters.

When Walters phoned Dick to tell him they wanted to build
a statue and had set an initial target of £35,000, the father cried.
An appeal was launched and Walters and his associates proved
indefatigably resourceful as they placed an ad in the paper for a
sculptor and set about raising the money.

'We started selling T-shirts and photographs,' he said. 'Our
daughters went around with buckets. The money came from the
Isle of Wight to Australia. I got a ten-guilder note from the
Netherlands. You know, it would have cost more to change it.
A band, Sugarhouse, did two shows for us. Some boy, just out
of work, said he only had a couple of quid but we could have
half and he sent a pound. It took two years, was a labour of
love and, to be quite frank, it cost all us who were involved
money, but it was an honour to do it for Johnny Owen.'

It would be the third boxing statue in Merthyr after those
honouring Eddie Thomas and Howard Winstone. In truth, there
should have been a fourth, but nobody had seen fit to honour
Jimmy Wilde, the best of the lot. All that was left was for
someone to unveil it. They bandied various names about, the
great and good of Merthyr, boxing celebrities, Welsh stars and
Dick Owens himself. And then Dick suggested Lupe Pintor.

He had often wondered what had become of Pintor, but
could never have guessed the intrigue and traumas of the interim
years.

Pintor's reign as champion was anything but smooth, and the king had suffered his inevitable fall. He spent his money on cars and horses and, according to Coti, other women.

'A girl over here, a girl over there,' she claimed. 'I realized what was going on and became bothered by it.'

Coti also claims the money began to dry up. A few ill-judged investments added to the friction of their home life, and they became mere co-habitants.

The next defence was against Jose Uziga, a rising star but one most people expected to be beaten soundly by the champion. Yet the fight at the Houston Coliseum went the distance and dragged Pintor through a mire of acute agony. Uziga managed to evade a flurry of rights in the sixth round, but one that glanced off his head contorted the champion's face.

'I broke the fourth metatarsal in my right hand,' Pintor said. 'I wasn't ready to lose the crown in such a stupid way, so I shut up and continued to throw punches, round after round, until the bell rang and it was over. Towards the end the pain was practically unbearable.'

Pintor shuffled to the referee's right so that, when he lifted his hand, he would hoist the left. It was a lop-sided, easy decision, but the fight took its toll.

'I got back to the dressing room and you can't imagine the size of the yelp when they took the bandage off.'

Hernandez knew a broken hand could end a career in an instant. At the very least, it would limit his power and lead to an enforced lay-off. He wanted to keep Pintor busy because he was at the peak of his powers, the money was good and the drama that surrounded him made him hugely marketable. He called Dr Plutarco Gatica, a leading surgeon, who studied the break. That night his forearm was put in plaster.

'You need to take a total break from exercise,' Gatica said.

Pintor did as he was told for three days. He stayed in bed and watched television, but the boredom drove him to distraction, so he sauntered down to the Atlas one afternoon and watched his friends go through their paces. Torres hugged him, but his expression soured when Pintor said he wanted to box.

'You can't, man,' Torres pleaded. 'You know what the doctor said.'

'But I need to,' he replied. 'I can tie my arm to my body with bandages and just use my left.'

'You're going to get me in trouble.'

'Come on Tony. Help me out.'

So they tied his right arm to his body and Pintor went to work on the punchbag.

At first it was just an outlet, but Torres quickly realized the routine was sharpening Pintor's left hand. Without the power of his right hook, he added speed, steel and accuracy to his left.

'I spent two months like that, shadow-boxing with just one hand,' he recalled. 'When I next defended my title, against Jovito Rengifo, five months after the fracture, I gave him a thorough going over with one hand. I knocked him out in the eighth. My right hand help up pretty well, but it became common for it to cause me trouble again and I ended up with more fractures. Luckily, I had a new weapon now, which was so powerful it became legendary.'

That is no hollow boast. Pintor did, indeed, become renowned for possessing one of the best left hands in the business, but his right was now flawed. He was also having problems making the 118 pound limit. On 3 June 1982, three years to the day since he had beaten Zarate to take the title, Pintor won a unanimous points decision against Seung Hoon Lee on his return to the Olympic Auditorium. By now he was considering his future and, having made eight successful defences, Pintor decided he wanted to step up in weight to the super-bantamweight class. He wanted to become a double world champion, and he wanted Wilfredo Gomez. And so, with one warm-up bout against Jorge Lujan under his belt, Pintor flew to the Superdome in New Orleans. And that was when the trouble really started.

Pintor weighed in for the fight at 121½ pounds, almost four pounds above his fighting best as a bantamweight. The additional ballast gave him extra power, but diminished his speed and agility. Nevertheless, the crowd in Louisiana witnessed one of the great fights. Some had come to watch Tommy Hearns, an American hero, take on Wilfred Benitez for the light middleweight title, but Pintor and Gomez stole the show. It was punishing, debilitating fare, especially for a man with a handicapped right, but Pintor wrought unprecedented damage on Gomez's face. His features were deformed and defiled, his eyes dykes in jellied tissue, but he summoned up some inveterate courage to floor Pintor in the fourteenth. 'I like to think that what I did was try to complete a masterpiece, and I don't regret how it ended at all,' Pintor said. 'There was some learning done, having lost a fight when I boxed better than ever. I learned that there's not even a whiff of defeat if you give everything you have, do your best and are aware that you have done so.

'People said I was too stubborn and obsessed with getting a knockout. They say that's why I lost. Maybe so. Without a doubt I could have taken the fight by going the distance in those final rounds, because my points advantage would have been too great. I don't think he thought I was going to go down when he unleashed that punch and that he was going to win. He didn't know where he was.'

Pintor left with his head held high, although a malicious rumour that the outcome had been determined by Mob influence began to circulate.

'I didn't throw the fight with Wilfredo,' Pintor insisted. 'Who in their right mind could think I'd try to fix a bout that could have opened the door to million-dollar purses? I'd have needed to be very foolish indeed. The truth is that guy had two hands, two feet, a brain and he could hit like no other boxer I ever faced. His image was of a cocky and conceited guy, but that was all the work of Don King. Wilfredo was, in fact, a really friendly person, generous and kind. Above all, his heart was in the right place.'

Pintor returned to Mexico without the title, and to an irreparable marriage. Coti's gripes about money increased and they existed in a state of shared distrust. Pintor was certainly not careful with his wealth, and bought a Kawasaki motorbike to add to his collection of sports cars. It had been his childhood dream to own a huge motorcycle, like the ones he had marvelled at as a boy. Then it had been a pipe dream for an ice seller; now it was a reminder of his triumph over life.

While out riding his Kawasaki one day, he spotted a girl at a bus stop. He pulled in to the side of the road and shouted: 'Hey, *nena*, you fancy a ride on my bike?'

The girl bristled at his arrogance.

'No way,' she sniffed, and watched incredulously as the man and machine shrank into the distance.

Coti alleged that things got even worse in the last days of their marriage.

'Money was always our problem,' she said. 'He only just gave me enough to eat and didn't give me anything for a good breakfast or a nice dinner. He says it's not true, but I lived it, felt it and, God knows, it's true. He bought me clothes when he got back from a fight, and that was meant to last me my whole life.'

Unbeknown to Coti, Pintor had become friendly with the parents of the young girl he had spotted while out riding. They were boxing fans and they loved talking to the former champion about his career and his fights. And the young girl came to realize that there was a soft centre beneath the front. She listened too, found herself being drawn to this man's power, and then, without her parents' knowledge, agreed to accompany the boxer on a date.

'You want to get some breakfast?' had been his chat-up line.

Pintor arrived an hour late. The girl, Virginia, noted how handsome he was, but also realized from his red eyes that he had slept in. He drove to Desierto de los Leones and, to her immense surprise, proposed.

'He never wasted any time,' she recalled.

After her surprise had faded sufficiently for her to declamp her jaw, she said: 'But you are already married.'

Pintor looked at her with his deep brown eyes. 'So what?'

The rain came and soaked them. Pintor invited Virginia back to his house to dry off and, while suspicious of the nature of his intentions, she accepted. Pintor handed her warm clothes and she left, her mind a potpourri of emotions, excited by the proposal, seduced by his charm, comforted by his gentlemanly demeanour and terrified of telling her parents.

Pintor was not looking forward to that himself, but after a week's courting went to meet Virginia's father.

'Listen, Rueben,' he began 'I want to have a chat about something, to make sure you think it's okay.'

'What is it?'

'Well.' Pintor swallowed and spoke quickly. 'I'm going out with your daughter.'

Rueben did not bat an eyelid. He remained silent for what seemed an eternity, and then said calmly: 'And what's wrong with that?'

Pintor realized that Rueben had misunderstood him. The old man had several daughters and was clearly not thinking of Virginia.

'No . . . well . . . I'm going out with your youngest daughter.'

A look of utter bemusement now flooded the old man's face. 'How can you be?' he said, almost to himself.

'I've been seeing her for a week,' Pintor started. 'I didn't want to hide anything from you.'

Rueben liked Pintor and understood Mexican men. He smiled softly. 'To be honest, I'm a man and I sympathize. But I don't know how prepared Virginia is for this. I'm not going to bawl you out, but I'm going to talk to her mother. Then we'll chat.'

Among the things to discuss was the fact Pintor was twenty-nine and Virginia barely sixteen.

That and the small matter of Coti.

Virginia's parents were sympathetic enough to take Pintor in when his life derailed shortly after the Gomez fight.

'I had just got in from the gym when the phone rang,' he said. 'I picked it up and it was my buddy saying, "Champ, I need you to pick me up and give me a hand because they want to take me to the nick." How could I refuse? But I never got there.'

The next time the telephone rang in the house, Coti answered and heard the strangled voice of her husband.

'I need you to get in the car and come over here,' he said. 'I've been hit.'

Coti did as she was told. She took the road to Toluca and

reined in her spiralling thoughts by reminding herself Pintor was at least well enough to make the call. Then she saw the squad car and the ambulance. She got out and saw her husband sprawled on the side of the road.

'Virgen Santa!' she cried.

Her husband had already seen her through a bloody eye. 'Help me,' he whispered. 'I'm picking up my teeth here.'

Her mercy mission notwithstanding, Coti's marriage to Pintor was over, and he moved in with Virginia's parents as he began his rehabilitation. He had been lucky to survive the crash after his Kawasaki slammed into the side of a car, but his jaw was crushed. It meant he did not fight for fourteen months, had three major operations and was forced to relinquish his bantamweight title.

'I mashed my jaw and arms and was in hospital for almost a year,' he said. 'The papers all said I was going hell for leather, but if I'd really been going as fast as they said then I'd have died.'

The accident reopened the door for Alberto Davila. After losing his third world title shot against Pintor, he had fallen out of love with boxing. Benny Georgino, his manager, had looked Davila in the eye soon after his disappointment in Vegas.

'Albert,' he said. 'It's not going to happen.'

'Whatever I do, Benny, whatever I do, I don't get the verdict.'

The look in the manager's eye went beyond sympathy. There was meaning and instruction in it, and so Davila quit. Young, gifted and washed-up.

He took a job driving for Coors Brewery.

'It was hard, physical work,' he said. 'Wherever I went, people would say, "Hey, you not boxing any more?" That was tough. I did it for a year and then I came around to thinking,

"Why?" I thought, "You know, I'm still young. This is wrong."
I felt I had so much more to give and I still felt I'd won the
Pintor fight.'

He spoke to Roberta and she understood. Then he called
Georgino.

'Sure, Albert,' he said. 'I'll help you if you really want to
come back.'

After thirteen months off, while still working at the brewery,
he came back at the Showboat Hotel in Vegas. The old fire was
there, the skills undiminished. And so he toiled, the thrill of the
dream negating the bad memories. He took six fights in 1982
alone and closed in on the endgame.

The bantamweight title was declared vacant as Pintor had
surgery on his mangled jaw and, when Davila beat Artemio
Ruiz in April, the stage was set for a fourth title bid. Davila's
place in the ring was a testimony to his past glories as much as
his recent wins.

His opponent that night would be Francisco Bejines. Everyone called Bejines 'Kiko'.

Almost three years to the day since Johnny Owen had
entered the Olympic, Davila was there in the same modest
dressing room, with its stale air and roof dripping conden-
sation, silently thinking of winning. Only winning. He knew
he could beat Kiko, but he knew that he had been robbed
before. If only it would all come right on the night. If only.
It was a big if.

By the end of the eleventh, one judge had the fight even,
while the others had Bejines winning by two and five points
respectively. Davila needed a big finish. Kiko was tiring, the
effects of a long lay-off catching up with him. The Olympic
Auditorium was a snarling cesspit of bias. It throbbed with
the sweaty sabre-rattling of hopes and dreams. Kiko ignored the

savage mien of the hateful crowd. This was his moment, this was his destiny. Then, blackness.

'I caught him real bad in the twelfth,' Davila said. 'He went down and I was so happy. I'd achieved my dream, the dream I'd had since I was a kid. I was celebrating and the place was going mad. And then I saw him struggling.'

Bejines had hit his head on the rope as he fell under a flurry of hard, accurate blows from Davila. The referee, Waldemar Schmidt, started counting. Bejines did make it to his feet, but Schmidt counted him out. Then Bejines fell again.

'I couldn't get carried away,' Davila said. 'I went to the hospital to see him. I remember leaving and trying to find my friends to celebrate with, but by that time it was late and nobody was around. I went for a meal with Roberta. It was strange. I'd become the world champion, it was everything I'd ever wanted, and it was bitter-sweet because of what happened. To have that glory snatched away.'

Bejines lasted three days on Hope Street before he died from his head injuries. Davila was a constant part of the vigil, spending much of his time in the same chapel where Pintor had prayed for Johnny Owen.

'It was hard when he passed away,' he said, his voice softening to a whisper. 'This was something I'd been working so hard for. Why do these things happen? You wonder that over and over again. All sorts of things go through your mind. You strive so hard and then things work out this way. I did this for me and my family, to better myself, so why? It was the biggest night of my life and I got all I wanted, but none of it mattered. I enjoyed it for about twenty seconds.'

Like Pintor, Davila fought in the same Olympic ring where a tragedy had unfolded beneath his fists within a matter of months. However, whereas Pintor felt the need to carry on,

Davila's heart chilled. The WBC stripped him of the title the following year due to his inactivity. Now, still married to Roberta, he works as a maintenance man for an air-conditioning firm. He appeared on television several times in the ensuing years and said how he regretted what happened and how he wished he could turn back the clock. He joined Pintor on the list of gruesome statistics – those boxers whose fists had caused another man's death.

Shortly after Bejines's death, Pintor had another operation on his jaw. With the media dismissing the champion and reclaiming him for the ordinary, his marriage stuttered to its messy conclusion. He set up a business with Virginia selling exhausts and mufflers – Mofles Pintor. According to Coti, that led to more problems, to the extent that the house she lived in was going to be repossessed because of an unpaid debt. Pintor told her to let the bailiffs have it, but she said she had nowhere to go. She claims she even locked herself and her son, Lupe, inside and only emerged when Pintor had promised to pay off the debt by selling two trucks. Money, though, was a matter of enduring concern.

'When he met that young girl, he started to spend it all,' Coti insisted. 'He started to sell up. He'd come in and tell me to sign papers because he was selling some plot of land. I'd say "Yes but give me a part of it."'

With both his personal and professional lives in trouble, Pintor hit his nadir. The papers wallowed in his decline, alleging that he was drinking too much and getting into sporadic trouble in bars. Eventually, his divorce came through and he was free to marry Virginia, but even that did not signal an immediate end to his problems.

'It was a rough patch and we lived like gypsies,' Virginia said.

The judge had said that Pintor and his first wife should share their assets, but added that Pintor had already spent his, so Pintor and Virginia lived a nomadic life in a string of homes, spending increasing periods with Virginia's parents. Even so, they tried to start a family of their own, but that endeavour was also plagued by difficulties and three months into her first pregnancy Virginia fell violently ill.

'I had a fever and my fingernails began to turn purple,' she said. 'Guada arrived home, grabbed hold of me and took me to the clinic. He took me from my parents' house on the back of his motorbike. My mother went a bit pale at that.'

At the hospital, the Pintors were told that the foetus had died a week earlier. Virginia would suffer two more miscarriages. They were tragedies that meant Pintor could empathize even more with how Dick Owens had felt in losing a son. It was a terrible parallel and he turned to his religion to survive it. His religion and his boxing.

He came back on 16 February 1984. He had been a professional for ten years.

It had been a decade of drama – the high of dethroning Zarate tempered by the low of Johnny Owen, the revenge against Davila by the enervating pain of Gomez. He had broken his hand and shattered his jaw, suffered the slings and arrows, but he was still only twenty-nine. Now he was fighting again. 'I still had a lot of energy,' he said. 'I felt the urge to fight and I wanted to prove to people that I could still do the business. I wanted to make the most of my life.'

He thought about the ice, the mayo jar, the night when Francisco had been held aloft by his fingertips. He thought about the beatings, the street and his mother. Of watching those crackly TV bouts with Francisco and his father. He thought of his children and his legacy.

'One fighter who always impressed me was Rocky Marciano,' he said. 'More than a warrior, the guy was like a hurricane, a madman, a bull. He only knew how to come forward, and he always ended up annihilating his opponents. Very few retire as world champion, but he did, and undefeated too.'

Pintor wanted to bow out at the top like Marciano, and that meant getting back into the ring. It would not be easy, given the injuries he had sustained, but Pintor craved the super bantamweight crown. To be a two-time champion, at different weights, after all he had been through, would be a noble achievement. So he returned to the Olympic, his spiritual home, and beat Ruben Solorio on points. In eighteen months he took six fights, a rigorous schedule for any comeback, and one which showed him he was not the fighter he had been.

'The quality of the other boxers had gone down, but youth was not on my side any more,' he said. 'I realized I wasn't the same.'

It was also hard to harness the fire after so many private wars. Mofles Pintor, the exhaust business he had set up with Virginia on the Acapulco coast, was a comforting distraction. They would open early and close early, watching the sunset together on the Caleta beach. The extra pounds he piled on were covered by the higher limit of the super bantams. Past his best, and settling into a contented home life, Pintor's record and reputation were nevertheless enough to land him another shot at the title. He had won six, drawn one and lost one. The defeat had come at the Olympic against Adriano Arreola, an LA boxer who had won on the undercard of the Pintor–Owen bout; the referee had been Marty Denkin. Life went on.

It was autumn 1985, three weeks to fight night, Tony Torres, Pintor's trusty trainer, went for a drink in the El Negrito bar in the Guerrero colony. The Atlas gym was only eight blocks away and some of the old boxers, Alfonso Zamora among them, drank there. Torres supped a beer and chatted to the barman before joining his friends. Torres was a popular figure, warm and excitable. Nobody has ever determined what happened and there was never an arrest, but it is clear Torres got into an argument. He was shot in the chest and died on the scene, another statistic in a country where life was cheap.

For Pintor, it was another motivation.

'I loved Tony,' he said. 'When I fought Kid Meza I knew I had to win, just as with Johnny. I was doing it for them. It hit me very hard, but that's the beautiful thing about boxing. You fight for a cause. You fight for your culture, the way you live your life, other people. There's nothing I would like more than to die in the ring. When boxers come together it is like titans clashing, and that is why people die. So I would have loved to have died in a great fight, right there in the ring, because that is where I felt most special.'

So when they left the car washes and the sweat-shops and the dusty barrios and piled into the Palacio de los Deportes in Tijuana, Pintor, by a vicious quirk of fate, was again fighting for the dead.

Juan 'Kid' Meza presented a daunting obstacle for Pintor. He had won forty-three of his forty-nine bouts and had a powerful punch. He had won the title after Gomez vacated it to move up to the featherweight division, and was tall and rangy. Most reasoned that this fight would be too much for a man on the comeback trail. Jose Camarillo, the boxing writer for *Esto*, recalled that Pintor was an almost sad figure at the weigh-in.

'The truth is he never made the 122 pound limit for the Kid Meza fight,' he claimed. 'Pintor was dried and exhausted, so Cuyo Hernandez begged Meza and his trainer, Jimmy Montoya, to ignore the excess. Jose Sulaiman, the WBC president, said it was up to them. Meza and Montoya thought Pintor was the living dead, so they said yes. And Pintor went on to give one of the best performances of his life.'

Meza had been concerned enough by Pintor's legend to ask for the judges not to be Mexican. Pintor was still a national icon, and Meza reasoned that he could not get a fair verdict from a Mexican jury. He was a champion himself, and had been born in Mexico before basing himself in LA, but Pintor's story had inspired the working classes. Meza was not prepared to take any chances.

Just as he had done five years earlier, Pintor sat in the changing room and thought of the departed. Then it had been Johnny Owen who occupied his thoughts, now it was Torres. The funeral had been difficult. The confusion over his murder made it hard to move on and find peace. All Pintor could do was fight and show Torres that all his hard work had not been in vain.

For four rounds Pintor slumped against the ropes, holding his arms tightly in front of his face and absorbing blows. The writers who had picked Meza to win by a stoppage looked like they were going to be proved right. And then came the fury. A left uppercut and a right cross staggered the champion. Pintor saw the opportunity and made sure the next left thundered into Meza's jaw. He fell to the canvas. Meza rose at eight and Pintor, urged on by the crowd, stalked him with the scent of blood in flared nostrils. Another left and right sent Meza sprawling to the floor again. The bell prolonged the agony.

The punches had wrought their damage, and Meza's strength was dripping away as the fight progressed, but he still won the seventh, eighth and ninth. In the tenth Pintor felled Meza for a third time. Uproar. Pintor's body ached and he was breathing hard, the extra weight and the days in Acapulco telling, but the sight of Meza struggling to beat the count was the best cure. The champion was game and brave. Somehow he hung on and, although his punches were now barren tokens, Pintor could not stop him. It went the distance, the full twelve rounds. The judges gave Pintor the verdict.

Suddenly, the decision to allow the fight to go ahead, despite the concerns about Pintor's weight, looked careless. Sulaiman's passive role in the decision did little for the sport's reputation, but Pintor had achieved the remarkable.

'To win in such a way gave me a lot of satisfaction,' he said. 'But even though I had passed the test I had set for myself and completed the objective, I knew my career was finished. The most important thing as a man is to understand and accept when you can't do certain things. I knew that night my career was finished. It was over.'

It was over, but he had already signed a deal to fight Samart Payakaroon in Bangkok. He wanted to emulate Marciano and bow out as the reigning champion, but money talked. He beat Billy White in a warm-up and then made the trip to the east in January 1986. It was a disaster. At the weigh-in, the Thai official claimed Pintor was over the limit. A row broke out, but the WBC delegate agreed. Pintor could not make the weight and therefore he would be stripped of the title. It was a farce, and one that meant he stepped into the ring knowing his career was over and having already lost his belt.

'There was a lot of pressure from the promoters to carry on with the fight because they had sold all the tickets,' he said. It was not surprising that, in those circumstances, he lost. When he was knocked down in the fifth, he still had something left, but his disillusionment left him on the floor.

'You can count to a hundred,' he said to the referee 'I'm not getting up.'

Some were not surprised. The previous year Camarillo, who topped up his income from working on *Esto* by doubling as Pintor's interpreter, had accompanied Pintor on a flight to Bangkok for the WBC annual convention. It was an eventful flight. Flustered after losing a diamond ring in the toilet, Pintor asked for a second meal. 'I always eat a lot,' he told a surprised Camarillo. The dedication was no longer what it had been in 1980.

'I knew I was finished, but I was a professional so I had to go to Thailand,' Pintor recalled. 'But when I got there these people were really dirty. They cheated me on the scale, so when I got into the ring I had a sense of injustice and lost motivation. My manager did not pay enough attention to what was going on at the weigh-in. They had robbed me of my title and I knew I was going to retire. I could have gone on another three years if it hadn't been for the motorbike crash, but on that night, for the first time, I didn't care if I won or lost.'

It was a sorry epilogue. In 1986 Pintor retired, turned his back on boxing and threw himself into his businesses. There was an inevitable void. Having been the idol of thousands in Mexico, he now sold mufflers. He had no regrets, but acclimatizing to the non-rarefied atmosphere was hard. For a while, they lived in Acapulco, where Pintor had often gone after his fights.

'Towards the end of my career my eyebrows were paper-thin,' he said. 'They nearly always split open, so after each bout I had to go and rest on a beach somewhere because wounds heal quicker at sea level.'

Champions rise and fall. Idols are supplanted and fade to half-memories. Pintor had to cope with being normal, an ice-seller turned muffler man. It was not always easy. A few years after his retirement Cuyo Hernandez died. Carlos Zarate was on the street, Johnny Owen was no more. The payments to Coti meant he did not have a life of luxury, although he was comfortable enough. He and Virginia moved back to Cuajimalpa, where the iron doors protecting his house were daubed with graffiti. The WBC belt sat unseen in the back of his cocktail cabinet.

Finally, in 1992, Virginia gave birth to a son. They named him Diego, after Diego Maradona, Pintor's favourite footballer. A year later Alexis followed, named in honour of Alexis Arguello, Pintor's friend and a world champion at three different weights. By the time Lupe junior arrived, in 1999, Pintor had made an ill-fated boxing comeback.

'I was having some trouble and had personal problems at the time,' he said. 'I needed the money and needed a way to let loose.'

So Pintor did what so many do and what he had told himself he must not – he came back, deceived by his legend and believing he could mould another extraordinary chapter and test another dream.

'I quickly realized that I'd chosen well to retire,' he said. 'There was nothing there for me any more.'

He actually fought for two more titles, the WBC Fecarbox lightweight and light welterweight crowns, but by now boxing was a fractured business, with devalued belts, a plethora of governing bodies and an absence of stars. They were messy, sad affairs. The end came on 21 July 1995 against Russell Mosely when Pintor was stopped in two rounds in Tijuana. He went home, hung up his gloves and became another ex-pro.

RESOLUTION

Two boys loitered on the corner of Milan Avenue, where cherry blossom and lavender were scattered on the pavement like confetti. Lupe Pintor parked his car, shook hands with his charges and went inside. The brown windows were cracked or shattered and the Virgin Mary had long faded to sepia on her perch in the corner. This was where it happened. This was his delivery room.

'Tempo,' he shouted, and the boys stopped. They spat out their gumshields and he squirted water into their gaping mouths. One gave him a smile, but Pintor knew he was nervous. The following night he had a fight; even those blessed with God-given gifts and inflatable egos have doubts. There were no showers, and the boy left for work at his father's shop. The thick-soled, heavy boots that he had danced in throughout the session were the same ones he would wear during the afternoon shift. Then, tomorrow, he would go to the Boxeo Coliseo and wonder.

Pintor drove home, tapping the customized chrome pedals with crocodile skin shoes. His eyes were hidden by Ray-Bans but the thick, bulbous hands betrayed his previous life. He was forty-six and, despite the nascent paunch was still a picture of health. It was 2002, and he knew that later that morning, he would have a visitor. Dick Owens was coming to see him. After twenty-two years they would meet again.

Dick still had his heart set on seeing Pintor unveil the statue to Johnny in the centre of Merthyr, but the first reunion had come out of the blue via a BBC documentary team, who wanted to make a film about the Merthyr Matchstick. Part of the film would see Dick travel to Mexico to meet Pintor. For Dick it was the perfect opportunity to deliver his invitation by hand. And that is how he came to be standing in front of graffiti-splattered iron doors in Cuajimalpa on a dust-dry day, alone with his hyperactive thoughts and bleary-eyed nostalgia.

He was tired from the flight. It had been hard to relax and he had kept drifting back into the past. But now they were here. It was hot and clammy and foreign. He checked with the producer, who wanted him to walk down the cracking road to the iron gates. Dick did as he was told. It was contrived, yet it was real. Inside, Pintor had showered and changed into a shirt. Then he heard the knock and kissed Virginia. He walked out into the courtyard and opened the gates to be met by a redder, older face, but nevertheless an unmistakable one. They hugged and went inside.

'I was nervous standing outside that gate,' Dick said. 'Then it opened slowly and there he was. It was difficult because we couldn't speak without an interpreter, but I think we were both happy. He was a nice man. Nothing was too much trouble. I felt better for having met him. I realized he was a decent person who had made something of his life. We fell into each other's arms and drank two bottles of whisky. He told me he had been carrying Johnny around in his heart all these years.'

Pintor was relieved too.

'The WBC got in touch with me and told me he was coming.

I was a bit worried at first about seeing him because of what had happened, but when I saw him, he was exactly the same guy that I remembered from all those years ago. Even though he told me he had some problems with depression, I believe in God and, eventually, that you get what you deserve. I don't know what faith Richard has, but if you fight for what you believe in and stay true, you will get rewarded for it. It is something life gives you, but you have to know how to value it.'

Pintor took Dick to see his young fighter in action the following day. For the Mexican, it was a chance to impress Dick with his stable, but his guest's mind was elsewhere. This was the first time he had been to a fight since Johnny had reached for the world title in 1980. Then Dick had been a middle-aged man. Now he was well into his seventies. His thoughts were jolted into the present when he was introduced to the crowd and applauded. It made Dick realize that the ugliness of the Olympic Auditorium was not the benchmark for Mexican sports fans; that, for all the vitriol imbedded in his memory it had been just one venue, one night and one way of behaving.

'It was bloody hard watching it, but at the end of the day I loved boxing and so did John,' he said.

In a flash it was time for Dick to go home. The documentary detailing the trip, *The Long Journey*, would win a BAFTA. Life returned to normal for a while. Lupe worked at the gym, alongside one of his sons. In the afternoons he sometimes took a trip with Virginia to Coyocan Park and ate ice-cream. Every week he would drive out of town, leaving the tumult of Mexico City behind, flanked by a reef of favelas and a hazy volcano, and lay flowers on his mother's grave. Then he would go to Faustino y Alicia's Consomme Barbecue stall in the covered market, watch the football cackling in the corner and eat his tacos. The woman behind the stall had metal teeth and gold eye-shadow and still called him 'champ'.

But the more important part of the reunion was still to come. Before leaving Mexico, Dick had asked Pintor to make a return trip and unveil Johnny's statue. Pintor had instantly agreed, but was unsure about the reception he would receive in Wales. After all, Johnny Owen had been a national hero and an icon. He arrived with Virginia on a rainy day in November. He met Dick and the family, and that was a difficult time. Kelvin had wondered whether he would even be able to shake Pintor's right hand.

'That was the one that delivered the fatal punch, so I was worried,' he said. 'But when it came to it I shook his hand without any hesitation. I was glad he had come.'

Shereen was also upset by the meeting, something Virginia could understand.

'She was really young at the time when it happened, and it must have affected her very strongly,' she said. 'We could appreciate that. Initially, we felt a bit of cold, a bit of rejection, but they began to warm to us more and more.'

Pintor could see that his presence must have induced a range of emotions in the minds of Dick and Edith and their children. He hoped that his visit proved enlightening, that it conveyed the ugly, simple truth that boxing would always be fraught with risks.

'Dick maybe felt guilty at forcing Johnny into something, but it was something Johnny wanted to do,' he said. 'That is just a factor of life. You have to do it. You don't give in. If you had asked Johnny in a combat situation, an attack situation, whether he was all right, he would have said yes.

'We were both out there chasing life. In a way, Johnny went

out there in search of his own death. He knew, just as I did, that it could happen. But he went for it. We both did. There was no reason for Dick to feel guilty about that. I understand that Dick got a bit lost afterwards, but he rediscovered life and that is good, because our fight was as much about life as it was about death.

'When he came to Mexico he really enjoyed it and he received a lot of love. When we went to Wales it was the same. We were treated very kindly. Although Johnny's sister didn't take it well I think, and hope, that at the end she accepted it. She saw that we were good people. I think by the time we left she was fine. That was the most important thing. We were able to feel happy that she accepted us. If she hadn't, there would have been a deep melancholy about it.'

Pintor visited the Labour Club, shook hands and signed pictures. Some people close to Johnny could not forget and stayed away, but the vast majority realized his very presence was born of good will, a need to show that the innate goodness of boxing runs deep, that in a way they were all the same.

'Johnny Owen was a warrior,' Pintor said. 'He was very brave and very strong. We were warriors together and then, afterwards, we were like brothers.'

As he signed his way through the hordes, there were those who felt a wave of respect for the Mexican. Graham Walters, one of those who had worked so hard to raise the money for the statue, said: 'Put yourself in Pintor's place. He was unable to speak a word of English and was going to the place where they had just put up a statue to the man he'd killed. He might have expected to have been hit, spat at or sworn at. But he sat in the Labour Club for eight hours solid. All he did was sign. Nothing was too much trouble for him – a true gentleman.'

In the Labour Club that day, Don James, Johnny's old trainer, got his autograph and was similarly impressed.

'I've seen fighters in the Hall of Fame in America, they sign a few autographs and say, "That's enough." When I met Pintor I watched him sign for hours. He had a quick break, a sandwich and a cup of coffee, and then he sat down again and carried on. He did not move until everyone was satisfied. I thought that was a true reflection of his character. To think Johnny had lost to a guy like that, well, somehow, it was not quite so bad.'

Pintor found himself enjoying the experience and the respect of the people of Merthyr. When the Mayor put his chain of office around his neck, he was genuinely touched.

'Another lady gave me a Welsh scarf,' he said. 'It was cold and wet and she wrapped it around my neck. I've still got it upstairs in my house. We couldn't understand anyone, but what happened went beyond words. The people were very sincere.'

Pintor attended a memorial service at the High Street chapel, where the Reverend David Protheroe said Johnny had won a world title by winning the hearts of his community. 'There is no bigger prize,' he said. On the Sunday, Lupe and Virginia had roast dinner with the Owens. Then, at the unveiling ceremony in the shopping centre, just around the corner from Howard Winstone's statue, the father and the boxer stood together and clasped hands. For once, clenched fists signified resolution rather than catharsis.

From humble, horrible beginnings, Lupe Pintor had fashioned a nice life for himself. He has admitted he made mistakes, but he has been happily married to Virginia for more than twenty years now, cocking a thumb at those who pointed to the age gap and said it would not last, and he is a devoted father. Jesus, one of his sons, is thin and bubbly and works with him in training his young fighters. They are another of boxing's father-and-son teams.

'I do it the same way that I did when I was a boxer,' Pintor said. 'I teach my fighters to be embarrassed to lose. I know I have a lot to learn about being a manager and relating to people, but I started in 1998 and will be involved in boxing now for the rest of my life. Nothing will be as good as being a boxer yourself, but this is something I can do to help people.'

Those he works with are impressed. In his gym there are no pictures of the former champion lauding past glories. He is defined by his past, but lives in the present. He has ten contracted boys. One, Edgar Rio Valle, he says will be a champion. He is just eighteen. Another, known as Lalo for short, said: 'Other trainers are in it for the money, but he is in it because he wants to make a world champion. You can tell by the way he puts so much more into it than others.'

Gerardo Aceves is a manager who likes his boys to work with Pintor ahead of others.

'Mexican trainers are not that great, but Lupe is very dedicated. He is strict about health matters and always has his fighters checked out. He has a holistic view – tactics, technique, vitamins, diet. He trains the way he used to in the old days.'

Whether he takes someone to the top or not, Pintor is happy in the small halls, where the seats are often empty, the prizes paltry and the dreams blinding. He says he would let his children box, although Virginia holds the opposite view. She is glad that Diego, their eldest, wants to be a diver.

'I would let them box if they were really focussed,' he said. 'If they had the determination to be a boxer and nothing else. But boxing is not a sport where you can take half measures. It is no good training once or twice a week. You need to do it every day, all or nothing. If they were prepared to make all the sacrifices and give all of themselves to it, then I would let them, but I would not allow them to just muck around.'

It is a the same view that Dick Owens held during his son's ascent.

In Pintor's house there are few signs that it is the home of a former world champion: a couple of trophies and a WBC belt that lies hidden. There are two bundles of photographs bound by string in a box in an upstairs cupboard. They are rarely seen. Pintor knows boxing is not about the prizes and the tokens of success, it is about stripping yourself to the core and answering the big if.

It was hard for Dick Owens to come to terms with what happened on 19 September 1980 and move on. His son was two or three fights from retiring, his dreams accomplished and his health intact. It was a struggle to move beyond the what-ifs. Johnny Owen was a very accomplished boxer, but, as Martyn Galleozzie said of him as a boy, it was his nature that really made him stand out. If boxing could do this to Johnny Owen, then was it worth it? Colin Hart had wrestled with that question and so have many more. This was not one of boxing's problem children, fighting to stop himself from spiralling out of control. He did not need the discipline to anchor him and, had he so chosen, could possibly have been a successful marathon runner. The debate is interminable, the conundrum unsolvable.

In 2005 Dick fell seriously ill. Among the stream of visitors to his bedside was Dai Gardiner. The differences that ruptured into a rift in Los Angeles meant the pair had barely exchanged words in a quarter of a century. But Graham Walters told Gardiner that Dick was ill and the old manager made the trip to the hospital. Finally, after all those years, Dick decided to let bygones be bygones and shook his hand.

In December 2005, just over twenty-five years after the death of his son, Dick passed away. Prior to his illness, Dick penned his own thoughts on Johnny Owen, Lupe Pintor and boxing. He recorded them on an old machine and then put them down on paper. This is the father's story:

When I was a trainer it was a great thrill for me to have a new boxer start in the gym. Usually he'd be very young, full of hope and dreams, wouldn't know his right hand from his left and couldn't skip or exercise or box. It was great to watch, and indeed I often did watch in wonder, as the discipline needed to become a boxer took hold and the young man became more and more proficient in his craft.

Apart from the sport's discipline it was also good to see the way boxing helped make real men and good citizens out of young and, very often, tearaway youths. It kept them off the streets, gave them great self-esteem and taught them respect for others, for those around them, and for those who knew a little about life. Boxing taught them to listen, to feel things, to be aware at all times.

Time and again I saw how boxing in this tough town turned out better human beings. It rarely failed. Some say boxing is a bit like national service in its outcome. The training is hard work, but when you get there, when it's all finished and done, you are a man, you know your power and you are able to control it. Very often this becomes the key to every success in life, the understanding of what you are and who you are and where you fit in.

But, as anyone who knows anything about boxing will tell you, it's a tough old sport. To get to the top a person has to be special. He must be one hundred per cent dedicated. One hundred per cent committed. One hundred per cent in tune with what is needed. That's to get to the top. To become a champion or a challenger to the champion one has to have something extra as well as all the dedication, commitment and insight. To be in the champion's league one has to have something indefinable. Something inside that is extra to everything else. I worked with only one such champion in my time as a trainer, my son John. Mark my words, he was special. Throughout his career and in every fight he gave everything he had and was tactically and mentally aware at all times during a bout. He trained hard, worked hard and maintained his diet and weight without ever complaining. Boxers like Johnny Owen are rare and are every trainer's dream.

Boxing is an art. We've all heard that said before. Each fight is different, each fight shows us something new and unique, each fight has its own drama and its own place in boxing history. Of course boxing can be brutal and not all its participants are artistic, but the overall idea is that the fight is settled in accordance with the rules and structure of the sport.

Yes, you must try and hit your opponent and not get hit yourself. And yes, you can get hit and hurt and cut and sometimes it can be downright dangerous and in extreme cases fatal. I know this only too well from my experience in the game. Though you must be aware of these dangers, you must not place them at the front of your mind. They must be placed far back where they are safe and do not hamper your performance.

Fatalities and accidents are as rare in boxing as they are in real life. Indeed boxing is a part of real life and getting in the ring is very similar to and no more dangerous than getting into a motorcar and heading down the motorway.

In this sport of boxing you go in the ring against one another. Once there you try to inflict harm on your opponent, knock him out if you can and generally endanger his very right to exist. But mostly, after the contest, you love one another like long-lost brothers and you forget all the pain you inflicted on each other.

This is fighter's respect. It is born out of an inner knowledge that each boxer has, that those outside the ring, those not truly involved, will never experience or gain access to. This knowledge is individual and different to each boxer and it is learned as they go along, as personal careers develop. No one can teach this. The boxers alone know how fast things are in that ring, how hard a punch can hurt, how difficult it is to be skilfully avoiding your opponent round after round and how much stamina is needed. They alone know of the courage they must draw on for such a fight, and courage is very often so difficult to summon. They are no different to any of us in that department.

All this knowledge brings them close to their opponent after the bout has ended. It is a gladiatorial respect that runs through the sport and it makes one proud to understand it and be a part of it all. Of course there is a lot more to boxing than even all of this. It takes a hell of a lot of hard work and pain to get your body fit between contests. You have to discipline your body, eat properly and avoid being overweight, and on top of everything we have spoken of so far add all the training, all of those endless days running the roads, skipping, exercising, sparring and learning the craft and working so hard, day in, day out.

If you want to box then please do, but do not give less than one hundred per cent. Eighty or ninety just will not do.

On the financial side of things, I can tell you that a life in boxing can be tough too. There is more money than ever in the game today, but this increase in income usually affects those at the top more than those in the middle and at the bottom, or those climbing or falling down the ladder. A boxer must have a personal trainer and we have discussed the workload and dedication needed already. On top of a personal trainer, and equally essential, the boxer must ideally also have a manager.

The manager will look after the boxer's interests outside of the ring. Help him with personal advice, guide his career, make sure he has no problems that might affect his performance and help him with looking after his finances. A manager will normally take twenty-five per cent of an arranged purse. That's just for starters. If you box abroad that turns into thirty-three per cent after expenses have been deducted. This is how it always was and to my knowledge it still is.

On top of those deductions there is the British Boxing Board of Control tax and personal tax – we all have to pay that, of course. What it means is that John earned a pre-tax £6,974 and 42 pence for fighting Lupe Pintor. Maybe things have changed, but I believe managers get a little too much out of their charges. Take a bit too much out of the game.

I have always been an advocate of fair play for the fighters themselves in matters of finance. Yes, the promoter and the manager play their part in securing the deal, but it is the boxers who drive the whole promotion and it is they who have to fight. I wished for many years for a new way of dealing with purses and maybe in some cases this is now happening. Perhaps the manager and the Boxing Board of Control might take a little less. The balance, plus a little more, could be automatically deducted from the boxer's purse and this could be set aside to help with the boxer's inevitable youthful retirement.

Most boxers have very little in their pockets when they retire and the financial side of the sport has always been its saddest. Boxing is a sport that uses dreams to realize its potential. In retirement all the dreams are gone and the boxer is no longer of use. It would be wonderful if we could find a way of ensuring that these spent and used-up dreams are rewarded with at least a small pension.

These are some of my views on boxing. I would hope they do not put anyone off entering the sport. I have not trained nor been involved in boxing since the death of my son in Los Angeles in 1980 after the bantamweight world championship bout with Lupe Pintor. During filming for a BBC documentary, I attended my first professional boxing bill since 1980. It was in Mexico City and I was there as the special guest of my son's opponent in that tragic title fight.

I had been asked to go to Mexico to meet him by the production team. I went but was very apprehensive when the time came to meet Lupe at his home in Mexico. I had neither seen nor spoken to him since 1980. The problems in the arena directly after the bout ended and the aftermath of that fight left me very embittered about the way the Mexican supporters treated us.

John was desperately ill almost immediately the fight ended. Everyone close by and in that ring knew it. I thought the crowd must have known that there were serious problems as the doctor came and went and then John was carried from the arena on a stretcher. The crowd chanted abusive slogans, were violent in deed and they rained empty beer cans down upon us. Some were not empty, but filled with urine and other liquids. It was very frustrating and annoying at the time and deeply upsetting. I was hurt for years afterwards and had very little good to say about the Mexican public.

But as the years of grieving for John went on, it gradually dawned on me that Lupe Pintor's supporters at that fight were just venting their feelings. They were different to us Welsh. They showed emotion in a very different way and had their own culture, of which boxing had become a very important part. They had a way of dealing with victory that was alien to those of us there from Merthyr Tydfil. I realized in time that just because they were different didn't mean that they were bad or evil, as many of us there felt they were at the time.

They meant us no real harm at all. It is doubtful if any of them really knew how badly hurt John was. Their man Lupe had won. He was champion yet again. And that was what they had come to witness and be a part of. I have come to terms with all of that now, but it still crossed my mind the night before meeting Lupe in Mexico. The next day I cast all doubts aside. The time had come to meet Lupe Pintor.

I'll never forget walking up to that big green door in Mexico City. Behind the door lay Lupe Pintor and the past. It was difficult. In the end I just knocked. It was Pintor himself who opened the door. The very first thing he did was to catch a tight hold on me. He hugged me and spoke in Spanish. There were tears in both our eyes. We entered his house and sat and had a drink and talked as men do after a long journey and a long absence. Thankfully, I was blessed with a damn good interpreter. Without him we'd have been all at sea.

Lupe told me that he had carried Johnny's spirit around with him in his heart for years and hoped that now, after our meeting, he could begin to lay it all to rest. He told me of how John was so strong, a warrior, someone whose courage prevented him from taking a backward step. He had never faced anyone like Johnny Owen, not before nor since.

Lupe was very happy I had come to meet him and he invited me to see a boxing bout in Mexico the next day. On the bill was one of his boys. Lupe was now a trainer. He was in my old job. I did go to the boxing bill and received a wonderful welcome from everyone involved. I was introduced to the crowd, both there and at home on television. That night, many in the audience shook my hand and passed on their good wishes. Some had been there in

Los Angeles on the night of September 19, 1980. They remembered.

The Mexicans showed, in their welcome and respect, what they thought of John and it helped me come to terms with many things, but most of all it restored my belief in the boxing fraternity. I shall never train or be involved in boxing again, but it is very pleasing to know that there are still many good people involved.

A statue has been carved in John's honour. It has been erected in the corner of Bethesda Street in Merthyr, with John facing home and Gellideg. I asked Lupe Pintor if he would come and unveil the monument. He said that he would be most honoured to do so. And so he did.

John now stands firm and proud on the very ground his great-grandfather was married on in 1868. He is home and recognized as one of Merthyr Tydfil's finest sons. That makes me very happy and proud. Lupe Pintor completed a great circle and ended a very painful journey for us all when he arrived in Merthyr to unveil the monument in November 2002.

John's legacy, not only as a boxer but also as a unique human being, must be preserved, and the lessons of John's life must be positive and learned well by the young people that will surely follow him. If that happens, then a value will have been placed upon my son's life beyond the priceless one he had for his family.

My wife, Edith, and I lost John at a very young age. We were, as indeed the whole family were and still are, heartbroken by the tragic turn of events that took our John away from us. The years, for me at least, have not diminished his memory in any way whatsoever. It is as painful now as it will always be. For a father to lose a son is the most difficult of events to accept, but I believe there is a truth here that we can take some comfort from. Perhaps it is better to depart reaching for the stars, doing what your life dictates, following the instincts of your heart, than to live to a hundred years and be forever miserable, disappointed and embittered.

Yes, John died young. But boxing was not to blame. Life is like that. You win some and you lose some. In boxing and in life this is always the case. We, that is, all of John's family and friends, and there are many friends, were winners just by having John as our son, brother, companion or whatever, for his lifetime. And that is what it was, no more, no less. It was a lifetime.

Boxing, the public and the wider world all lost out through John's early demise, as did we. There are no regrets now as I approach the end of my long life, just wonderful memories and a heart full of thanks to whoever may be up there for giving us Johnny Owen in the first place.